The Sociology of Education

The Sociology of Education

P. W. MUSGRAVE

METHUEN & CO LTD
11 NEW FETTER LANE LONDON EC4P 4EE

First published in 1965
Reprinted 1966 (twice), 1967 (twice),
1968 (twice), 1969, 1971

Second edition completely revised and reset 1972
SBN 416 28340 3

First published as a University Paperback 1972
SBN 416 28320 9

© 1972 Mrs R. Musgrave

Printed in Great Britain by
Butler & Tanner Ltd, Frome and London

Distributed in the USA by
HARPER & ROW PUBLISHERS, INC.
BARNES & NOBLE IMPORT DIVISION

Contents

Acknowledgements	*page* 7	
Preface to the Second Edition	9	
1	Introduction	11

PART I: THE CHILD AND SOCIETY

2	Socialization	17
3	The Family, Socialization and Education	32
4	Social Class and Socialization	53
5	The School	85
6	The Peer Group	104
7	Children and the Mass Media	120

PART II: THE SOCIOLOGY OF THE SCHOOL

8	The Teacher in a Profession	139
9	The Teacher in the School	160
10	The Curriculum	183
11	The Teacher in the Classroom	202
12	The Role of the Teacher	218

PART III: THE SOCIAL FUNCTIONS OF EDUCATION

13	Introduction	241
14	Stability and Change	244
15	The Political Function	267
16	The Selection Function	284
17	The Economic Function	312
	Name Index	351
	Subject Index	358

Acknowledgements

A book of this kind naturally owes much to a great many people, but I wish particularly to thank the following:

My teachers at the Institute of Education, the University of London, Dr G. Baron and Mrs J. E. Floud (now of Nuffield College, Oxford).

My students on the postgraduate and certificate courses at Homerton College, Cambridge during 1962–4, who left little unquestioned.

My colleagues at Homerton, who gave much assistance, often without knowing it, and particularly Dr N. K. Willson, who gave a great deal of her time to read and comment on the final draft.

My wife, for the typing of this book and much else besides.

Aberdeen, 1965   PWM

Preface to the Second Edition

Since 1965 when this book first went to press the reorganization of secondary education on a comprehensive basis has continued and the results of much new research have been published. I have taken account of both the structural changes and the new findings in this second edition in order that it may continue to serve as an introduction to this part of sociology for intending teachers. At the same time I have taken the opportunity of making some alterations suggested by various critics and by my own changing views of the whole field of sociology. Put briefly, the results of this rewriting are that Part I now focuses on the position of the child in society; much of the general introductory sociology that was included in the first edition has been omitted and chapters have been added on the school, the peer group and the mass media. Part II consists of the former Part III and deals with the sociology of the school; there is one new chapter here on the curriculum. The former Part II now forms Part III and this consideration of the social functions of education has been changed least of all.

I wish to add to the former list of acknowledgements: The staff and students of the Department of Sociology in the University of Aberdeen during the period 1965-9, who made me a rather better sociologist. The staff and students of the Faculty of Education in Monash University during 1970-1 who reminded me that I was also an educationist. My secretary, Mrs C. Stuart, who amongst other skills converts odd drafts into neat typescript.

Monash University, Melbourne, 1971   P W M

I

Introduction

Sociology is a social science. This implies that sociology is an attempt to build up a set of logical and consistent theories about the society in which we live. Its subject matter includes the institutions which mark our society; such are the family, the class system and the economy. One important institution in a modern society is the educational system. The increasing concern with education has led to a specialism within the larger field of sociology which deals with the sociology of education. In this branch of the subject a study is made of the relationship between education and society as a whole. This book in an introduction to this specialized field and, since it is intended for British readers, it will mainly be concerned with conditions in Britain, though comparative examples from other countries are useful for indicating more clearly what is happening in this country.

A science should contain no prejudice. Therefore, polemics must be avoided, though very often decisions on educational policy are the very stuff of politics. On the whole we shall be concerned with means and not ends, but sometimes we shall be brought to the point beyond which a sociologist can no longer go without taking up a moral position. This must and will be made clear. All teachers should realize when they are arguing from evidence and when their position is based on political or other beliefs.

There are two parts to our subject – society and education. To understand the sociology of education the student must learn something both of sociology itself and of education. Sociology often, but not always, demands statistics to demonstrate a truth, to indicate an order of magnitude, to make a point clear. These figures are not to be learnt parrotwise nor are they to be feared. They are only used where essential to the argument. Technical terms are used sparsely and are shown in italics on first use, being defined in the text at the same point. Footnotes have also been kept to a minimum. After each chapter there is a reading list to which references are made in the text by adding the date of publication to the author's name. Whenever a book exists in the Penguin or Pelican editions, this has been indicated.

The book has been divided into three parts. The first concentrates upon the way in which children become members of society. This process (Chapter 2) takes place to a great extent under the influence of their families (Chapter 3), though there are marked differences in the ways in which they develop according to the social class from which they come (Chapter 4). When considering the influence of the family and of social class some basic general sociology has been included upon which a sound sociology of education can be built. Finally, in the first part of the book three chapters analyse the main influences on the development of the child: of the school (Chapter 5), the group of friends with whom he mixes (Chapter 6) and the mass media (Chapter 7).

In the second part the position of teachers in the schools is considered on the grounds that teachers who have thoroughly examined the forces at work on themselves will be more effective in their vocation. Four facets of the teacher's position are examined. A teacher is a member of a profession (Chapter 8). He serves in a school where he is at the centre of a complex web of forces which act upon him both from outside and from inside the school (Chapter 9). Before continuing the examination of the teacher there is a consideration of what he teaches, namely of the curriculum (Chapter 10). Next the individual teacher's position in the classroom is examined; here he is the representative to the children of the aims implicit in the British educational system, and he is part of a definite social system together with the children in his class (Chapter 11). Finally, an attempt is made to answer the fascinating question, what does teaching do to the teacher (Chapter 12)?

The final part examines the relationship of the contemporary British educational system with other social institutions. The main concern here is with the schools, though higher education and other forms of education are mentioned. The functions of education in relation to certain important fields are analysed. An attempt is made to answer four questions. What part does education play in the balance between stability and change (Chapter 14), in maintaining a democratic political system (Chapter 15), in ensuring the full use of the talented people in our society (Chapter 16) and, finally, in supplying trained manpower to the economic system (Chapter 17)?

Though much work has now been done in this field there are still areas where the research that the topics warrant has not been done. An introductory textbook should avoid controversy and, therefore, an indication is given where facts are sparse. But a reasonably uncontroversial narrative has always been provided on the grounds that it is of overriding importance to give teachers and all others interested in education the analytical framework within which to view children, schools and teachers.

PART I

The Child and Society

2

Socialization

The members of any social group, whether it is as large as a nation or as small as a village darts club, have expectations of how those who join it should behave. If the group is to survive in its present form, they must somehow or other ensure that those who join their group learn the behaviour expected of them when they fill the new positions that they occupy as nationals or as darts club members. In the case of a nation, in the first place parents teach their children, often without conscious thought, how to be good Englishmen, Scots women, or Australians, whilst in a formal organization such as a sports club, frequently only those likely to conform are allowed to join, training prior to membership may be compulsory and clear rules specify what behaviour is normal for those filling the position of member. In all these cases where a situation is being defined or clarified to the new-comers to any group or where social arrangements exist to ensure that mutual behaviour expectations or *roles* are learnt, sociologists give to the process of induction the name of *socialization* (J. A. Clausen, 1968).

A. The Structural Perspective

In this chapter the process of socialization will be analysed from two points of view. Firstly, we shall look at the process as it takes place through time to see what roles are learnt as individuals during their life pass through the various positions available to them. Secondly, we shall examine the social process whereby individuals at any one moment learn through interaction with others how they are expected to behave. To the latter process we shall give the name of the *inter-personal perspective* and the former will be called the *structural perspective*.

Any group may be seen as made up of a number of social positions which interlock in a patterned way because the members have mutual expectations of each other. This is most clearly seen in military units where clear-cut expectations of behaviour based on accepted patterns of authority are known to all members, but similar patterns exist in all groups with any elements of permanence. This idea has been extended beyond such simple groups to whole societies, so that sociologists speak of the *social structure*. On this large scale there are numbers of positions that form possible routes or pathways through the social structure. These positions may cluster around similar activities. For example, around the family there are such positions as father, mother, son or daughter; within education there are the positions of teacher, inspector, pupil or school caretaker; in the economy the positions of manager, worker, doctor or plumber, and, finally, within political institutions such positions as prime minister, civil servant, mayor or voter. Any child may be expected to prepare himself so that when he is older he can play the roles successively of pupil, worker, father and voter. Any adult may be expected to behave at more or less the same time as a father, a worker and a voter. One very important effect of having to play successions of roles and several roles concurrently is that the social structure holds together in a more or less cohesive manner, since individuals have many connections with many different parts of the society of which they are members.

1. *The Life Cycle*

Anthropologists have given much attention to the ways in which different societies have divided up the succession of roles that are particularly associated with the family. In simple societies, and even in the rural sectors of more advanced societies, where the family forms the unit of subsistence, these roles are central to much of social life. This succession of divisions has been called the *life cycle*. Thus, in a study of a French village in the Vaucluse the following eight major positions with specific expectations of behaviour existed: baby, child, lad/maiden, newly married, father/mother, widow(er), old person, and, finally, that role for which we are all destined, deceased person.[1] To anyone who has been socialized into a Westernized

[1] L. Wylie, *Village in the Vaucluse*, New York, 1964.

urban society there is one obvious omission here, the role of a mother or father whose family has left home. This omission highlights the fact that the life cycle differs both between and within societies. There are rural and urban versions of the role which a boy or a girl in the USA must learn, but there are also differences in what is considered normal behaviour for an adult woman in the USA and in Britain.

2. *Age Grades*

These recognized divisions in the life cycle are sometimes known as *age grades* and very often important ceremonies mark the transition from one age grade to the next. The rites that mark the passage from being seen as a child to being seen as a young man or woman have been investigated by anthropologists in many societies. Such rites are very visible and often marked by physical scarring or the subsequent wearing of different clothes. In this way all will know just how anyone may be expected to behave and how in turn they should behave towards those they meet. In our own society there is much difficulty in knowing when transitions from one age grade to the next do occur. When those in mourning wore black for a year after their bereavement all knew who were to be treated with consideration as widows. Today it is very easy to cause distress by saying in good faith to the recently bereaved that her husband has not been in the local pub for a drink for a week or two.

The problem of knowing just what role a person is playing is particularly difficult in the case of the transition from childhood to adolescence and from adolescence to adulthood. Thus, children become adults at different ages along different dimensions. In Britain a child ceases to pay half fare on the railways at fourteen, is an adult as far as driving a car is concerned at seventeen, but may not vote till eighteen, or marry without parental consent till eighteen. In the last case, however, the age of adulthood is sixteen in Scotland, which once again points up the differences that exist between societies in the ages at which a child becomes an adult. Other examples may be quoted; in the state of Victoria in Australia a child becomes an adult on the railway at fifteen and may not yet vote till twenty-one, but in New Zealand a person of fifteen may drive a car. There are big differences in the social definition of the word 'precocious' between societies and in its application to various dimensions of behaviour.

3. *Ascribed and Achieved Roles*

There are some positions and roles which cannot, or cannot easily, be refused. Those filling these positions must behave as is expected of them. A very clear example is provided by the sex role. In every known society members must either be male or female and for physiological reasons it is difficult, though not impossible, to pass from one sex to the other. Another example, based on social rather than physical considerations, is that in a capitalist society a baby cannot avoid being born to parents who belong either to the middle or to the working class. In societies where social strata have other foundations than class a somewhat similar situation exists and babies are born to be sons of a ruling class or daughters of peasants and so on. Early, or indeed, any movement away from this inherited position is rare, though possible through the process of adoption. Such roles are termed *ascribed* by sociologists. They may be contrasted with roles which are not socially compulsory, but which may be *achieved* if one is able and so desires. Thus a man is ascribed maleness, but achieves the position of husband.

There is an important link between ascribed and achieved roles that is crucial in the context of this chapter. The future opportunities in life, or in the terms used here, the possible pathways through the social structure open to an individual, are largely determined by the nature of the social positions into which he is put willy-nilly. In other words the roles that he may achieve are in many cases constrained by his ascribed roles. In our society, though this is perhaps not so true of socialist societies, boys have more chance of becoming engineers or bus drivers than do girls, who in their turn are more likely to work as librarians or typists. There is also a greater probability that children born into the middle class will achieve an occupation of higher status than boys and girls of working-class parents. Basically these two examples draw our attention to the manner in which the social structure may be seen as providing tracks or pathways through life from which it is very difficult, though not impossible, to deviate.

4. The Dimensions of Socialization

Some behaviour is expected of us in all the settings into which we enter whilst we are expected to behave in certain other ways only in one specific position. The roles that we play all the time, for example, those concerning sex or social class, will be referred to here as *primary roles* and will be examined in more detail in the next two chapters. There are patterns of behaviour relating to such roles as that of a church sidesman at morning service on Sunday that are played in only one setting. These will be called *tertiary roles*. In addition there is a large number of roles that are played in some, but not all settings. These *secondary roles* form a large and important part of what we learn whilst being socialized. Some examples will be mentioned very briefly here, though further consideration will be given to such secondary roles in later chapters.

The way in which we analyse secondary socialization is determined by the nature of the social system, with which we are concerned. Thus, in advanced, urban societies such as Britain or Australia, there are clusters of closely interrelated roles that centre on economic and on political institutions, but members of these societies do not play these roles constantly. Such roles may, therefore, be considered as secondary roles, and much secondary socialization takes place in childhood. By the age at which adolescents leave school they already have learnt, partly at home and partly at school, an incomplete, but wide, knowledge of the occupational structure. In other words, their economic socialization as producers is well under way. At an earlier age they have learnt something of their national role, knowing who to support, for example, in a war or in an international sporting event. Similarly, children gradually learn their political roles so that they know not only such details of their own particular political system as how to vote, but also feel that they are part of it and have a greater or lesser degree of power to take part in and to influence political decisions that concern them.

5. Anticipatory Socialization

Clearly socialization is a forward-looking process. In the political and economic examples that have just been given the child was enabled to learn more efficiently the behaviour that was later expected of him because, whether consciously or not, prior preparation had been given to him. This preparation has been termed *anticipatory socialization*. The teaching of Social Studies at school is often a very relevant part of his preparation for the economic and political roles that the child will play in the future. The engaged couple rehearse together prior to marriage many of the behavioural patterns that they will later play as husband and wife. Likewise, the pregnant woman, at least mentally, prepares herself for her future role as a mother.

This process of anticipatory socialization is important in that, if it is apt, it eases the transition into future positions. The young person who has been taught at school to study in the more independent way expected of him at a university or college will more easily move from the role of secondary pupil to that of tertiary student. Discontinuities in behavioural expectations are to some degree eliminated. However, anticipatory socialization may be misplaced and thereby discontinuities may remain or even be increased. The child who does not achieve the particular occupation to which he has been led to aspire because either his parents or his school have unduly raised his hopes will have greater difficulties in moving into his economic role than might otherwise have been the case.

One final point must be made before completing this examination of socialization from the structural perspective. Since we can talk of a life cycle of roles through which individuals move, socialization must clearly be a lifelong process. In recent years, as sociologists have realized that this concept and the analytical tools associated with it are equally applicable to the learning of adult roles, much work on adult socialization has been done (O. G. Brim and S. Wheeler, 1966). Socialization is not something that happens only in childhood. New roles must be learnt, and often old behaviour must be forgotten because it is no longer apt for the new positions that are assumed or the new groups that are joined. This is particularly true as persons grow older. They are no longer expected to behave as young folk do. This is attested by the existence of such phrases as 'mutton dressed as lamb'. Adult socialization, however, builds greatly on the foundations laid in childhood mainly because, as psychologists have shown us, what we learn as children is more permanent in nature than what we learn in later life.

B. The Interpersonal Perspective

Behavioural expectations, or in the language of the sociologist roles, may be laid out in an interlocking pattern which can be conceptualized as the social structure, but how are they actually learnt? Learning has been seen very much as a part of the province of the psychologist. What has the sociologist to say about learning that is of help to the teacher (S. S. Boocock, 1966)? In beginning to answer these questions the focus of this chapter must be switched from looking at social structure to an examination of the manner in which people interact at a face-to-face or interpersonal level. Once something has been understood of the way in which learning takes place in a model situation where two people interact, then the possibility exists of extending this process to socialization in all parts of the social structure and at all stages of the life cycle. Basically, what has to be explained is how an individual indicates to another his definition of what social reality is in such a way that the other learns this version and makes it his own (P. L. Berger and T. Luckmann, 1967).

1. *Mutual Steering*
One useful model for examining the way in which socialization takes place at the interpersonal level is to use the idea of 'feed-back'. This concept may be applied to the way in which two persons steer each other as they interact with one another. Let us take as an example a teacher in a primary school. She has expectations of herself in her role as teacher and of the behaviour of the children aged, say, seven in her class. Her pupils likewise have expectations of their teacher and are willing to imitate or to obey her in order to learn what they take to be socially acceptable behaviour. They may be willing, and this is important, either because they value their teacher or because they see her as powerful enough to insist that they do as she wishes. In either case they interpret the cues that the teacher feeds back to them consequent upon any action that she observes or knows them to have made. The teacher signals to them by a nod or a smile that to throw papers into the waste paper basket is valued behaviour; it meets the value of tidiness which she wishes to teach to her pupils. But she may also indicate to them by a frown or by words of disapproval that

to throw paper darts even into the waste paper basket is not acceptable; it contradicts the value of orderliness upon which she puts
great emphasis and which she hopes will become a valued part of the
social reality that she will recreate in her pupils.

A point worth noting is that the range of behaviour tolerated in
any role is usually quite wide. There are strict and less strict, tidy
and less tidy teachers. Because of this each individual has some chance
to make, rather than just to take, his own role. When one remembers
the very large number of positions that any one person has to fill at
any point in his life – for example, son, customer, holiday-maker,
adolescent and so on – it is clear that there is considerable room for
individuality in the way in which interpretations of each role are
combined. Social devices do, however, exist to restrict the range of
tolerated behaviour in certain positions. Thus, many schools insist
that their pupils wear uniforms that ensure that they are highly
visible and cannot, therefore, easily deviate from the behaviour
desired by the school authorities.

2. Sanctions

The process of mutual steering may indicate to the learner how he is
to behave, but what has still not really been explained is why he
behaves as is desired. In any teaching situation, whether formal, as in
a school, or informal, as in a family or small group, the sanctions used
by the teacher or parent are crucial to the whole process since it is
because of them that he can make his definition of the role stick. The
term *sanction* is being used here in a non-emotional sense to cover all
measures used to ensure that an individual behaves as is desired.
Sanctions may be positive in the form of rewards or negative in the
form of punishments. They may take a physical form, e.g. corporal
punishment, or be material, e.g. prizes or fines, or immaterial, e.g.
the giving or withholding of love. The system of sanctions that a
teacher or parent selects from the wide battery available depends very
much upon his own background, the age and the sex of the child that
is being socialized. English evidence seems to show that corporal
punishment is more frequently used by working-class parents with
young children, whilst middle-class parents in their turn more often
use the threat that they will withdraw love. In all social classes girls
are treated somewhat differently from boys, but their fathers are more

indulgent of them than their mothers (J. & E. Newson, 1963). In somewhat stark contrast to these tendencies, prefects in independent schools for upper middle-class boys apparently still use corporal punishment more frequently as a sanction than their equivalents do in state schools for boys of the same age.

3. *Consensus or Conflict?*

The need to use sanctions to make a role stick has raised the question that has already been hinted at, namely the nature of the relationship between the teacher and the learner. Very often, particularly in the case of young children, the system of values held by the parent or the primary school teacher is absolutely unquestioned by the child. There is in effect a common system of values. The child wants to behave as the parent wishes him to do or to learn what the teacher has in mind for him. The sanctions, whether in the form of rewards or punishments, that the parent or teacher uses are seen as such by the child. The goals implicit in the behaviour are jointly held and the authority of the adult is accepted.

Suppose this were not the case. Immediately important questions of control are raised. Where there is no consensus on values, then some form of power must be used to make the child do as is expected of him. A middle-class child will accept the threat 'Mummy won't love you any more if you do that again' as a sanction because he values his mother, but a teacher may have to deal with children who do not either want to behave as he feels right or hold the same values as he does. In such a case, where immediate obedience is required, coercion or the use of power or at least the threat of it will often be used. Thus parents deprive their children of pocket money or physically force them to do what they want and teachers use systems of detentions or in some cases, even where supposedly this action is not permitted, use such physical punishment as blows with a ruler to force children to do what the teachers value highly.

In these latter cases the situation is one of conflict as opposed to those described beforehand where there was agreement. Recently there has been much more emphasis put in sociological writing on explaining situations in terms of conflict, since, especially perhaps in the field of the sociology of education, there has been a tendency to assume consensus. For this reason, the model of mutual steering, that has been outlined here as a way of analysing the process of socialization at an interpersonal level, has been developed in such a way that it may be used to examine situations that have the characteristic either of conflict or of consensus. This is apt, since situations of both types exist in whatever socialization takes place, whether in childhood or amongst adults.

4. Deviance

There is one last point before the main agents of socialization are considered very briefly. Despite the large arsenal of sanctions available to the apparently very powerful adults who socialize the young, there are those who are in some respects never socialized, who are in fact *deviants*. As used by sociologists this term has no overtones of condemnation, but merely refers to all those whose behaviour falls outside the tolerated range along whatever dimension is being considered. Thus, a boy may be normal in respect of his familial roles and be seen as a good son, but may be deviant at school and therefore seen as a bad pupil. Furthermore, deviance may be due to behaviour that falls outside either end of the range of tolerated behaviour. In, for example, the playing of religious roles, one may be a saint or a sinner. To a sociologist in his role of sociologist, whatever his view as a moral person, neither is good nor bad; both are deviant.

A great deal of work has been done recently on the topic of deviance (A. K. Cohen, 1966). However, in this book, though from time to time deviance will be mentioned, the main emphasis will be on normality, but it must never be forgotten that from the structural perspective a society may be so organized that some individuals follow pathways that perforce lead to deviance and that from the interpersonal perspective, some children and, indeed, adults, may be socialized in just the way analysed above into deviant roles. A vivid example of this process is found in Dickens' description of Fagin trying to make Oliver Twist into an efficient thief.

C. The Main Agents of Socialization

For the sake of completeness the main agents of socialization which form the subject of the rest of the first part of this book will be considered briefly as a conclusion to this chapter. In advanced, urban societies four agents seem crucial, namely the family, the school, the peer group and the mass media. Through these agents a version of social reality is created in the minds of the next generation which may match that of adults or may, along some dimensions, be deviant by their criteria.

1. *The Family*

In the past, and still in most simple societies, the family provided the main setting where roles of all types were learnt. As a result of experiences gained largely within the family the child became a loyal member of his tribe which was a political system in itself, a worker within the subsistence unit of his own family, and, in addition to this secondary socialization, he learnt from the members of his large, multi-generational family such primary roles as his sex role. In our contemporary society the family still acts as a powerful agent of socialization, especially for primary roles and for much of the knowledge of routine activities that has been called 'recipe knowledge'.[1]

With the growth of the capitalist economy the social class system has developed and different styles of life have evolved in various social groupings. These have been and are passed on from one generation to the next. One result of this is that whereas in simple societies most people knew very much the same, the stock of knowledge is now distributed differentially amongst the groupings within any complex society. This clearly will have important implications for education and a separate chapter must be set aside in which the differences between the manner of socialization in the main social classes will be considered. Whatever the social class, much of what is taught is passed to the next generation without any conscious thought. Often the main method of socializing the child would seem to be the regular presence of a role model to be imitated who has power or is highly valued and who persistently behaves in a consistent manner. Inconsistency, particularly with regard to sanctioning behaviour, muddles the child who often feels insecure since he does not know which actions are approved and which are not.

Unusual family structure has an effect on the way in which children

[1] P. L. Berger and T. Luckmann, *The Social Construction of Reality*, London, 1967, p. 56.

are socialized. Thus, children in families where due to bereavement or divorce there is only one parent undergo anomalous upbringings. Evidence shows that children of both sexes brought up by a mother alone tend to take more of a women's view of the world than is usual, and that in the more rare case where a man brings up his family alone the children interpret reality more from a man's viewpoint than is normally the case.[1] In this connection it could be of interest to study the children of fathers who have such occupations as trawlerman, commercial traveller or long-distance lorry driver.

2. *The School*

Not only does the way in which families differ in their life-style distribute certain kinds of knowledge differentially throughout society, but the very complex and specialized nature of contemporary economic roles also implies a further distribution of the stock of social knowledge. In addition, the educational demands of many occupations are such that very few parents are today capable of teaching their children what they need to know to play such roles. Many parents have difficulty helping their children with simple algebra or elementary science when set as homework, and would not know where to begin if asked to teach them quadratic equations or advanced physics.

Because families from different social classes differ in their values there is the likelihood that some children may come to school with values that clash with those held by their teachers. This can lead to a discontinuity between school and home. A clear and perhaps extreme case will indicate the nature of the problem. In Northwest Canada children from the Kwakiutl tribe of Eskimos are brought up so that the reality of time is very different for them from that of most Canadian children. For them the working day is longer in summer than in winter. Therefore, they find it hard to fit into a regular school routine that lasts from 9.00 to 4.00 all the year round regardless of the length of daylight. Furthermore, their fathers teach them to catch salmon, a main part of their traditional diet, by example rather than by verbal explanation, so that school seems to provide a very

[1] For some examples see E. Z. Dagar, 'Socialization and Personality Development in the Child', in H. T. Christensen (ed.), *Handbook of Marriage and the Family*, Chicago, 1964.

artificial way of learning. Also aggression is not punished at home, but is found to be most unacceptable at school.[1] This may seem to be an unreal case in the context of contemporary Britain, but we shall see that the differences between Kwakiutl and working-class children are not so great as may be thought.

Though the school can be a powerful agent of socialization, it is such constraints as those just mentioned that must be examined if the success or failure of socialization within formal educational organizations is to be assessed. Frequently counter-influences are encouraged by the presence within the school of groups of young persons who support each other in negating the influence of the school.

3. *The Peer Group*

Strictly, the term *peer group* should describe any group of equals according to some stated criterion, but sociologists usually apply it to groups made up of persons who are of the same age and most often to groups of children or of adolescents. A recent study (P. Willmott, 1969) has shown that in East London all the boys and most of the girls in this survey were in groups of two or more and that the average size of these groups was around five. Such small cliques should not be confused with gangs, which are frequently associated with deviance or even delinquency. The groups with which we are here concerned play a normal part in the process of socialization in most societies. They provide experience to those who are growing up of a type that are not available in their own families.

From children's point of view families are hierarchical since their parents are superior in power to them. Before children leave their families of origin to go to work and eventually to set up families of their own, they need to have certain experiences that they cannot experience in their own homes, but which will provide skills required in adult life. For example, they should mix in groups that do not have great differences in rank and where individuals may achieve status on their own behalf rather than be ascribed the status of an inferior member. Discontinuities between the role of child and that of adult will also be lessened by mixing with those of the appropriate

[1] R. P. Rohner, 'Factors influencing the Academic Performance of Kwakiutl Children in Canada', *Comparative Education Review*, October 1965.

sex who are not members of one's own family. Many adults look back with amused embarrassment on their first date, but they should remember that their awkwardness in meeting the opposite sex became less because of their membership in various peer groups.

Once again a social mechanism can be seen to function as an agent of socialization, though equally clearly no one doubts the spontaneous and real joy that individuals experience during the times that they spend with their young friends. There is something of a paradox here. The family, to which many people ascribe the duty of socializing the next generation, often does so without parents or other members of the family giving much thought to the process. Schools were established as formal organizations to socialize children because the task of recreating social reality was thought to have passed beyond the capability of the family, but nevertheless they are for one reason or another only partially successful. Yet the peer group, by nature a spontaneous group dedicated to leisure, is a powerful agent for socializing the young both by its own lights and even by some socially acceptable criteria.

4. *The Mass Media*

Over the last century the circulation of newspapers, magazines, comics and books has risen to match the rising spread of literacy. More recently films and the radio have become available to the majority of the population in advanced, urban societies. However, during the last twenty years the phrase 'the mass media' has become increasingly associated with one particular medium, namely television. This medium penetrates into almost every home in contemporary Britain and provides information, entertainment and role models of great apparent power to children. Examples are the currently fashionable pop stars and aggressive heroes, whose speech, habits and clothes are widely imitated, particularly by teenagers. What has to be considered in a later chapter is how and in what way television and other mass media influence the socialization of children.

D. Conclusion

The aim of this chapter has been to build up a theoretical framework which may be used to examine socialization in some detail. The process of socialization has been considered in two ways. Firstly, the passage of the child through the social structure was described and attention given to the various dimensions of behaviour which a member of a given society must learn as he becomes an adult. Secondly, the idea of a sociology of learning was introduced and attention was switched to the interpersonal level. At this level the important point was made that situations where learning occurred could be divided into firstly, those which were characterized by consensus and an agreed set of values and, secondly, those in which conflict was present so that coercive sanctions were often necessary to ensure that the desired behaviour occurred. These theoretical ideas will now be used in a more detailed consideration of the four main agents of socialization which were introduced in this chapter, in order to discover what is the nature of the social reality that they pass on to the next generation.

BIBLIOGRAPHY

P. L. Berger and T. Luckmann, *The Social Construction of Reality*, London, 1967.

S S. Boocock, 'Towards a Sociology of Learning', *Sociology of Education*, 39 (1), Winter 1966.

O. G. Brim and S. Wheeler, *Socialization After Childhood. Two Essays*, New York, 1966.

J. A. Clausen (ed.), *Socialization and Society*, Boston, 1968.

A. K. Cohen, *Deviance and Control*, New York, 1966.

J. and E. Newson, *Infant Care in an Urban Community*, London, 1963 (Penguin).

P. Willmott, *Adolescent Boys of East London*, London, 1969 (Penguin).

3

The Family,
Socialization and Education

In the first part of this chapter the family will be considered as a social institution. The aim will be to indicate the nature of family structures in Britain today (C. Harris, 1969). In the second part of the chapter the interpersonal perspective will be emphasized, so that the learning of the roles provided by the structure already described will be the focus, and, more particularly, of those roles that tend to influence how children will later fare at school. Social class differences will be mentioned occasionally here, but this is so important a topic that the whole of the next chapter will be given over to its consideration.

A. The Family as a Social Institution

How can we define the word *family*? To a sociologist the family is one of the many small face-to-face groups that he calls *primary groups*. It has certain peculiar characteristics that differentiate it from other common primary groups such as groups that work together or meet together regularly for some leisure pursuit. Firstly, it gives special recognition to the relationship between one male and one or more females or between one female and one or more males. The former case covers the common Western European or American family; the latter covers the case found in Tibet where one woman and a group of brothers form the family unit. This definition is influenced by the findings of anthropologists among primitive peoples, but it serves to remind us that the typical family pattern found in Britain is not the only one nor even the universal one in this country. The purposes that the family serves can be fulfilled in several ways. Temporary liaisons and men with several spouses, more frequently in succession than at the same time, are found in all social classes in the so-called civilized countries. These forms of family will give their offspring an upbringing of a quality very different from that given to children born into families of the more usual Western European pattern.

Anthropologists have found that some pattern of family organization is a common social institution even amongst peoples who do not understand the connection between the sex act and the birth of children. The theory held quite commonly in the nineteenth century that sexual communism was to be found amongst lower civilizations has not been substantiated. Even amongst those peoples who are ignorant of the significance of the sex act, there is a strong feeling between mother and child. The position of the father is less definite, as the part of the father in the family may be played by a 'social' father rather than by the biological father. However, here can be seen the second peculiar characteristic of the family, namely the stress given to kinship in the way that the family is organized.

1. The Functions of the Family

One of the main ways in which sociologists analyse any institution is by asking what are the functions that it is fulfilling. The first question that must be answered here is, therefore, what are the chief functions of the family? Traditionally, answers to this question have been given under three headings. Consideration has been given to the way that the family first fulfils the satisfaction of sex needs, secondly acts as an economic unit, and thirdly cares for the young and old. Each of these functions will be examined in turn, though it is to the way that the family cares for the young that most attention will be given because of its greater relevance to education.

(i) *Sex Needs.* There are very powerful impulses to sexual behaviour in most humans, and any organized society will wish to place this area of conduct under a form of control. Whatever family system is chosen, sex can be met in some way within the family. Today, amongst the more civilized peoples this function of the family has become more complex. In a modern industrial society marked by many impersonal contacts the individual could feel isolated and develop a personality insufficient to meet his problems, if he had not some secure base from which to venture forth and to which he might return. The family provides this security, giving the individual the affection and interest which are needed to sustain him in the many

T S E—B

brief and temporary contacts with the world at large. A person can often manage his psychological tensions if he can take his troubles home.

The institution of marriage has changed greatly over the last century; it is coming to be viewed today more as a partnership of equals than, as was the case, as a relationship between a dominant male and an almost servile female. The family has ceased to provide all the meals and most of the clothes, since many meals and clothes are now bought outside the family. The family has come to be used as a very specialized agency for providing the affection that helps to ensure the emotional stability needed if men and women are to manage their lives successfully under modern conditions.

(ii) *Economic*. The primitive family was a subsistence unit that organized the raising and getting of food. The family held and farmed the land. In countries where hunting and fishing were important means of food supply the family organized the labour for these purposes. Today, production of most goods and services is carried out in factories or outside the household, and members of the family are employed as individuals, not as one unit. Rewards in the form of money wages are paid to individuals who are often adolescents. Work and home or family have become separated. Different codes of values may rule in both, with the result that there is a loss of emotional unity within the family.

There is a further economic function that the family used to fulfil. Before the industrial revolution it was normal for the child, whether boy or girl, to learn his future occupation within the family; son usually followed father. This continuity is now no longer common, though in some of the professions there is evidence that this 'self-recruitment' of occupations still occurs.[1] The case may be cited of the sons of doctors following their fathers. Today the child does not learn the technical skills of the job from his father, but picks up the social skills and the background to the job. Again, in areas where one industry is predominant, such as in a mining village, the possibility that a son can do other than follow his father is remote. But the majority of children live today in urban areas that contain a diversity of industries and occupations. In these conditions the family cannot

[1] R. K. Kelsall, 'Self-recruitment in Four Professions', in D. V. Glass (ed.), *Social Mobility in Britain*, London, 1954.

fulfil its former function. Most parents can give neither the special-ized training necessary nor the advice that a child needs if he is to match his abilities and aptitudes to the local opportunities for em-ployment in the best possible way.

(iii) *Socialization.* Just as those who become members of any group must learn its ways, so must new members of the family be socialized into the roles relating to that stage of the life cycle through which they are passing. However, the family has a crucial position in the social structure since it is mainly through the family that society at large initiates its new recruits. It will be noticed that no consideration is here being given to one part of the third function of the family, namely the care of the old. This is of no less importance in itself, but the socialization of the young has a more direct relevance to education. Therefore in the context of this book socialization must be given the main emphasis.

Although any group must initiate its recruits, the family socializes its young in a different way because of its peculiar structure. This ensures that there is a difference in age between the older members – the parents, and the new recruits – the children. Thus, particularly where the children are young, the parents can exert great power over them. Secondly, except in those anomalous cases where only one parent is still living, families are bound to contain members of both sexes, unlike such groups as men's clubs. The family provides not only physical care, but also teaches to the children the parents' interpretation of social reality around them, and it is within the family that the child's personality is developed in the early and the formative years.

The family is not a necessary social institution from the biological point of view, since reproduction of the species does not demand such an organization. But within the limits set by hereditary poten-tiality the personality is formed, and in most contemporary societies this development takes place best through the socialization of the young within a small group such as the family (T. Parsons, 1956). The child learns the patterns of behaviour needed to exist in his environment. The young learn not just how to subsist but how to exist socially. Boys learn what to wear and how to treat other boys and girls. They learn what behaviour to expect from other children of the same and the other sex. They notice how their parents behave, often internalizing these patterns through their play, as, for example, when children dress up to play at weddings. It is important to note the complementary nature of any role, since it includes both the expected behaviour of that role and also the behaviour expected in others towards that role. Furthermore, to be fully competent in their social existence, children must ultimately learn the relevance of third parties to themselves and to the others with whom they interact. It is only by knowing each other's roles that we can cooperate with one another.

Children may play at roles like actors in the theatre, but ultimately they become these roles. The girl playing at mother takes on the characteristics of personality associated with women in that society; the personality expected in an American woman is different from that expected in an English woman. In their earliest years children are egocentric, but as they grow older they gradually achieve the capacity to put themselves in the positions of others. This process takes place mainly within the family. For example, the child comes to know that his mother may be too busy to attend to his immediate needs. In sociological terms he has begun to appreciate that roles are complementary. The child learns that age governs behaviour as he watches his mother and father. He comes to have a wider view of adult roles as he makes visits with his parents and observes other adults. He also learns from his parents and other adults the many occupational and leisure roles that are current in his environment.

As the child grows older the process becomes more complex. The older child or adolescent comes into contact at school or at work with values that may be very different from those held within his own family. His parents, as members of an older generation, may not change their values as quickly as the younger generation. There can, therefore, be discontinuities between the values of the family and its young. This becomes more possible after the adolescent has left school, as he meets an even wider range of values. The young worker can have encountered three different and conflicting codes of honesty, that of the home, of the school and of the factory. Thus it is that the process of socialization often ends in conflict and sometimes in rebellion by the adolescent. The educational problems that are inherent in this situation will be discussed later in this chapter.

2. Family Systems

Anthropologists have described many primitive societies which have very complex family structures so as to carry out the above functions. Some family units combine closely more than two generations, namely of adults and children stretching vertically over three or more generations. These families may also cover several degrees of kinship, stretching horizontally to include cousins and in-laws. The technical term given to this system of organization is the *extended family*. A form of this system was found in Britain before the industrial revolution, but under the impact of industrialization the extended family has gradually changed in character. Today in most industrial countries the family is thought of as a small unit consisting of parents and perhaps two children. To such a unit the name of the *nuclear family* has been given.

In the 1870s the average number of children in completed families in Britain was around six; by the 1900s it had dropped to three and by the 1920s to two (R. Fletcher, 1962). There were differences between the social classes, as can be seen from the following table:

Family size for women married in:	1900–9	1920–4
Non-manual husbands	2·81	1·90
Manual husbands	3·96	2·72
Average	3·53	2·42

The last column represents the size of families that must now be complete since the women concerned are past childbearing age. These figures clearly show both the decline in family size and the differences between the social classes.

Many advertisements show the nuclear family of 'mum, dad, and the kids'. This type of family has come to be considered as the norm by many, particularly perhaps among the middle-class occupations which include teachers and social workers. Hence, much of what is implied in the organization of the modern family and assumed to be a usual part of family life by many teachers may be peculiar to the middle class. A good example of this tendency is the value placed on the exclusive mother–child relationship, which is considered to have almost the universality of a biological law, but which may well be a local and temporary pattern. Those brought up in a nuclear family must beware of the parochialism that considers the extended family as a deviation from the norm.

Bott (1957) has pointed out that when considering the modern urban family the whole network of social relationships maintained by the family must be taken into account. She suggests the hypothesis that the closeness of the relationship between the husband and wife varies with the closeness of the tie between the family and its own social network. As a concrete case one may think of the working-class husband who goes out to the pub and leaves his wife at home with her relations. Here there is separation in the family of marriage directly offset by a close relationship by both husband and wife with the surrounding environment. But Bott points out that such a situation is not purely a matter of social class. In professional families also the relationship between husband and wife may be marked by distance. Though close-knit family systems are more likely in the social conditions under which the working class live, they are not universal or peculiar to those conditions.

Industrial societies allow various types of family system. Within Britain several ways of organizing the family have been reported, varying according to such factors as whether the environment is rural or urban, in Scotland or England, and what the prevailing local industry is.[1] However, the nuclear family does have some advantages in an industrialized society. Movement, both of a geographical nature and up or down the social class system, is probably easier for a small family with few local connections than for members of an extended family. These two types of movement, known as *geographical* and *social mobility*, are very necessary in the rapidly changing conditions of a modern industrial society.

We have taken the view of Talcott Parsons and his followers that the family is one particular type of small group. Parsons (1956) has gone a stage further and proposed a general theory of the family applicable to all family structures and covering all the local differences found by anthropologists. Briefly the theory is that the father's role is especially concerned with tasks and can be termed *instrumental*,

---

[1] Compare W. M. Williams, *The Sociology of an English Village: Gosforth*, London, 1956 (rural); W. Littlejohn, *Westrigg*, London, 1963 (Scottish rural); N. Dennis, F. Henriques and C. Slaughter, *Coal is our Life*, London, 1956 (a one-industry town). Also see the next section of this chapter.

whilst the mother's role is considered to be centred on the emotions and can be termed *expressive*. A good example may be seen in the setting of an industrial community where the father is out at work, whilst the mother gives most attention to the children and the home. The theory covers such cases which are common in Britain or America, but seems to be contradicted by anthropological evidence of peoples amongst whom the mother plays the roles more usually attributed to the father. In such societies descent is through the female, but it has been reported that another male, often the mother's brother, performs the roles played by the husband in our society, where both the nuclear family and the descent group are one. It would therefore seem that the general theory fits here, since the uncle and mother play the roles associated with the mother and father in our form of the nuclear family. Parsons' general theory notes that the family has sub-systems; such are the relationship between father and mother, child and child, mother and daughter, father and son, and so on. The relationships in some of these sub-systems will be of use later in this book. Any complete general theory of the family would have to cover all such sub-systems.

Parsons' theory gives a useful unity and provides tools for the analysis of the family, but social scientists offer also the concept of limiting cases. This section has indicated two such extreme cases, the nuclear and the extended family. We must now discover whether these types are found commonly in Britain today or whether the usual pattern of family organization is located in the continuum between the two limiting cases.

3. *The Facts*

Since 1945 there have been several investigations in Britain that have examined the family either as a main topic or as an important facet of the study. Here evidence will be cited from two famous studies, both of which contain corroboratory evidence from other British investigations and the results of which may, therefore, be taken as fairly representative descriptions of family life in Britain today. Young and Willmott (1957) described a predominantly working-class situation in Bethnal Green and also examined what happened to families moved from this environment to Endsleigh, a new housing estate in Essex. The same two authors subsequently studied family structure in the North London suburb of Woodford (Willmott and Young, 1960). This latter area is mainly middle class and provided an admirable comparison with their first study.

In Bethnal Green the extended family system was found still to be very much a reality. Families may be smaller now and the marriage partnership may be closer, but isolated nuclear families were not normal. Though nuclear families appeared to live in separate flats or houses, the actual social organization was found to be in units of three or even four generations with wide contacts between near relations. 'Mum' was the centre of a complex network of kin who maintained a very close relationship through constant visiting and meetings in the street, both of which were made easy by the confined physical space within which the kin lived. More particularly, there was a very close relationship between mothers and daughters. The sub-units of these extended families often merged to provide such services as meals or baby-minding, thereby enabling women to do part- or full-time work and to cope with illness more easily. There were even some cases of sons following fathers into the same occupation as, for instance, on the docks. In this 'village' in the midst of a city many people knew many others. The individual was given a position in the community because his kin were known, not because he had achieved status. Kin were the link between the individual and the community.

Amongst those on the housing estate there was much less visiting of kin because Bethnal Green was almost twenty miles away. The neighbours were not so well known. Mutual services became impossible, and this caused difficulties in times of illness or childbirth that in Bethnal Green the extended family could easily have taken in its stride. Husbands spent more time at home in the evenings and at the weekend. This meant a different quality of married life and a new relationship between father and children. The family became more home-centred. One result of this tendency was that position in the community came to be judged by the way the house was kept and furnished rather than by who one's kin were. Style of life came to be more important than in Bethnal Green. The nuclear family came to matter more than kin, though contact with kin was maintained by regular visits to Bethnal Green.

It was expected that in Woodford, an area predominantly middle-class in character, family organization would have moved even further towards the pattern of the nuclear family. This was not entirely true. Perhaps kinship mattered less and friendship more, yet there were similarities with working-class Bethnal Green. Old parents came to live with or near their children at retirement or on bereavement. In Bethnal Green the generations were together throughout life; in Woodford nearness depended upon the stage of the life cycle. The tie between mother and daughter, though not as close as in Bethnal Green, persisted. There was much friendliness, perhaps even more than on the housing estate, though it seemed to be of a different quality. There was less spontaneous friendship and more stress on conformity to social norms. An individual was not taken for granted because his kin were known; he had to prove himself.

4. *Conclusion*

It can be seen that for a very large proportion of the population it is still safe to use the extended family as a framework for analysis. Yet the nuclear family is growing in importance and is a useful tool for considering the process of socialization. It is this last function of the family that is of most interest when looking at the relationship between education and the family. At the simplest level, before the child starts his formal education he has already learnt much in the family that the school takes for granted. Even when the child is at school he spends more time in the family than with his teachers. It is for these reasons that knowledge of the family is important to the teacher, especially if the teacher's experience is of a different type of family structure from that of his pupils. We shall, therefore, now pass from examining family structure to the ways in which parents socialize their children.

B. Socialization within the Family and Education

Not all the analysis and information contained in the last section has direct implications for education. Some is essential background and some will be used in later parts of this book. If we consider the three functions of the family from the standpoint of the educational system, the first, the sex function, has little direct relevance. The economic function is of some importance though still in an indirect way. Since the nuclear family has lost this function in its pre-industrial form, some other social institution has had to take over. The teaching of the basic skills necessary to earn a living in a modern community has been handed to the educational system. Literacy is one such skill. In the same way schools can undertake much of the vocational guidance that is essential to steer a child into the job for which he is most suited. This task is unnecessary in a primitive village. These educational problems will be covered more fully later, particularly in the third part of this book. There remains the process of socialization. The interrelation between education and socialization will be discussed under three headings – early socialization, personality development, and the control of the adolescent.

1. *Early Socialization*

The patterns of behaviour that a society has to pass on to its new recruits are referred to as its *culture*. It must be stressed that this term will always be used in this its anthropological sense and never with any aesthetic connotation. In a primitive society the transmission of the culture was a major part of education. One of the most famous of contemporary anthropologists, Margaret Mead, studied the way children grew up in Samoa (Mead, 1928) and in New Guinea (Mead, 1930). Her accounts are based on life in one form of extended family and describe how the children of these peoples were given what we should call their primary education in the family without ever entering a school. The extended family did not need to hive off part of its function of socializing the child to a special educational institution. In our culture there are many patterns of living that are passed on in the same way, but the traditional peoples that Margaret Mead was describing did not yet have to cope with the rapidly changing culture that our children must do. The nuclear family can teach a child when to shake hands or how to eat a meal, but it cannot easily teach the child how to read or to do complicated mathematics, particularly if both parents go out to earn a living.

Two problems are at once raised. At what age should education outside the family begin and what alternatives should be available both at the start and later? These are administrative decisions and here the important point is that, by the age of five or six when children in most European countries start at school, the family has already done a great deal of an educational nature. Much of the culture has by this age been transmitted. Also, during the next few years when the majority of children are very malleable the school works alongside the family which still has a very potent influence. There is the possibility of a partnership of or a clash between the two institutions that are socializing the child. The danger of conflict is probably lessened by the fact that the school tends to stress the instrumental learning needed for future life in a complex industrial community, whilst the family on the whole stresses the expressive development of the personality and the emotions. However, certainly in Britain, the schools have come to consider that they have a pastoral care for their pupils. Therefore the values that the school tries to inculcate may be at odds with those that the family attempts to teach the child. For example, stealing may be thought very wrong by the teacher, but no one may prevent a country child from taking apples from an orchard or a city child from taking fruit from a lorry moving through his playground, the streets (J. B. Mays, 1951).

The children in Samoa and New Guinea, whose upbringing was described by Margaret Mead, could learn all the roles that they had to play from the education that they received as they were socialized within the extended family. But the roles that an adult in contemporary Britain needs to learn cannot all be taught within the nuclear family. A very simple example will show this to be true. A nuclear family is of one social class and mainly meets members of the same or almost the same social class. In industry, however, a manager or a workman must meet all social classes and know how he is expected to behave in each different social situation. The school can provide experience of a wider range of adult roles in a less emotional frame of reference than the family. This opening of the world to the child is one important function of the school that is often forgotten by teachers in their stress on sheer knowledge and on the inculcation of moral virtues.

Yet though the family cannot do everything and may clash with the school it does much more than teachers are sometimes prepared to admit. Children come to learn what is expected of them and of others. 'You're a big boy now, you mustn't cry.' 'You don't do that to smaller children, do you?' They begin to learn how their family views adults of other social classes that impinge on them; the middle-class child who imitates his mother's telephone voice when she orders from the local grocer has begun to learn something of the social class system. Vocational aspirations may be mainly of an unrealistic type in very young children. 'I want to be a fireman.' But, when the child is older, the family has been found to have a very strong influence on occupational choice, and often this power is exercised without the more precise knowledge that the school could give. Sex roles are learnt, as are views on modesty, the latter often in the process of toilet training. The nursery rhymes that are sung, first at home and then at infant school, begin to stress the moral virtues. Bo Peep found the lost sheep and the Knave of Hearts was punished for stealing the tarts. In the type of single class environment common in suburbia or on housing estates, differences in cultures between social classes are reinforced, since the children's playgroups are homogeneous. 'I wouldn't play with that Tommy if I were you, he's not a nice boy', or 'he's stuck up'.

There are, however, more subtle forces at work. Several large-scale and thorough investigations have shown that measured intelligence (IQ) varies directly with the size of the family. This tendency operates at each social class level. In 1947 a survey was made of all children born in Scotland in 1936, out of which a smaller and representative sample was chosen containing the 7,380 children born in the first three days of each of the twelve months in the year. The evidence from this survey showed the connection between family size and IQ at all social class levels very clearly, as can be seen in the table opposite. Furthermore, it should be noted that ordinal position within any size of family apparently plays no part in these differences in IQ.[1] More recently Douglas' work (1964) has given evidence of the same trend. His sample consisted of 5,362 children living in England, Scotland and Wales born in the first week of March 1946. As in the Scottish survey he found that there was not a dramatic fall in IQ in middle-class families until the family contained four or more children, but there was no group of middle-class families

[1] From *Social Implications of the 1947 Scottish Mental Survey*, London, 1953, p. 49, Table XXIV; R. Illsley, 'Family Growth and its Effect on the Relationship between Obstetric Factors and Child Functioning', in R. Platt and J. S. Parkes, *Social and Genetic Influences on Life and Death*, Edinburgh, 1967, p. 39.

where size did not have some influence on the IQ score of the children.

Mean test score by occupational class by size of family

Occupation	Size of family				
	1	2	3	4	5
Professional and large employers	52·5	52·3	53·7	51·3	43·1
Skilled manual workers	41·7	40·7	39·4	35·8	33·4
Unskilled manual workers	34·6	36·1	33·1	32·8	29·4

(Maximum score possible = 76)

There has been much speculation as to the exact reason for this connection between size of family and IQ. The argument has usually run that parents of low IQ have large families and that, since there is a correlation (of about 0·5) between the IQ of parent and child, the children of these larger families will tend to have a low IQ. Yet this does not account for the incidence of this effect at all social class levels. Recently it has been argued that the causation runs in the opposite direction. The large family results in the low IQ, mainly because the younger infants in a large family, in which the children are closely spaced in age, are not given sufficient time and attention by their mother so that their inherited intellectual capabilities can be developed to the full.

There is some evidence to back this view. In the Scottish Mental Survey the 974 pairs of twins were found to have an IQ on average five points lower than that of only children. A French investigation has shown that the IQ of children in families whose ages are well spaced is on average higher than in closely spaced families. But an additional factor must be taken into account, namely that variations in both family size and in IQ may be affected by a common causative factor. Thus it is known that there are certain important differences in values between those who have large and those who have small families. The ability to defer present pleasures into the future is one such value that is differentially held. The hypothesis that there is a common cause, namely the pattern of values held by parents, that influences both family size and the IQ of children, has been tested and appears to be true.[1] It would seem that, whatever the cause,

[1] For an account of this problem see J. McV. Hunt, *Intelligence and Experience*, New York, 1961, pp. 337–43. For Scottish evidence see J. Nisbet,

the quality of life in large families does influence measured intelligence and perhaps even attitudes towards school. These tendencies in their turn will have a vital bearing on success at school, more especially in the process of selection for secondary education.

The family teaches the child a great deal, both consciously and unconsciously, during the first few years. Later the school takes over part of the task, but few teachers come to influence a child as deeply as his parents do. This deep influence does not only extend to the transmission of the outward signs of the culture. It has already been pointed out that the child tends to become the roles that he plays. The connection between the family and personality therefore requires examination.[1]

2. *Personality*

There are inherited determinants of personality which put limits on the moulding that society can do. These, if anything, form the core of individuality in a person. But how is it that individuals show their singularity against a basic personality that is common to their own culture and different from other cultures? Why is it that a Cockney or a Scot is credited with a certain type of personality? (J. Klein, 1965.)

Anthropologists have reported some of the most significant cases of such differences. Margaret Mead described two tribes in New Guinea who lived in relatively close physical proximity, but who did not meet due to the impenetrable nature of the intervening country. In one tribe the men cared for the children, whilst the women did the hunting and the food gathering. Each sex had the personality characteristics that one would associate with the tasks allocated to it. In the neighbouring tribe the pattern of tasks and of personalities was more akin to that in our own culture. As in these two cases, each society ensures that its members have a substantial degree of con-

'Family Environment and Intelligence', in A. H. Halsey, J. E. Floud and C. A. Anderson (eds.), *Education, Economy and Society*, New York, 1961. For the hypothesis of a common causative factor, see D. Oldman, B. Bytheway, G. Horobin, 'Family Structure and Educational Achievement', *Journal of Biosocial Science*, Supplement 3, 1971, pp. 81–91.

[1] For a fascinating account by a novelist of how easily the effects of early socialization may be sloughed off under certain conditions, see W. Golding, *Lord of the Flies*, London, 1954 (Penguin).

formity in this respect, so that individual personalities fall within the permitted range. In this process the link between the community and the personality is the family.

There is a basic psychological need for the child to attach himself to others, especially to adults. The nature of such attachments is very general. The child loves its mother, not any of her specific acts. The loved adult becomes a model that the child will imitate. He will attempt to imitate all the different roles that the adult plays. These roles are structured differently in each individual, and the emphases put on different parts of the role structure are different from that in other individuals. The child internalizes these systems of roles to lay the foundation of his own personality. Personalities come to differ because of varying inherited potentialities and because the experiences that are met, even in early life, are not common to all members of society. But the traits of personality that are common to any one country can be understood to have their beginnings within the family. It is worth adding here that evidence will be produced in the next chapter to show that such inter-cultural differences in personality exist between social classes as well as between nationalities.

There exist very few technically sound empirical studies by sociologists of the ways in which children in early childhood learn. This is probably because of the great difficulties of employing the usual sociological methods with subjects of this age. However, recently the results of research done in an underprivileged area of Sydney have supported the aptness of applying the model of mutual steering to the socialization of very young children.[1] A sample of 108 mothers and their children aged three to five, some of whom were at nursery school, completed a number of tests to discover whether the children learnt certain values that their mothers held. The mothers were found to hold an integrated cluster of values that emphasized self-reliance, cooperation and compliance, as did the nursery school teachers concerned. The children also held these same values in a similarly integrated way, but where their mothers held these values more strongly, and where the child went to nursery school, the values were held more firmly. In addition, the more accepting of her child

---

[1] E. Scott, 'Social Value Acquisition in Pre-school Aged Children', I, II and III, *Sociological Quarterly*, Summer and Fall 1969, and Winter 1970.

the mother was, the more fully did the child appear to learn the appropriate values. It seemed also that the children developed a personality paralleling this cluster of values that they had learnt by conforming to the expectations of the valued others with whom they interacted. Here the personality of the pre-school child was being formed through a process of mutual steering.

Although the development of personality is a process that continues throughout life, the foundations are laid before the child goes to school. By the age of five or six the child has begun to learn within the family how to cope with the many tensions and frustrations that are inescapable in life with others; how, for example, to control his anger or how to postpone his immediate desires. After the child goes to school, his teacher may become the model that is imitated and hence a potent influence upon the development of the child's personality. In this respect teachers and the school once again can reinforce or conflict with the foundations laid in the family. Under modern conditions, however, there is one particular way in which the educational system can be of great assistance in the development of personality.

Smaller families and the physical isolation inherent in living in, for example, high-rise flats or semi-detached suburban houses can cut children off from other adults and more particularly from an ample experience of other children. This can result in an exclusive and over-intense relationship between the adults in the nuclear family, especially the mother, and the children, who may develop overdependent personalities. This tendency can be corrected by sending the children to nursery schools, where they must learn to live with other children who conflict with them. Today in Britain the supply of nursery schools does not meet the demand for them. The contemporary demand appears to have two sources. There are middle-class parents who realize that they cannot give their children the best environment in which to develop their personalities. Secondly, there is a demand from the working class for a place to leave their children when mother goes out to work. In as much as this demand is met, the mothers are unconsciously allowing their children a fuller chance of developing the personality through coming into contact with the wider range of children who attend the nursery school.[1]

[1] For some doubts as to whether children who go to kindergarten ultimately

3. Control of the Adolescent

The nuclear family offers enough scope for the young child, but as he grows older he needs to go outside this narrow circle, not just to learn the social skills that he will need as an adult, but to fulfil the psychological needs that come with adolescence. The most obvious need is to experiment with sexual roles amongst those of the same age. By convention this is impossible within the family. However, as soon as the child becomes attached to a group of his own age outside the family, his conduct, which was relatively easy to determine within the family, becomes far less capable of control. Such groups of adolescents have, or rapidly evolve, codes of values and of behaviour of their own which, as will be seen in Chapters 5 and 6, will in all probability be very different from those of either the family or the school. This makes for conflict, but when social change is rapid there is a further cause of difficulty. The code of values evolved in the group may not only be at odds with the home and the school, but will also almost certainly differ from the code that was common amongst the adolescent groups of twenty-five years ago, when the parents and teachers of today's adolescents were young. There are various reasons for this gap in values. The major causes are that there have been big changes in the generally held moral code over the last generation and that there are very different ways open to the young today to spend their spare time in our wealthier society.

One of the most important attitudes involved in this problem is that towards authority. A fully developed adult personality will be able to obey those in authority, cooperate easily with his equals and, if necessary, assume some authority. To a certain extent these three abilities can be learnt within the family, though the stress put on each will change as the child grows older. The ready obedience expected from a five-year-old cannot be exacted from a fourteen-year-old. Schools are supposedly arranged to achieve this same purpose as the chances of assuming authority rise as the child nears leaving age. In the past there were social institutions organized so that there was a smooth transition in this respect from childhood to

---

have any social and intellectual advantage over those who do not, see J. W. B. Douglas and J. M. Ross, 'The Later Educational Progress and Emotional Adjustment of Children who went to Nursery School or Classes', *Educational Research*, November 1964.

full adult status. The training to become a medieval knight or the apprenticeship system in pre-industrial days are good examples.

Where there is not a smooth transition from family to school, or from either of these social institutions to work or to adult life, a discontinuity is said to exist and there is the possibility of conflict. Where this occurs, possibly because the family or school does not fully meet the needs of the adolescent, children will create or find the spontaneous type of youth group that is often called 'a gang'. Youth organizations, such as Youth Clubs, may be started by educational authorities or by adults interested in the welfare of the young, such as religious bodies, but they are often rejected by the adolescents for whom they are intended because of their connection with adults and with authority (S. N. Eisenstadt, 1956).

This latter tendency raises a problem inherent in the notion of the continuity of socialization. Continuity implies that the roles of the growing child are fairly rigidly defined at each stage and that this knowledge is widely known. In the primitive tribes described by the anthropologists there was no doubt about this, as the movement from stage to stage was marked by such 'rites of passage' as initiation ceremonies. In contemporary Britain no one is clear when a child becomes an adolescent. Even the word 'teenager' does not mean what it would seem to indicate. There is no clear universal agreement as to what the rights and privileges of an adolescent are. In different families, social classes and schools, and at different times, childhood has had a different duration.[1] This lack of clarity in defining the role of the adolescent is bound to lead to conflict both within the family and at school as the child grows up. Sex will often be the centre of this conflict because of the strength of the biological forces involved, though to the family the difficulty may seem to be the hour at which the child must return home, or to the school how much homework is to be done.

The spirit of rebellion implicit here can have the result that these spontaneous gangs become totally dissociated from school and even feel themselves to be against all that school stands for. Under these conditions culture transmission in the school is very difficult. One of

[1] P. W. Musgrave, 'The Relationship between the Family and Education in England: A Sociological Account', *British Journal of Educational Studies*, February 1971.

the more serious effects may be that the rebellion is expressed in actual crime. The peak rate for juvenile delinquency amongst boys is in the last year at school, and the incidence is far greater amongst boys than girls. At the age of fourteen the number of crimes, excluding motoring and other non-indictable offences, is double that committed by those between seventeen and twenty-one and almost three times that for those between twenty-one and thirty.[1] Whilst this problem must not be minimized, it can be seen as a passing phase of adolescence.

That this problem of discontinuity in the process of socialization is peculiar to contemporary urban communities can be seen clearly by comparing a rural community. In Gosforth,[2] an isolated village in Cumberland, the young, especially if brought up on a farm, are members of families that provide for their psychological needs as they grow older. There is no great discontinuity. The children gradually learn more of their future adult roles; in the school holidays and the long summer evenings there are plenty of interesting odd jobs around the farm to hold their attention and at the same time prepare them for adult life. The result is that, though there are groups of youths who meet together, there is nothing equivalent to the urban youth culture. The same point was shown to be true in Israel in an investigation that is about as near to laboratory conditions as the social scientist is likely to come. In Israel there are two types of cooperative farm, both of which have approximately the same school system, but which have very different family organizations. In the Moshavim the family is the basic unit of production, whilst in the Kibbutzim this is not so and living is on a more communal basis. The very different family systems seem to be the reason for the comparative lack of youth activity in the Moshavim and the intense youth activity in the Kibbutzim.[3]

[1] D. J. West, *The Young Offender*, London, 1967 (Pelican), pp. 14 and 19–24.

[2] W. M. Williams, *op. cit.*

[3] S. N. Eisenstadt, 'Youth, Culture and Social Structure in Israel', *British Journal of Sociology*, June 1951. For supporting evidence from the USA see R. I. Hough, G. F. Summers and J. O'Meara, 'Parental Influences, Youth Contraculture and Rural Adolescent Attitudes towards Minority Groups', *Rural Sociology*, September 1969.

4. *Conclusion*

From the individual's point of view the way that the family is
organized and the direction in which the family system is changing
are important. The family moulds the personality of the child before
he goes to school and is a potent influence on the child throughout
his school life. Culture is transmitted within the family, and this
helps to form national character within the limits imposed by
biological inheritance. From the point of view of the State and the
school one of the most important functions of the family is to assist
in taking the child through the stage of adolescence with the minimum possible anti-social behaviour and yet in such a way that the
child's personality is not warped by any undue repression.

BIBLIOGRAPHY

E. Bott, *Family and Social Network*, London, 1957.
J. W. B. Douglas, *The Home and The School*, London, 1964.
S. N. Eisenstadt, *From Generation to Generation*, London, 1956.
R. Fletcher, *The Family and Marriage*, London, 1962 (Penguin).
C. Harris, *The Family*, London, 1969.
J. Klein, *Samples from English Cultures*, London, 1965.
J. B. Mays, *Growing Up in a City*, Liverpool, 1951.
M. Mead, *Coming of Age in Samoa*, London, 1928 (Pelican).
M. Mead, *Growing up in New Guinea*, London, 1930 (Pelican).
T. Parsons, *Family, Socialization and Interaction Process*, London,
    1956.
P. Willmott and M. Young, *Family and Class in a London Suburb*,
    London, 1960.
M. Young and P. Willmott, *Family and Kinship in East London*,
    London, 1957 (Pelican).

4

Social Class and Socialization

Already social class[1] has been mentioned on several occasions, but in the interests of simplicity no detailed attention was given to the differences between the social classes either in family structure or in their ways of socializing children. However, so important are these differences, particularly in their effect on the chances that children have of benefiting from educational opportunities, that a separate chapter must be devoted to this topic. The procedure will be as in the last chapter. A brief introduction to the sociological work on social class will precede a consideration of the ways in which differences between the social classes affect the socialization of children.

A. Social Class

The idea of social class is a relatively simple one. There are many common forces influencing the behaviour of all who fill the same social position in any society. A rather extreme example was the medieval monk. So similar were the lives of monks throughout Christian Europe that they were probably more like each other, regardless of their place of birth, than they were like the peasants who came from their own home districts. Under contemporary conditions the social constraints at work on any person as he fills his economic role as a producer are of crucial importance because this position gives him his livelihood and, in any society above the subsistence level, his standard of life. In a capitalist society the majority are workers with little property other than their own capacity to work, whilst the minority are either owners of businesses or salaried

[1] In this book the full term 'social class' will be used in this connection except where the context is clear, in order to avoid any confusion with the educational term, 'the school class', i.e. a group of children taught together.

employees, often of professional status, both categories having considerable security and often much property. Since the time of Karl Marx much has been written of the effects, implicit in a capitalist society, on those filling such positions. In a rather similar fashion to the example of the monk, capitalists in, for example, the United Kingdom, Australia and Germany are probably more alike in many of their attitudes and in their style of life because of the similarity of their economic roles than they are like the workers whom they employ in their own national communities. This idea of classes based on the similarity of social experience is relatively easily understood, but it has proved very difficult to isolate such categories in statistical terms or, to express this in a different way, to put the concept of social class into operation in sociological research.

1. *Indices of Social Class*

Many attempts have been made to discover what proportion of the population are in the different social classes. In any such investigation indices must be defined and used to represent the concept under examination. Several have been used. Firstly, the investigator may ask a question of the following type, 'To what social class do you belong?' The answer will be purely subjective. Answers to such questions vary according to the wording of the question. Thus a higher proportion of respondents will say that they are members of 'the working class' than will admit to belonging to 'the lower class'. The timing of the question also seems to influence the answers. An American survey conducted immediately after the accession to power of the British Labour Party in 1945 found that a higher proportion claimed to be working class than in a strictly comparable survey a few months earlier. Again, to ask a person's friends to what social class he belongs may bring a number of different answers. When people ascribe others to social classes they take account of many imponderable details, typical of which is accent. In different parts of this country varying weight will be placed upon whether a person speaks with or without an accent. It is probably true to say that in the south of England someone with a well-educated Scottish accent will be put into a higher social class than will a person with a well-educated Yorkshire or Lancashire accent.

Because of the obvious difficulties in attempts based on subjective measures of social class, sociologists have tended to use objective indices more frequently, particularly where statistical work is necessary. Since social class rests primarily on economic foundations, the objective indices most often used are of an economic nature. Occupation is perhaps the commonest, though there are problems even here. Children can be included with their parents. The retired may be allocated to the occupation that they followed last, though this may not have been their life's career. But the thorniest problem is how to allocate women, many of whom work at occupations which are of a lower social class than that to which they clearly belong. In fact, wives are usually included in their husband's class regardless of their own occupations; the position of spinsters is, however, difficult to solve. Another possible objective index is income; the problem here is to decide whether it is individual or family income that is the more important determinant of social class.

An index that is rarely used is the pattern of consumption. How is the income spent? Many people earn £1,500, but they may spend it in very different ways. To be specific, some dockers and some teachers earn the same income, but their expenditure follows different patterns, and these consumption patterns are the outward signs of their different social class position. Each individual expresses the pattern of values that he holds in the way that he spends his money. The teacher may be buying his house and spending a considerable amount on his children's education, whilst the docker lives in a council house and owns a car. These different patterns of values are vital in determining social class. Aggregates of individuals with the same or nearly the same income are clearly not necessarily of the same social class, though it must also be stressed that even groups consisting of individuals who hold the same values are not a class until they are conscious of having important common values and interests. Class consciousness makes a mere aggregate into a social class.

The ownership of wealth plays an important part in determining social class, since an unequal distribution of wealth leads to the unequal incomes that make it possible to give children a more advantageous start in life. Despite the very high rates at which death duties are now levied, there are still big inequalities of inherited wealth. However, income does seem to be less unevenly distributed than fifty years ago, although this is an area of investigation in which economists are far from reaching complete agreement. A policy aimed at achieving a fairer distribution of incomes has been pursued over recent decades by means of measures affecting the extremes of the income structure. High incomes have been taxed heavily and part of the proceeds transferred to the lower income groups, often in the form of social services and welfare benefits. By 1939 this had levelled out some inequality (J. R. Hicks, 1960). During the 1939–45 war there seems to have been a rise in the proportion of the national income that went to wage earners as opposed to salary earners and those living on unearned income. In the years since the war the *real income* (the amount of goods and services that the money income will buy) of the working class has undoubtedly risen, but the proportion of the national income that they earn seems to have been stationary through the 1950s and has perhaps declined slightly in the 1960s.[1]

There have been a number of attempts to construct measures of social class using one or a combination of the indices mentioned above (D. C. Marsh, 1965). Probably the most used divisions of social class in Britain are those employed by the Registrar General in the Government's decennial Census of Population. The five broad categories (I to V) are socio-economic in character and may be termed I – Professional and similar occupations, e.g. lawyers, doctors, professional engineers; II – Intermediate occupations, e.g. farmers, retailers, teachers; III – Skilled and clerical workers, e.g. most factory workers, shop assistants, most clerical workers; IV – Partly skilled occupations, e.g. bus conductors, domestic servants, window cleaners; V – Unskilled occupations, e.g. dock labourers, watchmen and most kinds of labourers. Slight changes in the allocation of occupations to the five categories have been made from one Census to the next so that the results are not quite comparable. However, using the data gathered it is possible to give, as in the table opposite, a rough indication of the distribution of the population by socio-economic status or, to speak less accurately, by social class, both through time and at the most recent Census.

The careful reader will have noticed that as yet no definition of 'social class' has been made. Throughout the discussion of class a number of interlocking strands have been traced. To summarize

[1] See D. Seers, *The Levelling of Incomes since 1938*, London, 1951, and 'Salaries', *The Economist*, 23 May and 30 May 1964.

Social class of occupied and retired males in England and Wales

		1931	1951	1961
I	(Professional)	2	3	4
II	(Intermediate)	13	14	15
III	(Skilled and clerical)	49	52	51
IV	(Semi-skilled)	18	16	21
V	(Unskilled)	18	15	9
		100	100	100

Source: D. C. Marsh, *op. cit.*, p. 198.

briefly, the first of these is economic. Occupation is vital here, mainly in that it yields an income, though wealth can also provide this. Different sizes of income lead to differences in life chances. The second strand is that of status, which measures the prestige accorded to an individual. Status tends to vary with economic criteria such as occupation or income, but this is not always the case. The status of a professional footballer or a popular singer may not be measured directly by his income. Thirdly, there is the underlying strand of power, which can be defined as the ability to control the behaviour of others. This usually varies directly with economic criteria, but there are again awkward exceptions; top civil servants or the leaders of trade unions have much greater power as defined above than their incomes might lead one to expect.

It is, therefore, very difficult to know just what is meant by the term 'social class'. It would perhaps be best to use the term 'class' only in the strict Marxian sense, that is to refer to social conflict and to analyse both the groups involved in such conflict and the attendant social change. Today in Britain the conflict between these groups is not over property ownership nor economic conditions as Marx assumed, but is rather over the exercise of power. As pointed out above, these groups only become social classes when they realize that they hold interests in common. Thus the working class has come to acknowledge a common set of interests and values and works for power so as to preserve and extend these values through such institutions as the Labour Party and the trade unions. In this sense 'class' remains, as with Marx, a tool for the analysis of social change (R. Dahrendorf, 1959).

However, for convenience we continue to talk about the upper, the middle and the working classes (and even of sub-divisions within these classes) in contexts other than a strictly Marxian one. In this book the main relevant problem will concern the relationship between social class and education. The focus will, therefore, be on the ways in which membership of social classes can influence likelihood of benefiting from education. Much of the work quoted will be based on indices of social class and it must be remembered that any such index is being used to represent the quality of a lived situation in which persons have experienced similar social realities because they are filling similar social positions.

2. *Social Mobility*

When assigning an individual to a social class, stress has come to be put on what he has achieved rather than the position to which he was ascribed by birth into his family. Naturally his family will influence what he achieves, but the vital difference between the social class system and such other modes of stratification as the Hindu caste system is that relatively greater movement is possible between the strata. This movement between social classes is termed *social mobility* and can be in either an upward or a downward direction. The analysis of social mobility has come to be one of the central problems of sociology. Theoretically it is a useful concept in studying the formation of social classes. In the context of this book social mobility assumes great importance since under modern conditions it is mainly through education that movement up the social class system is possible. In general it is difficult today to be considered a member of the middle class unless one has an occupation for which a relatively high level of education is the prerequisite.

The more movement between the social classes there is, the more socially mobile that society is said to be. Comparisons are made between social mobility in, for instance, the USA and Britain. The generally held beliefs about these two societies are opposite ones. The American system is reputed to provide ample opportunity for upward mobility, whereas in Britain it is supposed to be difficult to 'get on'. However, recent authoritative work (S. M. Lipset and R. Bendix, 1959) shows that between 1900 and 1939 social mobility, measured by movement across the line dividing manual from non-manual occupations, seems to have been as great in Britain and several other Western European countries as in the USA. Certainly it is part of the contemporary democratic ideal that there should be as much social mobility as possible. Today in Britain a large measure of equality has been gained in many fields, for example between the sexes or before the law. Yet, though it is probably true that over the last century upward social mobility has become more possible for the lower classes, it will be shown that for various reasons there are not equal chances to gain political power or access to occupations carrying the higher incomes. One of the root causes of this inequality is to be found in the way that the educational system works.

The accurate measurement of social mobility is difficult. It is not sufficient merely to know how many individuals move up and down the social class system. For a true picture the changes in the numbers of the positions at each class level must be known. For instance, it has been said that there is a permanent tendency to upward social mobility under contemporary conditions, since in a modern economy there is a growing number of managerial and administrative positions that carry high social status and whose occupants are considered middle class. Some indication of this process can be seen in the changing proportion of the various classes in the table on page 57 above. As these new middle-class positions are filled, it may be said that upward social mobility has increased. But before a true account can be given as to whether the actual chances of social mobility have become greater or less than at some former date, allowance must be made for those changes in the occupational structure of a country that alter the relative numbers of the available positions at each social class level (D. V. Glass, 1954).

For women one possible avenue of upward social mobility is to marry a husband of a higher social class than themselves. The role of a woman in our contemporary society contains skills that are very 'portable'. Such are the skills of housekeeping and childrearing. The role of a man is more heavily weighted towards occupational skill and upward social mobility must usually be achieved through success in a man's occupation. It has been shown that women do marry 'above themselves' significantly more often than men.[1] This fact must be remembered when mothers' attitudes towards their children's education are discussed.

[1] D. V. Glass (ed.), *Social Mobility in Britain*, London, 1954, p. 327.

Another important concept is that of *social distance*. This refers to the imagined distance between the social classes. It is generally held that over the last century the classes have moved much closer together. Greater wealth has been distributed somewhat more evenly. Many material possessions which even twenty years ago were symbols of status are now too common to bring the prestige associated with scarcity. A good example is the spread in ownership of cars. Again, the clothes worn by all classes are now much more uniform and do not provide a reliable guide to membership of social class unless one has a very detailed and up-to-date knowledge of fashion.

Taken together these two tendencies, the lessening in social distance and the increase in social mobility, can combine to bring for some a heightened awareness of social class. The upper strata see themselves more threatened by the lower classes and feel the need to defend their social position. Since the change in the chances of upward social mobility are in the main due to the increase in provision of education and to the more egalitarian ways of entry to secondary education, middle-class defensiveness can take the form of opposition to educational reform (W. G. Runciman, 1966). This was certainly the case in Germany around 1900, as in that country then there was a very strong sense, particularly among the middle class, of 'Stand', which can roughly be translated as social position.

3. *Social Class in Britain Today*

The combination of a growing national income and its somewhat more equal distribution has enabled the British working class to lead a more affluent way of life in recent years. Some writers have held that this has brought a change in attitudes towards social class. It is said that the worker now considers himself to be middle class. This trend has been called the *embourgeoisement* of the worker. The main basis upon which this analysis has rested is economic. Statistics can be quoted to show that many members of the working class must own expensive pieces of household equipment. Thus by the middle of 1962 eight out of every ten households in Britain had a television set, three out of five a vacuum cleaner, and two out of five a washing machine. In 1961 there were about six million private cars on the roads, a fair proportion of which must have been owned by members of the working class. The Government report that gave these figures was entitled *Social Changes in Britain*. It concluded that this country could not lapse back into the working-class poverty of the 1930s and that the average man had made a great investment in his future 'as a middle-class citizen'.[1]

It has been convincingly argued (J. H. Goldthorpe, D. Lockwood, F. Bechhofer, J. Platt, 1969)[2] that this is not in fact a true picture of what has taken place. The economic fact of greater wealth cannot be disputed and a more even distribution of incomes can be accepted. But interpretations of these developments can differ. The teacher and the docker may earn the same income and perhaps even own the same household equipment, but the teacher has a higher degree of security of employment and a much greater chance of promotion during his career. A study through time of the pattern of a typical middle-class career would yield a very different picture from that of a member of the working class. The latter usually reaches his maximum income early and, despite changes in his job, will rarely raise his real income after the age of twenty-one. This is a very different picture from the normal step-like progression of the member of the middle class. In fact the chances of rising above the supervisory level, for example above the job of foreman, are actually declining in contemporary British industry and, if upward social mobility through the educational system increases, the traditional 'hard way up' is bound to assume less importance, since the more able members of the working class will have already achieved middle-class status through the educational system.

However, the main criticism of the thesis of the embourgeoisement of the worker is not on economic grounds. If the worker has become middle class, he should have taken on the norms or the pattern of values and beliefs of that class. The type of evidence used to indicate that this has happened is drawn from the social surveys already quoted. For example, it is said that in moving from Bethnal Green to Endsleigh the worker has left the sociability of the pub and corner shop for the loneliness and status-seeking of the housing estate. The move has been from a community-centred to a home-centred life and

---

[1] This report was never published officially, but is reproduced in *New Society*, 27 December 1962.

[2] For a concise version of the argument see J. H. Goldthorpe and D. Lockwood, 'Not So Bourgeois After All', *New Society*, 18 October 1962.

is therefore seen as a move from a life typical to the working class to one more usually associated with the middle class. Yet the same social surveys provide evidence of almost the opposite point of view. The home in Bethnal Green was always a private place into which only the closest kin ever penetrated. In addition, there was status amongst the working class in Gosforth where there were 'respected' and 'rough' sections of the lower class. Even in Woodford, where the working class seemed to imitate their middle-class neighbours, they did not go as far as joining clubs or holding parties at home to the same extent that the middle class did.

It would therefore appear a more valid interpretation of the evidence to say that certain parts of the existing working-class culture have come to be given more emphasis under contemporary social and economic conditions. To summarize, it seems doubtful that the working class has in fact assumed middle-class attitudes. Statistical evidence of the poll type has also been used to support the thesis of embourgeoisement; between 10 and 40 per cent of manual workers in various recent studies have claimed themselves to be middle class. It has been indicated above that there is great difficulty in accepting such subjective estimates of social class position. However, evidence from a very carefully designed survey of the poll type made in 1961-2 has been used to back Goldthorpe and others' refutation of the thesis of embourgeoisement.[1] In this investigation an examination was made of the type of definition given to the term 'middle class' by the 33 per cent of the men or their wives who by an objective index were in manual occupations but who claimed to be middle class. It was found that, though the majority may have been conscious of being in some sense different from the traditional working class, yet their definitions of middle class seemed to show no definite sense of belonging to the non-manual category of occupations that is here termed middle class.

There is a further point to consider. Even if the working class has taken over middle-class norms, has the middle class accepted these new recruits to its own social class? It has already been suggested that a lessening of social distance may have led to an increase in middle-class defensiveness. Certainly there has been great difficulty

[1] W. G. Runciman, 'Embourgeoisement: Self-Rated Class and Party Preference', *The Sociological Review*, July 1964.

in creating socially mixed communities on new housing estates. The middle class will not remain in predominantly working-class communities. This same tendency can be seen more clearly in industry; the status distinctions between managers and workers are as rigid as any in contemporary Britain and are institutionalized by separate canteens which may number as many as four of descending status in some large-scale factories. Yet it must be pointed out that there are also changes amongst the middle class. The professional part of the middle class seems to have left the extremely individualistic stance usually associated with this class in Britain and to be readier than formerly to use cooperative action almost of a trade union type.

It is this last point that leads us to a truer interpretation of what may be happening. The two classes are changing independently under the impact of the same social and economic forces. At a time of full employment the working class may have become more individualistic, whilst the growth in the size of industrial units may have made the middle-class professional man more cooperative. The result may ultimately be a convergence into a new class. Both classes are changing. It is not a true picture to concentrate only on the changes that affect one class, the working class.

B. Socialization and the Social Class System

1. *Children and Social Class*

Wealth can be inherited and, despite death duties, some inequality of income perpetuated. A high income enables parents to give to their children the advantages that money can buy. It is a great help to a child to live in pleasant surroundings, be provided with educational toys,[1] to go to a private school with a low staffing ratio, to receive stimulating experiences such as foreign travel in adolescence, and to have the entry into the 'right circle'. In the words of the German sociologist, Max Weber, such children are receiving better 'life chances' than the children of poorer parents. The family not only transmits material benefits to its offspring, but also passes on some of the more indefinable and immaterial aspects of social class. The child

[1] B. Bernstein and D. Young, 'Social Class Differences in Conceptions of the Use of Toys', *Sociology*, May 1967.

undergoes social experiences of power and prestige upon which his ideas of class are built. The way in which his parents treat others and are treated by them give him the cues as to how he should later deal with his superiors and inferiors in class position.

Children of primary school age seem to mix very freely with children who to adults appear to be obviously of another social class. In rather the same way they ignore such adult caste boundaries as colour in choosing their playmates. In both cases, however, it appears that they recognize that there are differences but do not know the social customs associated with these differences. An interesting experiment was carried out with 179 children between six and ten years of age in Glasgow. Drawings were prepared that showed adults of obviously different social classes in incongruous circumstances. The children usually spotted this. For instance, when a picture of a workman wearing overalls and shaking hands with a man in a suit carrying a briefcase was shown to a child he commented that men dressed in that way do not shake each other's hands.[1]

A study has also been made of the views of British adolescents on social class. This survey was carried out in the early 1950s amongst boys from both grammar and secondary modern schools. When asked if they knew what social class meant, 60 per cent (49 per cent grammar, 73 per cent secondary modern school) said that they did not know, but it was found that they had already acquired a thorough understanding of our social class system. Their views were very like those of adults and had been picked up unconsciously in their ordinary day-to-day life. Amongst those who understood the term 'social class' the usual frame of reference was wealth or consumption pattern, unlike adults, for almost three-quarters of whom the frame of reference seems to be occupation. A third of these boys were aware of the importance of status symbols; they appreciated that a man may be judged by how he dresses or by his accent. They also had an understanding of the idea of social mobility; 60 per cent considered that upward mobility was associated with achievement, intelligence and personality, though those middle-class boys who were in secondary modern schools laid more stress on manners, dress and speech. Adults of all classes stressed education much more and

[1] G. Jahoda, 'Development of the Perception of Social Differences in Children from Six to Ten', *British Journal of Psychology*, May 1959.

manners hardly at all. Boys of below average intelligence spoke just as easily about social class.[1]

Evidence gathered in Sydney late in the 1960s has shown something of how children learn their social class roles. Though the content of the Australian social class system is somewhat different from that of Britain, yet the process of socialization being influenced by similar psychological constraints is probably very much the same. Between the ages of about five and eight, these Australian children saw social class in terms of dramatic contrast; an uncle was a 'millionaire', but Mum was 'poor'. In the next stage up to the age of around twelve the structure of the class system was grasped, but in very concrete terms; the garbageman earned very little money, whilst others had luxuries, clothes and cars. By sixteen children seemed to hold detailed, complex and more abstract versions of the class structure with all its attendant subtle nuances related to areas of residence, types of school and snobbery. They were now able to relate individuals to this system, particularly in terms of careers, through the various pathways of positions that it made available. It would seem that a knowledge of class is gained mainly through the process of familial socialization, one more indication of the important social role played by the family.[2]

2. Social Class Learning

Each social class has its own particular way of life. Many examples could be given of the differences between the middle and the working class. What is considered right behaviour varies; for example, each social class treats its womenfolk in a different way. Table manners and what is eaten and drunk vary greatly. It is possible to view each class as having a culture of its own. Strictly these ways of life can be seen as sub-cultures of the overall British culture. Each sub-culture will entail a separate pattern of socialization very different in some respects from that undergone by the children in the

[1] H. T. Himmelweit, A. H. Halsey and A. N. Oppenheim, 'The Views of Adolescents on Some Aspects of the Social Class Structure', *British Journal of Sociology*, June 1952; F. M. Martin, in D. V. Glass (ed.), *op. cit.*, pp. 59–61 and 74.

[2] R. W. Connell, 'Class Consciousness in Childhood', *Australian and New Zealand Journal of Sociology*, October 1970.

families of another social class. These sub-cultures are characterized most obviously by the differing outward behaviour, such as the drinking of tea at the evening meal instead of water, or the watching of a game of soccer instead of the playing of a game of golf. But it will be shown in this section that at a deeper level there are differences even in the basic personality patterns and modes of thought found in the social classes. The transmission of all these differences is a special case of the process of socialization described earlier in this book, but in view of its importance and the interest that it has raised it has come to be analysed separately and has been given the name of 'social class learning'. It is this process and its implications for education that will be examined here.

As might be expected social class learning leads to a differential ability to benefit from formal education. This is less so amongst really able children, but becomes more the case as one considers children of lower measured intelligence. Likewise this differential tendency becomes of more importance the higher up the educational system one goes, and is therefore more pronounced at university level than in the sixth form and at eighteen than at sixteen years of age. This can be seen clearly from the following table, which refers to the large sample of children born in 1940–1 in England and Wales that was investigated by the Robbins Committee on Higher Education.

Academic achievement of children at maintained grammar schools (percentages)

IQ at eleven plus	Father's Occupation	Degree Level Course	At least 2 'A' levels	At least 5 'O' levels
130 and over	A. Non-manual	37	43	73
	B. Manual	18	30	75
	A divided by B	2·06	1·43	0·97
115–129	A. Non-manual	17	23	56
	B. Manual	8	14	45
	A divided by B	2·12	1·64	1·24
100–114	A. Non-manual	6	9	37
	B. Manual	2	2	22
	A divided by B	3·00	1·50	1·68

Source: Higher Education, 1963, Appendix One, from Table 5, p. 43.

If one considers the relative *social class chances* as measured here by the line 'A divided by B', it is clear that the children of non-manual fathers have better chances than those of manual workers of gaining a given standard of education as successively lower IQ bands are taken, for example 3·00 times as against 2·06 in the case of university courses. Again, holding IQ constant, the middle class, as measured here, have a greater chance of reaching each level of education than the working class, for example in the lowest IQ category 3·00 times as against 1·68. The exception to this last generalization is the expected one, namely that the class chances for the ablest category of gaining five 'O' levels are more or less equal.

In interpreting these figures it must be remembered that they only refer to those who have already entered a grammar school. Entrance to these schools is also linked to social class. Thus J. W. B. Douglas (1964) found that below the children who were in the top 2 per cent of measured intelligence, social background was an important factor in entrance to the grammar school. Thus for those with an IQ level of between 107·5 and 110·5 at eight years of age, the rate of entry to grammar school at eleven that was achieved by the different social class divisions was as follows – the upper middle class 51 per cent, the lower middle class 34 per cent, the upper working class 21 per cent and the lower working class 22 per cent. It must be realized that the minimum IQ for entry to grammar school is in the region of 114, though great regional differences occur. The results quoted are in an IQ band well below the top 2 per cent of ability and hence much influenced by differences in social class learning.

3. *Infant Behaviour*

One of the pioneer investigations in the field of social class learning was that of the American, Allison Davis, carried out in the early 1940s.[1] Conclusions from American evidence cannot be transferred directly to British situations, but they can be guides in examining our own similar problems. Davis showed that there were great differences between the social classes in the child's learning in such basic areas of behaviour as eating, aggression and sex. He traced these social class variations in behaviour and personality to very different patterns of mothering in infancy. More particularly

[1] A. Davis, *Social Class Influences on Learning*, Cambridge, Mass., 1948.

he analysed the social class patterns of breast feeding and toilet training.

A longitudinal survey (J. & E. Newson, 1963 and 1968) is being made of how some 700 mothers bring up their children in the city of Nottingham. The object is to investigate contemporary ways of caring for children as they grow older, and the survey provides evidence that is comparable with that of Davis. It was found that although middle-class mothers were definitely more progressive in their attitude to child care, the influence of more enlightened methods was spreading down the social scale. But there were some major differences in approach. For example, the idea of what was meant by 'a spoilt child' varied. Basically the answer depended upon what each social class would indulge. The middle-class mother would put up with tantrums but would not feed an endless supply of sweets to her child; the working-class mother would not indulge her child's tantrums, but would give him sweets when he wanted them. The middle-class mother put up with more crying at night before going to comfort her child or giving him a feed. The question of sanctions has also been considered. How were the parents to ensure conformity? When a child offended, the working-class mother tended to use smacking immediately, though particularly in the case of mothers in unskilled workers' families, not very consistently, whilst the middle-class mother preferred to try 'to love her child out of it'.

Discontinuities can be built into the process of socialization and this is especially true in the matter of discipline. It is probable that authority is wielded in a working-class family in a very different way from that in a middle-class family. The working-class parent will often make his child do what he wants more by a gesture than by a verbal command backed by the reason for the order argued at the child's level of understanding. Punishment in the working-class home is probably more often based on the consequence of the wrong done rather than on the intent of the action.[1] The child who is brought up with a working-class notion of authority will note great discontinuity when he enters the world of school which tends to be governed by middle-class attitudes. The more formal the atmosphere

[1] B. Bernstein, 'Social Class and Psycho-Therapy', *British Journal of Sociology*, March 1963, espec. pp. 58–63.

of the school becomes, more particularly when he reaches secondary school, the greater will the discontinuity become between the idea of authority learnt at home and that which he meets at school. The child can react in a number of defensive ways. Wrong-doing may be automatically denied. Feelings of guilt may in these circumstances become dissociated from many anti-social acts.

The Newsons also found that feeding habits differed greatly. All the children had ample chance to suck, but in different ways according to their social class. The middle-class child was more often breast fed, but was weaned earlier; the working-class child was bottle fed for longer and was allowed a dummy. There was little thumbsucking amongst the children (only 8 per cent), but, as may be expected, it was more pronounced amongst the earlier-weaned middle-class babies. The middle class began potty training earlier and were more successful at it; unskilled workers' wives were very much later than others. Genital play was stopped by working-class mothers, but permitted or diverted by the middle class.

4. Personality Differences

The overall impression of the Newsons' evidence, though not all the details, is much the same as that of Davis. The working-class mode of infant care was characterized by a pattern of indulgence that in Davis' view led to a lack of self-discipline in older working-class children and adults. These very different ways of socialization led to markedly different patterns of personality. Davis noted that the working class did not control their basic psychological drives in the same way as the middle class did. The working class tended to extremes. When money was available, they overate and overheated their rooms. They used aggressive action much more often, and this was particularly so with regard to sex. These ways of behaviour were approved as normal among the working class, whereas the middle class directed the identical drives into channels that were socially approved in their sub-culture. Working-class aggression became middle-class initiative; the same psychological drive could take the form in a working-class child of actually striking a teacher and in the middle-class child of hard work leading to good school marks that would earn him the name of 'teacher's pet'.

What evidence is there for similar personality differences in

ain? In the early 1950s B. M. Spinley (1953) investigated the
slopment of personality in English children. She compared the
upbringing and personalities of two contrasted groups of boys and
girls, one from a London slum environment and the other from
public schools. In the case of the slum group she collected evidence
from interviews with mothers and social workers in the area and
from participant observation in various roles in local clubs; for the
public school group she collected life histories of her sample and
interviewed nursery nurses in training about the methods of infant
care. She administered a personality test (Rorschach) to both groups.
From this evidence Spinley was able to establish a different basic
personality pattern for each sub-culture that she was considering.
She attributed the differences to their particular patterns of socialization. It must be stressed again here that within the limits set by
inherited temperamental differences personality is formed by the experiences that the child and later the adult undergoes. The personality of an individual is part of his mode of survival; it will within
the genetic limits fit his environment or he will not easily be able to
survive within his own particular culture.

Spinley found that the members of the slum group were basically
insecure, since a newborn infant was made much of till the next came
along or till it grew into a child and then almost put on one side. The
children in this group rebelled against authority, since it had been
weak and inconsistent in their own experience. They were sexually
disturbed, as the male figure in their families was weak and often
changed. They had an underdeveloped conscience and were unable
to postpone immediate desires or tackle difficult problems, which
they tended to brush to one side. To children with this type of personality school poses many problems. The teacher is not liked as he
is seen as a representative of authority who is trying to impose an
alien code of moral behaviour and who sets difficult problems. Likewise the teacher has difficulties with these children beyond the
obvious one of mere communication. It is hard to pass on a code of
morals or impart religious instruction to rebellious children with
weak consciences. These children have such totally different standards from their teachers that the instruction must unconsciously,
but almost inevitably, become a criticism of the whole ethos from
which the children come. Yet the personality which these children

display by their behaviour is not a deviant one at home; it only becomes deviant at school where they spend a minority of their time. These children are exposed to living in two environments, each of which views the other as deviant. The clearest example of this is Spinley's discovery that the boys played football by the rules under the supervision of the teacher, but did not do so at home in the street, because no child observing the rules could survive in the free-for-all version of football played away from school.

The public school group provided almost a copybook contrast. The children were secure in their home lives. They had developed a satisfactory adjustment to their own and to the other sex. They had strong consciences and had achieved a balance of respect for and criticism of authority which was to be invaluable to them in the move from schoolchild to prefect and from assistant manager to manager in their later careers. To these children the worlds of home and school were not in conflict; both were striving to form the same personality type. Hence there was a much greater chance of success at school for this group.

The Nottingham sample used by the Newsons was much more representative of the general population than that examined by Spinley, which rather provided limiting cases at the extremes of the social spectrum. But the two opposing personality types that Spinley found are in a large measure what might be expected from the patterns of indulgence noted by the Newsons. The self-discipline that Spinley's public school group exhibited through possessing a conscience and in their more balanced attitude to authority can be traced back to the pattern of middle-class infant care found by the Newsons. Its foundations lay partly in the early patterns imposed with regard to feeding habits and toilet training and in the way the mother tried to love her child out of wrong-doing. The opposite personality traits in Spinley's slum group have counterparts in the opposite habits of infant care found in the working-class part of the Newsons' sample. Therefore, although such extremes in type of personality cannot be assigned outright to the broad bands that make up the working and the middle classes, yet it seems likely that Spinley's two types are approximate descriptions of the basic personality found among many in the middle class and among certainly a large proportion of the lower working class. In between these social classes it seems likely that there is a continuum with the basic personality tending towards one or other of the extremes according to the social class being considered. The teacher, who is more often than not from the middle class, has to deal mainly with children from the working class and may well find that one of the main demands put upon him, if he is to achieve success, is the adjustment that he must make in order to teach children the majority of whom have a very different pattern of personality from his own. Neither pattern is deviant in any moral sense; both were formed through the normal process of social class learning.

There is one dimension of personality that is much more directly related to success in education than the important, but general characteristics so far discussed. This is the need felt by an individual for achievement (D. F. Swift, 1966). One tradition of research, stemming from the work of McClelland,[1] has shown that the need for achievement is learnt very early during the process of socialization. Parents put before the child frames of reference defining what is thought to be excellent and encourage the child to refer to these standards in all he does. Children who have already been found by other tests to have a high need for achievement tend to take calculated risks when given games to play in which there is the chance of failure; they neither take the easy way nor trust to luck. The parents of such children tend to set problems for them that are not too difficult, but that are just beyond their present capabilities, and to encourage them warmly without actually interfering whilst their children are seeking solutions.

McClelland's work links with another tradition of research, namely that on the achievement syndrome. This latter work has been closely related to social class. It has suggested that there is a cluster of attitudes relating to achievement. Especial attention is given in this syndrome to three sets of opposing viewpoints. There is, firstly, the priority that the individual gives to himself as opposed to the groups with whom he interacts and particularly his own family. Next, there is the belief held about how much control over his immediate en-

[1] D. C. McClelland, *The Achieving Society*, Princeton, NJ, 1961; for a concise, but complete, account of relevant work see D. C. McClelland, 'The Achievement Motive in Economic Growth', in B. F. Hoselitz and W. E. Moore (eds.), *Industrialization and Society*, UNESCO, 1963.

vironment an individual sees himself to have as opposed to the view
that things just happen to him because of luck or chance. Lastly,
there is the willingness that a person has to put off present satisfaction to the future in preference to living for the immediate
moment. Clearly the child who has been taught the syndrome that
has been shown to be a middle-class characteristic, namely to defer
present gratification, to believe that his present efforts or lack of them
will be rewarded or punished in the future and to rate his own interest above that of the group, is more likely to do well at school.

Much research in this tradition has been done in the USA, but
studies have shown that this syndrome apparently also exists in
Britain. Thus, in a study of children aged eleven or twelve recently
undertaken in Aberdeen, boys seemed to hold to the middle-class
syndrome more strongly than girls. At the time that they were
questioned these children already knew which of them had been
chosen to go to selective secondary school and those with a high IQ
displayed the middle-class version of the achievement syndrome
more strongly than those with an IQ of less than 115. A similar
finding for children aged fifteen has been reported in the London
area. However, differences between the social classes were not as
clear in Aberdeen as expected, except on the dimension of looking
to the future. Questions may, therefore, be raised concerning the age
at which these roles are learnt and about whether a traditional and
relatively staunch Presbyterian city such as Aberdeen is typical in
this respect.[1]

A crucial determinant in this respect seems to be the extent to
which the family religion stresses individual, as against ritual, contact with the deity. The Protestant ethic with its emphasis on an
individual approach to God can be seen as a special case of the
general law here, since McClelland's work has shown that certain
pre-literate, non-Christian societies fit this same pattern. Self-
reliance appears to be an essential trait. This and such Protestant
economic virtues as hard work are character traits that can be stressed
either in church or at home and in both cases are likely to influence
the way in which children fare at school.

[1] P. W. Musgrave and G. R. B. Reid, 'Some Measures of Children's
Values', *Social Science Information*, March 1971, espec. pp. 147–9.

5. *Attitudes towards Education*

So far it has been shown that social class learning can result in children with a personality type that is not sympathetic towards school. Clearly the attitudes that parents show towards their children's schooling can offset or reinforce this tendency. In an investigation carried out in southwest Hertfordshire and Middlesbrough during 1952–3 (J. E. Floud, A. H. Halsey and F. M. Martin, 1956) it was shown that the chances of a working-class child entering a grammar school were greater if he came from a home rated as having poor material conditions but where attitudes towards education were favourable, than if he came from a good material environment but where the attitudes were unfavourable to education. Only 9 per cent in southwest Hertfordshire and 12 per cent in Middlesbrough of children from homes with poor attitudes but good material conditions gained grammar school places, whereas the figures were 23 per cent and 15 per cent respectively for those from homes with favourable attitudes but poor material conditions.[1]

Edu
X

It is true that not all middle-class parents have attitudes entirely favourable towards their children's education, but it seems that fewer parents of lower social class have attitudes favourable in this respect. F. M. Martin found that in 1952 in southwest Hertfordshire concern with secondary education varied directly with social class. Of fathers in professional occupations 82 per cent had thought a lot about their children's secondary education as against 38·3 per cent of fathers who were unskilled workers. Similarly 81·7 per cent of fathers in professional occupations preferred their children to go to grammar school compared with 43·4 per cent of fathers in unskilled work. Douglas found comparable results in his national sample. But in addition he found that the mother's interest in her child's school progress varied by social class and seemed to be of great 'importance' in deciding chances of entry to a grammar school. Thus, if measured intelligence is held constant, children with mothers who are undecided get 8 per cent fewer places than expected, whilst the children of mothers wanting them to go to a secondary modern school and

---

[1] J. E. Floud and others, *op. cit.*, pp. 91–5. The position in Middlesbrough is complicated by differences for the Roman Catholic part of the population; see ibid., p. 138.

leave at the minimum legal age have 60 per cent fewer grammar school places than expected.[1]

Some children from the working class against whom the educational cards seem to be stacked do better in the educational system than might be expected. Why are some children so different in this respect? Work in both the USA and Britain gives one possible structural explanation of the source of these deviants. In Huddersfield (B. Jackson and D. Marsden, 1962) there was a strong connection between success in the eleven-plus examination amongst working-class children and whether or not their mothers were downwardly socially mobile. These 'sunken middle-class' mothers held values different from the social class in which they were now located and, therefore, to pass to the interpersonal perspective were likely to socialize their children into deviant values. Other work, this time done in Lancashire, has supported findings from the USA that the children of fathers who are foremen or mothers who have been secretaries have a more than proportionate share of children who pass the eleven plus. Such parents seem by virtue of their closeness to the middle-class role models that they meet at work to be able, for example, to look further into the future than the parents of children who do not manage to go to selective secondary schools.[2] The implication is that certain children located in the working class are socialized into a set of values deviant for that class, but which enable them to succeed at school, and that this occurs because the experiences of their parents are atypical of the working class. Sometimes, for apparently idiosyncratic reasons, a child comes to be seen by his teachers and parents as clever. It may be as Jackson and Marsden found in one or two cases that he is 'literary early'. There is evidence to support the view that in such cases this success leads to the parents subsequently forming aspirations for their child that support him in his deviant role.[3] In this perhaps relatively infrequent case the direction of causation is reversed. It is not the child who is caused to

[1] F. M. Martin, in D. V. Glass (ed.), op. cit., pp. 162–3 and J. W. B. Douglas, op. cit., pp. 21–2 and 45.

[2] D. F. Swift, 'Social Class, Mobility-ideology and Eleven Plus Success', British Journal of Sociology, June 1967.

[3] D. M. Toomey, 'Home-centred Working Class Parents' Attitudes towards their Sons' Education and Careers', Sociology, September 1969, p. 314.

succeed because of his parents' aspirations, but rather the parents change their values because of their child's success.

Once a child has gained entry to a grammar school his success there can be much influenced by his parents' attitudes towards education. Himmelweit found in 1951 that working-class boys were less successful in certain London grammar schools than were middle-class boys, despite the fact that they realized that their present efforts at school were related to their probable future success in life. A major contributory cause seemed to be lack of parental support for working-class boys. Middle-class parents visited the school more often and came to watch school games or plays more frequently. The middle-class boys themselves thought that their parents were more interested in their progress at school. Their parents more often supervised homework.[1] Douglas reported that the possession of a separate room for homework varied directly with social class. This is partly, but not entirely, a matter of the type of house that can be afforded, and in this connection overcrowding is much more common under working-class than middle-class housing conditions. Homework in a crowded room with a television set turned on is very difficult.

A very thorough investigation of the effects of home environment on success at school was carried out in Aberdeen in the early 1950s (E. Fraser, 1959). The results were particularly interesting because the survey was planned so that the measured intelligence of the large sample of twelve- and thirteen-year-old children was held constant and the variation in academic attainments could be related directly to differences in the home environment. Of the four areas studied, namely cultural, material, emotional and motivational, only the last is directly relevant here. Fraser found that consistent parental encouragement was most important in providing the incentive to effort that resulted in achievement at school. Such encouragement was born in attitudes favourable towards education.

There is a growing tendency for children to stay on at school after the present legal minimum leaving age of fifteen. This must to a large extent be due to parental encouragement. Douglas found that there was no real difference between older and younger parents in this respect and concluded that the change must be a general one that

[1] See H. T. Himmelweit, 'Social Status and Secondary Education since the 1944 Act: Some Data for London', in D. V. Glass (ed.), *op. cit.*

affected parents of all ages. It is commonly held that this trend is due to the growing numbers of parents who have themselves undergone higher education and secondary education beyond the minimum legal leaving age. If such educational experience is 'infective' one would expect a growing number of the children of these parents to stay on longer in the educational system. This impression is reinforced by the following figures, which cover the Robbins Committee sample of children born in 1940–1. If children of parents of whom one or both have had selective education are compared with those of parents of whom neither has had selective education, it is found that 5·9 times as many achieved entry to degree level courses, 5·2 times as many two 'A' levels, 3·5 times as many five 'O' levels, and 2·4 times as many entered selective secondary schools.[1]

This last tendency is only indirectly related to social class in that in the past selective education has been more of a middle-class prerogative, and therefore the infective process did not spread far. It had more the nature of a feed-back system. However, it can be seen that attitudes towards education are an important determinant of chances of success in secondary education. Since favourable attitudes are found more often in the higher social classes, they reinforce the effects of social class learning on educational success that were discussed earlier in the present chapter.

6. *Thinking*

So far in this chapter we have been considering the effect of different social class patterns of learning on the personality of children and thereby on their chances of success in school. But as a result of recent work it now seems that social class learning has an important effect on the actual development of intelligence and perception. In recent years the generally accepted notion of intelligence has changed greatly (P. E. Vernon, 1969). The work of two psychologists, namely the Swiss Jean Piaget and the American D. O. Hebb, has been of particular influence.[2] Piaget has stressed the developmental aspects

---

[1] J. W. B. Douglas, *op. cit.*, pp. 50–1; *Higher Education* (Robbins), 1963, Appendix One, p. 57.

[2] For Piaget see J. H. Flavell, *The Developmental Psychology of Jean Piaget*, Princeton, NJ, 1963; see also D. O. Hebb, *The Organization of Behaviour*, New York, 1961.

of intelligence, and Hebb has made the valuable distinction between inherited potential and present mental efficiency. The analysis here is based on the importance of language learning in the development of intelligence and of ways of thinking. Most thinking is done verbally. The work of Bernstein and his associates (D. Lawton, 1968) has shown that sub-cultures transmit different modes of speech and hence different modes of thinking.

Bernstein has worked with middle- and working-class boys in London and found that in the working-class sub-culture there is on the whole a particular mode of speech that is characterized by its very restricted nature. Sentences are short, dependent clauses are rare, vocabulary is small, adjectives few and not used with fine discrimination, abstract ideas are infrequently used, and, finally, gesture is commonly used in addition to or in place of speech. This syntactically simple language may be called 'restricted code' and those who are brought up to speak this code will automatically be brought to think in the same uncomplicated way regardless of whether they are genetically capable of far more complex thought. To those who can use a more complex code of speech there will not be the same limit to mental development. In the middle-class sub-culture children hear the speech of their parents who put a very high value on verbalization (J. & E. Newson, 1968) and on answering their children's questions.[1] Since they are encouraged by adequate rewards, children in the middle class imitate their parents' linguistic code. This tends to be a more elaborate mode of speech; sentences are long and contain a complicated structure of dependent clauses, many subtly chosen adjectives are used, the words 'it' and 'one' are common, abstract nouns are found, and gesture assumes a much less important place in communication. This is termed 'elaborated code' by Bernstein and gives its speakers the possibility of thinking of a much more complex and abstract quality than is open to those who speak in restricted code. The middle-class child can understand both codes, but the working-class child is brought up to a restricted code and finds great difficulty in translating elaborated code into something that he can understand. It should perhaps again be added that the

[1] W. P. Robinson and S. J. Rackstraw, 'Variations in Mothers' Answers to Children's Questions, as a Function of Social Class, Verbal Intelligence Test Scores, and Sex', *Sociology*, September 1967.

account given here for ease of exposition covers limiting cases. Between these limits there will exist combinations of the two extremes.

Evidence for this theory is provided by examining the results of members of the working and middle classes in intelligence tests. Bernstein gave a verbal and non-verbal intelligence test to two groups.[1] The first consisted of sixty-one Post Office messenger boys aged fifteen to eighteen, none of whom had been to a grammar school. This group could safely be considered as working class. The second group was made up of forty-five boys from a major public school who were matched for age with the first group. This was the middle-class group. For the working-class group the results on the verbal test clustered around an IQ of 100, whereas on the non-verbal test thirty-six out of sixty-one had an IQ greater than 110. For the middle-class group the results on both tests were all above an IQ of 100 and the distribution of results in the two tests were closely matched. If the mean scores were extrapolated for a mean age of sixteen, then the difference on the non-verbal test between the two groups was 8–10 points of IQ, but it was 23·24 points on the verbal test; that is, it was more than twice as great as for the non-verbal test.

To summarize, the language scores of the working-class group were depressed in relation to the scores at the higher ranges of the non-verbal test, but this was not the case for the group from the public school. It would seem that the mental operations necessary to do non-verbal tests are available to both the working and the middle classes but that the mental operations necessary for understanding the more complex parts of the verbal tests are only available to the middle class and have not become a part of the mental equipment of the working class.[2] Two things follow. Firstly, purely because of differences in social class learning the middle class have more facility in the mental operations necessary to pass the verbal intelligence

[1] B. Bernstein, 'Language and Social Class', *British Journal of Sociology*, September 1960.

[2] J. W. B. Douglas, *op. cit.*, p. 46 found a slight tendency for the middle class to do better in verbal and the working class in non-verbal tests. The difference was not statistically significant, but certainly confirms other studies.

tests mainly used for entrance to grammar schools, but, secondly, there must be many working-class children who have high innate mental ability, but who cannot have this potential developed since the mode of speech they learn in their sub-culture is of too restricted a nature to furnish them with the mental equipment that is necessary and that they could have possessed. No firm answer can be given in the present state of psychological knowledge to the question of how late a child may delay the development of his innate potential mental capacity and not damage his chances of ultimately catching up.[1]

Therefore the working-class child may well come to school with a twofold handicap. His innate intelligence is underdeveloped in certain aspects that are important for success in our educational system as it is now organized, and his personality is so structured that he is unlikely to do well in school. It is to a fuller examination of the effect of this personality structure on the child's perception of the school situation that we must now turn.[2] The working-class child has not had his spare time carefully organized for him, as is often the case with middle-class children. He has a very general notion of the future and is incapable of pursuing long-term goals. This reinforces the already mentioned difficulty of postponing his present whims. To such children arbitrary luck rather than rigorously planned work appears to be the reason for success. On the other hand, the middle-class child comes to school with his intelligence developed in the direction required for success. In addition his personality has been moulded in a very different social setting so that he sees the importance of long-term goals and perceives that he himself, rather than good fortune, is the main influence on his chances of achieving such goals. The working-class child largely has his social role assigned to him, whilst the middle-class child is accorded discretion to achieve his social role.[3] These two ways of perceiving the school situation that are due to personality differences may explain the previously quoted paradoxical finding of Himmelweit, in her survey of London

[1] See J. McV. Hunt, *Intelligence and Experience*, New York, 1961, for an account of this problem.

[2] B. Bernstein, 'Some Sociological Determinants of Perception', *British Journal of Sociology*, June 1958.

[3] B. Bernstein and D. Henderson, 'Social Class Differences in the Relevance of Language to Socialization', *Sociology*, January 1969, p. 17.

grammar schools, where working-class boys did not do as well as middle-class boys despite the fact that they knew that their success at school could influence their long-term chances in life.

The description of social class learning that has been given here has stressed limiting cases. It can be appreciated that such cases are useful tools of sociological analysis, yielding results from which it is possible to work. But in the world of the school all is not so clear cut. The situation is blurred by the existence of 'illiterate' middle-class parents, who care little for their children and do not provide an environment favourable to their full development, and also of working-class parents who, perhaps through extensive further education, have come to value education and who can speak in both codes. It can, however, be appreciated that a knowledge of the extreme effects of differential social class learning on the personality and intellect of children will be of great assistance to all who work in schools.

Perhaps the most succinct summary to most of what has been said here concerning social class learning is provided by some answers given by respondents in a survey amongst mothers of American five-year-olds who were about to go to school.[1] They were asked, 'Suppose your child was starting school tomorrow for the first time. What would you tell him? How would you prepare him for school?' One middle-class mother replied, 'First of all, I would remind her that she was going to school to learn, that her teacher would take my place, and that she would be expected to follow instructions. Also, that her time was to be spent mostly in the classroom with other children, and that any questions or any problems that she might have she could consult with her teacher for assistance.' When prompted, 'Anything else?', she replied, 'No. Anything else would probably be confusing for her at her particular age.' Here the message given to the child is assured and informative; school is shown as paralleling the home and as a place involving the personal relationships of almost near equals, the teacher and the pupil; and the classroom is defined as a place of learning.

The working-class mother replied to the same question in the

[1] R. D. Hess and V. C. Shipman, 'Early Experience and the Socialization of Cognitive Modes in Children', *Child Development*, September 1965, pp. 876–7.

following way: 'Well, John, it's time to go to school now. You must
know how to behave. The first day at school you should be a good
boy and should do just what the teacher tells you to do.' In marked
contrast to the middle-class case this child is being socialized in
anticipation of his going to school in such a way that his role is
defined as passive rather than active; the roles central to the situation
are seen as about authority and instruction rather than about help
and near equality; the relationships in the school are presented as
impersonal rather than close and friendly; and, lastly, the message
given to the child is restricted and vague rather than ample and specific.

C. Conclusion

Social class is a topic to which sociologists have given much attention.
Yet to define the term is very difficult, and for our purposes here
the important point is that those ascribed at birth to different social
classes are largely socialized into different sub-cultures within which
there are different patterns of learning. Social class learning affects
three psychological concepts – personality, perception and thinking,
and, perhaps of more importance, it implies a differential distribution
of knowledge, skills and competence that varies by social class. The
transmission of the different styles of life associated within each class
takes place in the main, especially in early childhood, through the
family. In this way social class position is normally passed from
generation to generation and whole classes may be seen as self-
recruiting.

Yet the key to the class system in comparison to such other modes
of social differentiation, as, for example, the caste system, is the
relative case of social mobility between the various levels. Such
mobility in Britain today takes place mainly by means of the educational system. This must be the case in an industrial system with a
strong egalitarian tradition. The political outcomes of this democratic philosophy in the form, for example, of the welfare state,
together with certain economic developments such as the growth of
a wealthy group of salaried employees, have helped to temper
capitalism so that the prediction made by Marx that the divide
between rich and poor would grow so great that a socialist revolution
would occur has not yet proved true.

Yet the process of social class learning outlined here, which is implicit in the contemporary structure of society, clearly prevents children brought up in the working class from achieving their full potential in the school at a time when success at school is almost a necessity for entry into many occupations. In an egalitarian age this tendency raises the problem of whether it is possible to diminish these social class differences. The educational problems implicit in this issue will be raised again both in Chapter 5, when the comprehensive school is considered, and in Chapter 16, when the selection function of education is examined.

BIBLIOGRAPHY

R. Dahrendorf, *Class and Class Conflict in an Industrial Society*, London, 1959.

J. W. B. Douglas, *The Home and the School*, London, 1964.

J. E. Floud, A. H. Halsey and F. M. Martin, *Social Class and Educational Opportunity*, London, 1956.

E. Fraser, *Home Environment and the School*, London, 1959.

D. V. Glass (ed.), *Social Mobility in Britain*, London, 1954.

J. H. Goldthorpe, D. Lockwood, F. Bechhofer and J. Platt, *The Affluent Worker in the Class Structure*, London, 1969.

J. R. Hicks, *The Social Framework* (3rd ed.), Oxford, 1960 (espec. Ch. XVII).

B. Jackson and D. Marsden, *Education and the Working Class*, London, 1962 (Pelican).

D. Lawton, *Social Class, Language and Education*, London, 1968.

S. M. Lipset and R. Bendix, *Social Mobility in Industrial Society*, London, 1959.

D. C. Marsh, *The Changing Social Structure of England and Wales, 1871–1961* (2nd ed.), London, 1965, Ch. VII, 'Social Classes and Educational Opportunities'.

J. & E. Newson, *Infant Care in an Urban Community*, London, 1963 (Pelican).

J. & E. Newson, *Four Years Old in an Urban Community*, London, 1968 (Pelican).

W. G. Runciman, *Relative Deprivation and Social Justice*, London, 1966.

B. M. Spinley, *The Deprived and the Privileged*, London, 1953.

D. F. Swift, 'Social Class and Achievement Motivation', *Educational Research*, February 1966.

P. E. Vernon, *Intelligence and Cultural Environment*, London, 1969.

5

The School

There has been a growth in the importance of the school as a socializing agency over the last two hundred years, mainly because of two interconnected social changes. Firstly, the family has been given a lower priority in this connection and, secondly, the structure of knowledge has grown much more complex, particularly over the last century, as science has been applied more fully in the economy. It is largely because of the greater weight given to education in formal institutions, as opposed to the former methods of socialization by informal means mainly within the family, that a separate sociology of education has come into being. One of the principal interests of such a sociology must be the school and the whole of Part II in this book consists of a sociological analysis of the school. Here, however, consideration will be given to the structure of the British educational system and the cultures that exist within various types of schools. The emphasis here is on possible pathways through the formal educational system and the behaviour expected in the positions concerned, rather than on the interaction between pupils and teachers which will be considered in the next Part.

A. The School System

I. *The Foundation of the Contemporary Structure*
The way in which the British educational system[1] is organized is very largely determined by its historical growth (P. W. Musgrave, 1968). There is, firstly, an important division between the independent schools and those provided by the State. In January 1969,

[1] Throughout this book, except where otherwise mentioned, the position is taken that there is a fairly uniform British educational system. For some of the differences between English and Scottish schools, see P. W. Musgrave, *The School as an Organisation*, London, 1968 (Ch. 2).

5 per cent of all children were in independent schools (3·6 per cent were in independent schools recognized as efficient), but the existence of these schools has political and economic consequences out of all proportion to the numbers attending them because of their connections with the higher ranks of the social class system. In addition, the ethos of these schools, especially those secondary boarding schools known as public schools, has had a powerful impact upon the way in which the State secondary schools have developed.

Until the 1902 Education Act the schools provided by the State were in the main giving schooling to children up to the age of fourteen under the Elementary Code. The curriculum was narrow and almost entirely restricted to the 3 Rs. The flavour of these schools was that of a cheap and minimal education provided for the working class almost out of charity. Around the turn of the century the growing power of organized labour and the more complicated nature of the economy forced a reconsideration of the structure of British education. Initially as a result of the Act of 1902, grammar schools were provided by the State to which able children from the working class were admitted in growing numbers through a system of scholarships. However, the civil servants in the (then) Board of Education, administrators at the local level, headmasters and apparently many of the staff recruited to these new schools, were all perforce drawn from the existing schools, namely those of the elite independent system. Thus the aims, curricula and methods of these new grammar schools came to be very like those of the existing independent schools which were so closely linked with the upper and upper-middle classes.

In terms of the social structure the result was that by 1939 two main pathways existed through the educational system. These were formed by the elementary schools which led in the main to the lower levels of the social hierarchy and by the system of independent and State-provided grammar schools that 'sponsored' their pupils to social positions of high status.[1] For the working class there was

---

[1] R. H. Turner, 'Sponsored and Context Mobility in the School System', *American Sociological Review*, December 1960 (also in A. H. Halsey, J. E. Floud and C. A. Anderson (eds.), *Education, Economy and Society*, New York, 1961).

a narrow track connecting the two pathways through a scholarship examination at the age of about eleven or twelve.[1] Differences between the two systems in expectations of social behaviour and in the formal curricula ensured that a definite pattern of social and academic knowledge existed. The schools reinforced and perpetuated the existing distribution of knowledge.

2. Contemporary Ideological Changes

As early as 1897 the first demand came from the Trades Union Congress for 'Secondary Education for All'. Initially the answer was seen by all political parties and by the educationists to be the greater provision of scholarships allowing entry to the grammar school for children from the working class. It was felt that this would create chances for upward social mobility by opening the way to jobs in the economy carrying high social status. This view was strengthened by the development in the inter-war years of psychological testing, since these tests were widely believed to provide an accurate measure of innate intellectual ability so that able children from the working class could be discovered and helped to the grammar school. This view strongly influenced the way in which the educational system was reorganized as a result of the 1944 Act.

By the second world war there was a feeling that the educational provision of the State should be reconstructed to meet the growing demands for a more egalitarian system. This view was strengthened by the idealism engendered in the war which supported such attempts to plan a fairer society as the Beveridge Report of 1942, that formed the basis of much of the post-war legislation concerning social welfare, and in the field of education the 1944 Education Act. This Act had two important results for the structure of British education. Firstly, the Elementary Code was abolished so that the State schools were now divided into two sections by age rather than by status. There now exist primary schools for children between five and eleven (twelve in Scotland) and secondary schools for those over eleven (or twelve). Before the 1944 Act the division was between the low-status elementary schools and the high-status secondary

[1] For the way in which this age became the most common see J. D. Nisbet and N. J. Entwistle, *The Age of Transfer to Secondary Education*, London, 1966.

schools; in the higher age levels of both systems of schools the same curriculum was taught, but facilities were worse in the former than in the latter. However, secondly, though the Act itself laid down nothing about the structure of secondary education, the newly established (then) Ministry of Education indicated in 1945 that three types of school with 'parity of esteem' were envisaged, namely the secondary grammar, technical and modern schools. Strong criticisms of this structure, which came to be called the tripartite system, led by 1947 to the official recognition of the comprehensive school, a common school for all the children in a given catchment area apart from those whose parents sent them to private schools. Despite the changing policies of various governments, this last type of school has grown so important that in January 1969, out of 5,454 secondary schools, 962 (21·4 per cent) were comprehensive and 26·3 per cent of all secondary pupils were in such schools.

Any examination of the contemporary structure of British education must, therefore, take account of the existence of an independent and a State sector, and within the latter, of primary and secondary schools. The secondary schools, furthermore, are of four main types, the comprehensive school and the three types of school found in the tripartite system. Clearly, the culture of each type of school will be influenced by the history of its development, but all organizations, and perhaps especially educational organizations, are slow to react to social change and therefore certain forces may be at work on the contemporary structure which have only recently begun to influence the schools, but which could well have a great ultimate effect. To single out any one contemporary social force for consideration is dangerous in that a prediction is being made about the likely direction of social change, but one change, which has great theoretical interest, seems important enough for this to be done.

The main drive for structural change has in the past come from the demand to create new pathways through the educational system, so that anyone of whatever social origins, who by certain criteria of ability and achievement was considered capable, could achieve high status. There was a growing realization that the success of working-class children in primary schools was constrained in the ways outlined in the last chapter by their background, but the feeling was that this problem could be solved without radical restructuring by, for example, such positive discrimination as led the Plowden Committee to recommend the creation of Educational Priority Areas.[1] In other words, anyone should have the chance to acquire the knowledge and the social behaviour appropriate to, and currently on the whole only available to, those high in the social hierarchy. Recently, however, an ideological change seems to have occurred so that a much greater emphasis is coming to be put upon developing the individual than upon teaching him to be a member of the society to which he belongs. Many of the appeals made by students and others against 'the system' are symptomatic of this change. In many schools curricular changes have been made in line with this ideological shift. Individual differences and predispositions are given more weight. Thus a choice of what material shall be studied in, for example, social studies, history or English is allowed particularly to older pupils, and especially at the tertiary level of education. One implication of these freer courses is that the whole of any school class does not necessarily cover the same syllabus. A consequence of these changes, if they become common, is that what is taught within the schools will not reproduce the present social distribution of knowledge. This may be the manifest aim of new curricula of this type, but it may also be a latent and unplanned consequence. In the past, schools have largely seen themselves, and been seen, as agents that transmitted the contemporary culture much as it was, but there are some today who wish the schools to act to change the culture.[2] What are the cultures that are passed on by the various parts of the British educational system as it exists today?

B. British Schools and Their Cultures

Some parents send their children to school to acquire a specific pattern of behaviour, attitudes and knowledge. In the case of those children who go to independent schools their parents are often willing to make great material sacrifices to pay the fees involved. A few parents will not permit their children to take up their places in

[1] Children and Their Primary Schools (Plowden), Vol. I, London, HMSO, 1967, Ch. 5, 'Educational Priority Areas'.
[2] P. W. Musgrave, 'Two Contemporary Curricular Ideologies', in R. J. W. Selleck (ed.), Melbourne Studies in Education, 1972, Melbourne, 1972.

selective secondary schools because 'that's not for the likes of us', in other words, they reject a pattern of behaviour offered to them. Others again without any great thought allow their children to go to school knowing that they will learn something, though it may, as far as they are concerned, be much or little. In all cases the children are being socialized with more or less success into one of a number of possible cultures according to the route they take through the educational system.

In recent years research into the cultures of British schools has begun and results are now available, but very often reliance has to be put on one or two studies so that this analysis must be largely in terms of what Weber called *ideal types*. Such ideal types are analytical constructs which have the aim of furthering the clarification of what is really taking place. In all likelihood any one ideal typical account may be shown by future work to be incomplete or even biassed, owing to our current ideological blinkers or to contemporary sociological ignorance. However, the construction of such ideal types does enable us to give some account of contemporary social reality in the different types of British school.

1. *The Primary School*

Here three main cultures may be specified (W. A. L. Blyth, 1965). Within the British primary schools there are two main traditions at work, which may be called in the terms of common usage the traditional and the progressive, each of which generates very different school cultures. In addition, there is the rather different culture specific to the independent preparatory schools that cater for a somewhat similar age group.

(i) *The Traditional Culture.* The primary school is in some ways a direct descendant of the former elementary school since it is based on the age range from five to eleven whose education formed the major responsibility of the older type of school. Therefore it is reasonable to expect some historical residues in the new primary school. However, it is not often that a contemporary primary school exhibits the worst features of the old type, those associated with cheapness and nastiness – cheap in as much as it provided minimal facilities for teachers and children, and nasty in as much as the discipline was repressive, and such was largely the case because of the feeling that this was good enough for the working class. The great changes that have taken place may be seen in a study by Jackson that describes a good example of the traditional culture in a contemporary primary school.[1] The school buildings were new, modern in architectural style and brightly decorated; the teachers had excellent materials and used some up-to-date methods. Yet the characteristics of the traditional culture predominated over the trappings of modern education. Success in the academic field was all important, not as in the nineteenth-century elementary school in the sound learning of the 3 Rs, but in achieving success in the eleven-plus examination for selection to grammar school. Though corporal punishment was rarely used, very powerful sanctions, often of a punitive nature, were brought to bear by the staff and by the parents of the pupils to achieve the desired academic results. Furthermore, though the children seemed bright and full of ideas, there was an underlying trend of conformity to those behavioural and academic patterns that were perceived by the children as right for future members of the elite. These tendencies influenced the whole school and not only the 'A' stream, most of whom could expect to go to grammar school. In the primary schools, to use the terms of the structural perspective, teachers often create such permanent positions as 'members of number one, two or three group', or 'form captain', which imply behaviour, whether intellectual or social, of a hier-archical nature. In short, the culture of these schools is centred on academic learning, conceived in a rather formal manner and usually achieved in a competitive way, on status along various dimensions and on negative sanctions or punishment.

(ii) *The Progressive Culture.* Very different are those primary schools whose aim is to create a culture based on the child learning rather more of what interests him than what the teacher feels is right for him, on an interpretation of equality that implies each child shall have as many experiences as possible, and, finally, on a pattern of sanctions based upon using reward rather than punishment. There may well be a degree of double-thinking in the attempt to focus on children's interests, since learning at any age, but especially in the primary school, is fundamentally a situation based on authority and

[1] B. Jackson, *Streaming: An Educational System in Miniature*, London, 1964.

the teacher may well use children's interests as a means of motivation to teach what he has already planned that the child shall learn. But the progressive culture is rooted in the writing of such educational theorists as Froebel and Montessori, and such educational psychologists as Piaget. There is, therefore, a strong tendency to see education in developmental terms. The stress is put on the child's step-by-step progression under his own motivation, rather than upon the class learning given chunks of knowledge under threat of punishment from the teacher with strong support from home.

Structurally a classroom organized in this tradition will have many positions offering varied types of experience through most of which many, but not all, of the children will pass. Furthermore, the positions will probably all carry similar status. This week a child will be book monitor, the next week in charge of the flowers, and the following week look after the blackboard. The children – in such a situation one can hardly call them 'pupils' – will be grouped in a number of different ways for their various experiences and these groups will be so arranged that all the class will work with each other and so that no status is attached to any one group. Such primary schools will attend to individual differences. The teacher will be open to pupils' suggestions and the curriculum will be broadly based, reaching out into the environment of the school and the children's homes. The culture could be described as egalitarian, non-repressive, developmental and non-competitive in comparison with the traditional classroom.

(iii) *The Preparatory Tradition.* Entry to the major independent schools has for a long time been at the age of thirteen or fourteen. Because of this, during the early part of the nineteenth century special schools evolved in answer to a demand from those who wanted and could afford to send their children to the public schools, which were then becoming more popular. Today these preparatory schools take pupils usually at about eight and prepare them to take the Common Entrance Examination which is the hurdle that those wishing to go to public school must pass. Thus the curriculum of the preparatory schools is largely governed by the fact that their pupils must have reached by the age of about thirteen certain academic standards in, for example, Latin, mathematics and science. Again, the public schools have a very strong sporting tradition. Thus, though not strictly necessary, pupils will suffer less discontinuity if they can play such games as rugby football or fives before going to their public school. Many of the preparatory schools are boarding schools and can, therefore, have a much fuller control over the life of their pupils than in the normal day primary school. In addition, their pupils are homogeneous in nature in that they are drawn from middle-class houses with a very similar set of values which will support the school in term-time and will not seriously undermine its efforts during the holidays. The pupils come from families with high social status where notions of hierarchy and duty are strong; they are going to schools of which the same may be said. Therefore, prefect systems with formal sanctions under the control of the pupils themselves and permanent captains of games teams are common. Under such cir-cumstances the preparatory schools have a rather extreme version of the traditional culture, in which academic learning and status in a hierarchy are given high priority and in both cases are achieved through competition of one sort or another. A major additional element in comparison to the traditional primary school is that there is a strong emphasis on the playing of competitive games.

2. Secondary Schools

(i) *Independent Schools.* The essential features of the independent schools are seen in their fullest form in those public schools whose tradition is firmly based in the past and in the historical connection between such private education and the upper middle class. For over a century now these schools have been popular with those of high social status who have delegated a large part of the socialization of their sons, and less often of their daughters, to teachers, who, though usually themselves of somewhat lower social status, were yet experts at teaching 'elite role behaviour' (I. Weinberg, 1967).

The schools themselves were rigidly hierarchical. New boys joined the ranks of fags and passed gradually upwards through a series of such junior offices with minor responsibilities as head of a bedroom for a few younger boys to the top of the scale of status when they filled the positions of prefects. This progression was seen by all concerned as an apt preparation for a career in the professions, the civil service, the armed forces or, as times changed, even in industry. In all of these occupations organization was based on the readiness of the majority, even in the junior managerial ranks, to obey and of the few to command. The sanctions available in such schools were many, but the means of physical coercion were commonly available to both staff and senior boys. The lessons that the schools had to teach were easily learnt in a boarding school largely closed to outside influence.

Competition was encouraged especially on the games field both with other schools and between the houses into which the schools were usually organized. Though there were always a minority who were keenly interested in things academic and the teaching, especially of the classics, was at the higher levels often inspired, yet it was very largely in the playing of games that those responsible thought that many of the qualities of the gentleman could be best learnt. Such qualities were the easy bearing of authority, loyalty to one's peers, and the display of courage, physical and moral, in adversity, and of easy good manners on all occasions.[1]

Under contemporary conditions, those running the public schools have made serious attempts to offset their social isolation so that they attempt to have their pupils move into the local community and also almost perforce allow them to import many outside influences into the schools. Yet much of their traditional culture remains, like many British institutions, subtly unaltered by changes made to meet today's world. Fagging may either be abolished or exist in a more humane form, but there is still a marked pattern of hierarchy and authority, often reinforced by such traditional elements of ritual as house assemblies, ceremonies associated with awarding colours, or rules about, for example, who may wear certain jacket buttons undone. Academic results may be given more emphasis in an age where success in examinations seems important, but the main lessons of the public schools are still seen to be the learning of those rather intangible qualities of the gentleman that are imparted outside the classroom. The educational world at large may be more democratic, but the public schools remain closely linked to the elite, both because the parents of their pupils are drawn from the upper middle class and because most of their pupils will ultimately achieve that level

[1] R. H. Wilkinson, 'The Gentleman Elite and the Maintenance of a Political Elite', *Sociology of Education*, Fall 1963 (also in P. W. Musgrave (ed.), *Sociology, History and Education*, London, 1970).

during their careers. The culture that these schools appear to transmit to the majority of their pupils is, as has been the case for many years, one based on duty, responsibility, loyalty, self-reliance, and one which aims to translate these characteristics into actions with the minimum of intended publicity.

(ii) *The Grammar School.* There were grammar schools in England and burgh schools in Scotland before the public schools ever achieved their great popularity in the nineteenth century, but, as already indicated, the State grammar schools grew up in the twentieth century as an imitation of the nineteenth-century version of the public school. In a recent study King (1969) has examined one such school in the London area. The teachers aimed to create a specific culture in the school and to transmit this to their pupils. In many respects they wished to create an atmosphere similar to that in the public schools. They put a high emphasis on the development of personality or, to use their evaluative term, character. They expected the boys to aim for positions of leadership in the professions rather than in industry and not necessarily to go for a job that was well paid, since the intrinsic worth of work was more important in their view than the monetary reward. Academic work was given great emphasis, partly because examinations must be passed to enter the occupations which today carry high status, but also because much knowledge was seen by the staff as good in itself.

However, the majority of the boys in the school did not subscribe to the values of their teachers and certainly those who left before entering the sixth form did not learn the values that their teachers hoped to impart. They saw themselves as an intellectual elite by virtue of their success in the eleven-plus examination and hence considered that they ought ultimately to earn more than those who had not been selected for a place in a grammar school. Furthermore, they were more attracted than the school hoped to the teenage culture about which more will be said in the next two chapters. The boys who entered the sixth form were largely those from middle-class homes that had the same values as the teachers and that supported the school in its efforts. Thus, in the sixth form the school did succeed in some measure in creating the intended culture in which a feeling of responsibility, for what went on in the lower school, academic excellence in a few subjects oriented towards the universities and the intellectural discipleship involved in intensive work in small classes with a specialist teacher, were highly valued by the pupils.[1]

The study by King, when taken in the context of this analysis, poses a number of questions. For example, which culture was that of the school – that of the staff or that of the boys who left early? Can we then speak of a school having one culture? Clearly in this school, as is probably the case in most grammar schools, there was an intended official culture in which high priority was given to many values found in the public schools. But there was also a culture that was outside the control of the staff, being that of many of the boys and of their world beyond the walls of the school to which they returned each evening and at weekends. This second culture was in many ways less akin to that of the public school than to that of the secondary modern school to which we now turn.

(iii) *The Secondary Modern School.* The secondary modern school is directly descended from the upper age levels of the old elementary school, but, since it was born at a time of high idealism during and just after the second world war, it was given the aim of parity of esteem. As Taylor (1963) has shown, the hope of many teachers was to recreate at the secondary level the progressive type of education found in many primary schools. This intention was frustrated by the social forces that constrained the way in which the secondary modern school developed during the late 1940s and throughout the 1950s. Parity of esteem was not granted to these schools which typically occupied the premises of a former elementary school but had been given a new name, because most of their pupils came from the working class and left school to enter jobs that had low social status. Therefore, the schools set out to earn esteem by imitating the grammar schools and in many areas were supported by parents who had hoped that their children would gain places in selective secondary schools. In many such schools the children who were thought to be the abler pupils were entered for external examinations. In this way traditional academic aims and curricula came to take the place of progressive intentions. Heads established school uniforms, systems of houses and prefects, prize days and many of the rituals associated with schools of higher status.

[1] For a brief account of the culture of the sixth form see *15 to 18* (Crowther), Vol. I, London, HMSO, 1959, Ch. 21, 'The Marks of a Sixth Form'.

Though forces outside the secondary modern schools gave strong support to these developments, yet for many children school was a place at best to be borne and at worst to be hated or attacked. Hargreaves (1967) studied a typical mixed secondary modern school in urban Lancashire in which there were four streams. The range of reactions to school among its pupils was great and may best be seen by a brief account of the findings concerning the children in 4A and 4D. The children in 4A wore uniform, behaved largely as expected by their teachers both at work and at play, and aimed to do well in external examinations at sixteen. A modified version of the culture of the grammar school existed here. However, in 4D things were very different. The children did not wear the school uniform, did not meet the behavioural expectations of their teachers and did little or no work. Indeed, for them the system of sanctions used in the school had no avail. To offer a pupil who did a good piece of work the reward of praise or of possible promotion resulted in bad work in future as the child did not wish to be normatively or physically isolated from his friends. To censure bad work or behaviour led to further bad behaviour, since censure indicated that the teacher was annoyed and this was the intention of the original action. Here again there were two cultures in the school. One was the official one, valued and sanctioned by the staff and in turn valued by a few pupils, most of whom were successful by the criteria of the school. The other was a culture generated, valued and sanctioned by the pupils and opposed to that of the staff. The proportions of the pupils who learn either of the cultures will vary from school to school and depend upon such factors as the nature of the catchment area, the predominant social class of the children, the aims and qualities of the staff and the leadership exercised by the headmaster.[1]

(iv) *The Secondary Technical School.* The secondary technical school grew out of the junior technical school, founded in that form in 1913. The aim was to build a secondary education around the basis of one broad group of occupations such as the engineering or the building trades. These schools never became as common as the other types of

[1] For an analysis of the influence of these factors on the development of one secondary modern school see C. M. Turner, 'An Organisational Analysis of a Secondary Modern School', *Sociological Review*, March 1969.

T S E—D

secondary schools. In January 1969, only 1·9 per cent of secondary pupils were in this category of school. Furthermore, their original aim was perverted when the eleven-plus examination became important, since the technical schools came to be seen as a second chance for entry to occupations of relatively high social status for those who had failed to be selected for the grammar school. This position is complicated by the fact that recruitment, or to be more exact selection, to some of these schools is at the age of eleven, while to others it is at thirteen. There is a strong possibility that technical schools with an entry at eleven approximate to grammar schools in many ways and that this may also be true, though to a lesser extent, of those with entry at thirteen, because of the presence of many pupils whose parents see the latter type of school as a second, and even final, chance for their children to enter or to remain in the middle class. In schools with either age of entry there is some emphasis put on such vocational subjects as technical drawing and there are usually well-equipped workshops. However, in one study of two technical schools, one to which entry was at eleven and the other at thirteen, it was found that, although the pupils preferred the technical to the modern school, they were somewhat critical of technical education and would have preferred more emphasis to be put on the elements of the curriculum that were common with the grammar school.[1] The culture of the secondary technical school, about which even less is known than that of the other types of British schools, would seem to be in many ways more akin to the grammar than to the modern school, namely a somewhat academic atmosphere with a technical basis, and with strong support for the school from both pupils and parents.

(v) *The Comprehensive School.* Increasingly over the years, but especially since the 1930s, there have been criticisms of the existence of the strong connection in Britain between the schools and the system of social stratification. One constant target for criticism in this respect has been the continuing popularity of the public schools, though this has so far had little apparent effect. Initially the main drive for reform of the State schools was directed towards widening the social class composition of the entry to grammar school. More

[1] P. J. Kemeny, 'Dualism in Secondary Technical Education', *British Journal of Sociology*, March 1970.

scholarships were granted to defray the costs of secondary education for able children from the working class and eventually all secondary education in State schools was declared free by the 1944 Act. However, despite the initial trust in psychological testing there was a growing realization after 1945 that such means of selection as the eleven-plus examination in its various forms, though relatively accurate, were not absolutely reliable and, furthermore, that the determinants of IQ were, as Bernstein's work described in Chapter 4 shows, in many ways as much social as genetic. In addition there was growing political criticism of the tripartite system and this soon settled into a demand for some form of common or comprehensive school for all the children in a given catchment area, including those who went to independent schools if the latter were ever abolished.

Though the comprehensive school came to be seen as the answer to the faults of the tripartite system, the argument for a common school was rarely put in an articulated or testable form. However, there seem to have been two main strings to the case. The first intention seems to have been to create a school in which the children could learn a unified and integrated culture which would overcome those divisions of social class that separate schools linked to specific social classes seemed to perpetuate. This argument was tacitly assumed in the claim made that these schools would lead to social cohesion. The second main argument for the creation of a system of comprehensive secondary schools concerned the wastage of talent in the secondary modern schools, since it was hoped that more of the able children from the working class who now left school early would be encouraged to stay on longer and attain the jobs for which their talent made them capable. In addition, this claim drew attention to the way in which the secondary modern school tended to become a school for failures in which the children, by virtue of not achieving selection to a grammar school, lowered their aspirations and aimed almost entirely for occupations of low status regardless of what their actual capabilities might be. In other words, the argument was that the schools in the tripartite system were closely linked to and perpetuated a social class system divisive in nature, and that in one common school the children could learn a less divided culture and aspire to positions that matched their capabilities. The vision of 'one nation', which was the dream of Disraeli, the nine-teenth-century politician and founder of the modern Conservative Party, was to be translated into reality by a reorganization of the secondary schools, largely supported by the Labour Party.

A number of studies have now been made upon which the success to date of the comprehensive school may be judged. The most complete is that by Ford (1969), who compared a coeducational comprehensive school in the inner London area, chosen to be representative of such schools in general, with a grammar and a modern school in the same area, having, as far as was possible, characteristics similar to those of the comprehensive school. In the matter of reducing the wastage of talented children, Ford reported that on the evidence of these three schools there was still a persistence of class bias in educational attainment within the comprehensive system. This finding is in some respects perhaps over-pessimistic in the light of Eggleston's large survey of a number of local education areas in the Midlands, where the rate of staying on beyond the minimum leaving age of fifteen was higher in comprehensive schools than in the tripartite system. Yet even in this survey the increase in the proportions of children staying on was greater amongst children from the middle class than from working-class families.[1] As has so often been the case in Britain, the middle class seem more able and more willing to take advantage of all the increased facilities offered by the various branches of the welfare state.

In the matter of social cohesion Ford found that the children in the comprehensive school showed the same tendency to mix with children of their own social class that was found in the grammar school and the modern school that she investigated. Furthermore, the pupils at the comprehensive school did not appear to learn occupational aspirations that were very different from those learnt in the tripartite schools; the large group of children from the working class expected to enter occupations of low social status, while a small group of children largely from the middle class hoped for careers in the higher reaches of the occupational structure. With continuing divisions of this nature it is hardly surprising that the children in the comprehensive school did not hold a more flexible

[1] S. J. Eggleston, 'Some Environmental Correlates of Extended Secondary Education in England', *Comparative Education*, March 1967.

view of the social class system than those in the grammar school and the modern school.

These findings would perhaps be expected in view of the way in which comprehensive schools are usually organized. Classes are still largely streamed by academic capability, which varies directly with social class. Thus, the cultures of the middle class and the grammar school tend to be recreated in the upper streams of the comprehensive school, whilst those of the working class and the secondary modern school are found in the lower streams. The findings of research in a comprehensive school in Birmingham support this interpretation, since in this school there were variations by stream in attitudes towards religious and racial tolerance and also towards specific school subjects. These differences matched existing social class differences. The upper streams were more tolerant and favoured academic, rather than directly vocational, subjects, whilst the lower streams, which contained a higher proportion of working-class pupils, were less tolerant and more in favour of, for example, work in handicrafts.[1] Again, to use the structural perspective, such positions of responsibility as that of prefect, which should ideally in such a school be open to children of all social classes, seem to be filled largely by those from the middle class,[2] so that the hierarchy of social status outside the school is still in some measure reinforced within the school.

In general, those running the comprehensive schools do not seem to have created one common culture to pass on to all their pupils. As these schools are now usually organized they have tended to recreate the grammar and the modern cultures, in as much as these are identifiable, within the one school. The social background of the children, particularly in relation to sub-cultures of the various social classes, has largely overcome the influence of the school, which has not acted as an agent of social change as was intended.

C. Conclusion

The educational system is structured in such a way that children may pass through a number of possible pathways. In the positions

[1] T. W. G. Miller, *Values in the Comprehensive School*, Edinburgh, 1961.
[2] D. N. Holly, 'Profiting from a Comprehensive School: Class, Sex, and Ability', *British Journal of Sociology*, June 1965.

in the various types of schools there are differing expectations of behaviour for the pupils. These patterns may be seen as cultures clustered around certain central values. This analysis is nearer to reality in the public schools and the primary schools, though in the latter case there are three main versions of the culture. In the tripartite system each type of school seems to contain more than one culture, largely because of the power of the roles connected with social class into which the pupils have been socialized at home, but which they play in a latent fashion at school. Although its aim is to overcome these divisions, the comprehensive school does not seem to have achieved one common culture that is learnt by all its pupils and this seems once again to be due to the power of the family in the process of socialization.

A question may be asked at this point to which no research worker has yet been able to give an answer, namely how much of what a child learns during his socialization may be attributed to the influence of the family, and how much to the school. The next two chapters pose the question of whether the additional influences of the peer group and the mass media must also be considered. However, in a recent report of a longitudinal study, Himmelweit and Swift have begun to show us one way of answering such questions. They studied a group of children at the age of fourteen in four grammar schools and five secondary modern schools in the London area and interviewed this sample again at the age of twenty-five when their education was complete and they had settled into a job. The aim was to examine the nature of the pathways through which various categories of persons had passed and to judge the influence of these routes on the groups of individuals. Their main finding was that the school was a powerful socializing agency that overcame external influences under certain specific conditions, but the irony of their work in the contemporary ideological setting is that these conditions were in a real sense parallel to those provided by the tripartite system. Thus, the schools that could select, rather than merely accept, pupils had the greatest socializing effect. Again, the use of such organizational strategies as streaming could 'offset the poor motivation generated by a family that is little interested in education'.[1] In our present state of knowledge the school, it seems,

[1] H. T. Himmelweit and B. Swift, 'A Model for the Understanding of the

can cause some, but not all, of those that believe in different values and hold different patterns of behaviour, to change, but only when given favourable conditions.

BIBLIOGRAPHY

W. A. L. Blyth, *English Primary Education*, Vols. I and II, London, 1965.

J. Ford, *Social Class and the Comprehensive School*, London, 1969.

D. Hargreaves, *Social Relations in a Secondary School*, London, 1967.

R. King, *Values and Involvement in a Grammar School*, London, 1969.

P. W. Musgrave, *Society and Education in England since 1800*, London, 1968.

W. Taylor, *The Secondary Modern School*, London, 1963.

I. Weinberg, *The English Public Schools*, New York, 1967.

School as a Socializing Agency', in P. H. Mussen, J. Langer and M. Covington (eds.), *Trends and Issues in Developmental Psychology*, New York, 1969, p. 178.

6

The Peer Group

This chapter is concerned solely with the influence of groups of equals upon children and adolescents, though such groups do affect the behaviour of such subsequent age grades as university students or old age pensioners. The actual process of socialization is the same in the peer group as it is in the family or the school and the analysis must, therefore, centre on roles and sanctions. The justification for giving so much space to this topic is that children spend much time both in and out of school hours mixing in groups which have been shown to have considerable influence on their behaviour and attitudes in general, as well as on their capacity for education. In addition, as children grow older they move away from their families and begin to relate more to their peers. Furthermore, in most contemporary societies the time allowed to the young to pass through the stages of preparation for adulthood seems to be lengthening. For an increasing number today the age of starting work has been postponed until at least twenty-one. In this connection Musgrove (1964) has shown that the adolescent was invented by the late eighteenth century. Perhaps the contribution of the late twentieth century has been to complicate the process of socialization further by popularizing the role of the student. This longer preparation for adulthood has become possible largely because of the greater wealth in such societies as the USA, Britain and Australia. However, this same increase has made the influence of peer groups more complex, since affluence allows more choice to the contemporary young than was possible for previous generations. Conflict over the way in which these choices are made is therefore likely between the representatives of older generations, namely parents and teachers, and those moving away from the influence of the family and the school into the ambit of various groups of peers.

A. The Functions of Peer Groups

In the family or at school the child is in a situation of subservience, where power can be exercised over him. In both situations the child is in a heterogeneous age group (Eisenstadt, 1956) where some, by virtue of a position based largely on their age, are more powerful than others. However, a peer group is a homogeneous age group. All the members are of the same or very similar age. Therefore, in such a group a child can gain certain experiences that he cannot possibly have in the normal family, particularly in the small-sized nuclear family usual in contemporary industrialized societies. The experience of mixing with equals is an essential preparation for adult life, since at work or at leisure much time must be spent and many important actions must be undertaken in company with one's peers. He who during adolescence does not master the social skills of mixing with his peers will not be able to lead a normal adult life.

Perhaps the most important set of social roles that cannot be learnt completely within the family are those concerning sex. Young persons may learn something of their sex role if they have one or more siblings of the opposite sex in their families, but they must mix with boys and girls other than their close relations if they are to learn how to treat the opposite sex in the socially approved manner so that they have the social skills needed for courtship and a stable marriage. Despite contemporary changes in the nature of marriage, continuing relationship based on love still seems to be the normally approved system in most Western societies. However, the age of marriage is tending to fall whilst there is a tendency for the time spent at school to lengthen, so that parents and teachers are more likely to come into conflict with adolescents over the matter of their relationship with the opposite sex. It is while amongst their peers and usually away from the control of their elders that adolescent boys and girls can try out the behaviour expected of them towards the opposite sex and move from apparent gaucherie to greater sophistication. They learn how to approach and to talk with those of the opposite sex and how much of themselves to invest emotionally in each other so that they have some chance of becoming more able to make a reasonable choice of marriage partner by early adulthood.

Another important consequence of the existence of peer groups is that the individual learns to achieve and accept status in a group on his own account rather than because of his ascribed position in his family. In a society where social and geographical mobility is common, in taking up a new job or at holiday times, movement away from the family is frequent and individuals must mix with others who do not know them. The social skills involved in 'keeping one's end up', learnt in the peer group, enable the achievement of social ease outside the circle of normal acquaintance.

There are social, as well as individual, functions of peer groups, though these are of familial and political, rather than direct educational, importance. The family, even in the extended form, does not usually provide marriage partners, whereas the peer group mixes those from many family groupings and thereby spreads the possible scope of friendship. This same process, particularly in small-scale societies, facilitates the integration of social systems since the network of those who know each other becomes very complex through mixing in groups at school, church, work and in clubs or societies. An important example of this process is the way in which the old boys' clubs of British and Australian public schools, cross-cutting profession and occupation, political party and often national boundary, help to integrate the upper middle classes within those two countries.

B. The Formation of Adolescent Groups

Some idea of how peer groups develop and change through the period of adolescence may be drawn from two recent reports. In the first Willmott (1966) looked at the life of 279 adolescent boys aged between fourteen and twenty in Bethnal Green (London) during 1964, and in the second Dunphy (1969) examined the structure and formation of adolescent groups, made up of both sexes, in Sydney, NSW, during the period between 1958 and 1960. In both projects the research workers relied rather more on participant observation than on the use of questionnaires and were able to come very close to the teenagers whom they were studying. Dunphy found that in his sample of 303 boys and girls aged thirteen to eighteen there were forty-four 'cliques', containing between three and nine members, but with an average size of 6·2 persons. Similar groups of about five boys were found in Bethnal Green. These cliques were linked into twelve 'crowds' of between fifteen and thirty members, and averaged 20·2 teenagers. 'The crowd (was) essentially an association of cliques', as there were between two and four (average 3·1) cliques per crowd. Only four of the forty-four cliques were not linked with any crowd.

One common misconception is that such crowds are 'gangs'. This was neither the case in Sydney nor in Bethnal Green. Although these cliques and crowds persisted over a number of years, most of the other features usually associated with a gang were absent. There was, for example, no pronounced division of labour within the groups such that roles with specific tasks were allocated to members. There were no signs of warfare over territory or of organized law breaking, although a certain amount of minor law breaking, and especially in Bethnal Green of theft among the younger boys, was a sub-cultural norm. Above all there was no hierarchy; on the contrary the members of the groups saw each other as true equals. However, the larger groups in Bethnal Green and the crowds in Sydney were known by the names of a prominent member, although the members claimed that he was not really a leader. In order to understand his position and function, the life history of the system of cliques and crowds must be described.

During the early teens peer groups are made up entirely of boys or of girls and these small single-sex groups are isolated from one another. At about fifteen, though to specify an exact age is impossible, the members of the single-sex cliques begin to interact with each other and the leaders in each group seem to be the first to intermingle with the opposite sex. There is, therefore, a period during which the isolated single-sex cliques are being transferred into a linked system, the crowd, made up of cliques, now containing both sexes. However, by the late teens the process of disintegration is likely to have begun as the members of the new cliques become engaged or married and tend to drift away from the very loosely organized activities of the crowd.

The crowd is the focus, especially at weekends, for the more organized social activities such as parties or visits in large numbers to beaches or entertainments, whilst the cliques in both Sydney and

Bethnal Green were mainly used by their members for 'hanging around' or for conversation, particularly in weekday evenings, when no activity was organized for the crowd as a whole but when there was the need, normally felt by these adolescents, to be away from their families. Though, as noted above, the members of all these groups claimed that there were no leaders, each group was structured around one member, who was the best known outside the group. In Sydney it was through him that the clique was linked to the crowd. As is usually the case in any type of group, this leader displayed the norms of the group in their clearest form. In Sydney this meant that leaders 'were invariably more advanced in their relationship with the opposite sex than were their fellows'. 'Going steady', for instance, was more common amongst leaders than followers. In Bethnal Green leaders appeared to be the toughest member of the group, though this implied the adoption of a style of bravado rather than the use of physical violence. It is worth noting that members of all these groups had to live up to the norms expected of group members. The reward for such behaviour was acceptance and the punishment for a falling away was exclusion, a severe sanction when an entrée to the culture of the teenage group is as strongly desired as is usually the case today.

Another aspect of leadership in the groups in Sydney might also have been predicted from what is known about the structure of small groups. There were often two leaders, though it is possible that one person could have done the work of both. The one on whom the discussion has so far turned is termed the instrumental leader, and he tends to be responsible for seeing that the group achieves its main purpose. In the case of the Sydney groups this implied the arranging of occasions when boys and girls could meet and in the case of the groups in Bethnal Green the organizing of entertainment or sports, and by sixteen, the age after which in Britain motor cycles may legally be ridden, the organization of group cycle activities.

Though in both studies the adolescents used youth clubs, more attention was given to this aspect by Willmott. At the time of his survey two-fifths of the boys were members of a club, but the greatest incidence was at about sixteen or seventeen, whilst by the age of twenty only one in seven were still members. By that age 90 per cent of the boys had been members of a youth club at some time.

In a large sample representative of Britain, Douglas found that only 16 per cent of the boys and 15 per cent of the girls never joined a club, though there were differences by social class with the lower working-class adolescents showing the lowest percentage, namely 21 for boys and 19 for girls.[1] Although these clubs were run by adults and were criticized as 'strict' by the adolescents in this sample, they did seem to fill the necessary purpose of being 'meeting places' or 'somewhere to go' outside the family. In fact Willmott says that 'every youth club – and for that matter, every Scout Group or Cadet Corps – is really a federation of peer groups'. In other words, the older generation have provided an institution where adolescents may organize 'a crowd'. Ultimately members left these clubs as they grew older and began to go steady, or because they 'lost interest'. In neither case had the clubs failed. They had helped in the process of socialization by easing the transition to adulthood.

C. Some Attributes Influencing Peer Groups

Those who join any group may be expected to conform to the norms of that particular group, but they also play other roles elsewhere in the social structure. There are certain behavioural expectations such as those relating to sex roles that have a very powerful influence on how persons act in whatever social setting they find themselves. These primary roles, as they were called in Chapter 2, are brought from outside the groups and, though apparently latent, may to some extent constrain how an individual acts whilst a member of a group. Clearly, different behaviour is expected from a boy and from a girl as members of the peer groups that have so far been considered in this chapter. Here we shall examine three important latent roles. In addition to the sex role, those concerned with age and social class will be discussed.

1. Age

The older a child grows, the more he seeks group activity outside the family and also the more likely it is that he is influenced by groups that are outside the full control of those in charge of the

[1] J. W. B. Douglas, J. M. Ross and H. R. Simpson, *All Our Future*, London, 1968, p. 101.

school, even though the activities of the group may take place largely within the boundaries of the school. Exact ages are hard to link to types of group structure, but in view of the progression from family-based activity through school to peer group-based activity, age roles will be considered here according to the three broad stages of schooling.

(i) *Pre-schooling.* Very young children tend to play by themselves a great deal and when they start to relate to other children they rarely form groups, but tend to play usually in pairs. Though deep and lasting friendships can be found between pairs of children, temporary pairings seem more common except where the social situation is such that the availability of possible playmates is limited, as may be the case in such remote country areas as the Scottish highlands and islands or the Australian outback. At this age friendships and those small groups of shifting membership that do temporarily exist are based on both sexes. Boys and girls intermingle without thought or restriction. Spontaneous group activity as such is rare with one possible exception. Young children may gang up on one child and temporarily cast him in the role of scapegoat, though even this form of group activity is rare and not very lasting. Children at this age are learning how to behave towards others and hence seem to be experimenting with their relationships towards their peers. Thus, the characteristics of all groups at this early stage are their small scale, impermanence, and cross-sex nature. John is friends with Ian today, Jenny tomorrow and Ian again next week.

(ii) *The Primary Stage.* There is some evidence concerning the nature of groups amongst children as they pass through the primary age range. This is based on a number of studies done in English primary schools (W. A. L. Blyth, 1960). Around the age of seven, peer groups seem to be rather unstructured and still unstable in that membership changes quite substantially even within a school year. There is, however, the beginning of the division that has already been noted into single sex groups. By the age of eight or nine this division is more marked and after nine quite separate groups of boys and girls appear. Boys by this stage will not be seen dead playing with girls and vice versa, and powerful sanctions operate within the peer group so that each sex conforms to the behaviour expected of it. The groups of boys are larger and more closely structured than those of the girls, who have a tendency to form pairs or trios. These small groups of girls are less closely linked together compared with the bigger groups of boys. The latter gather around a leader who may have one or more henchmen. The leader is often the captain of a class team or an able child, so that the informal structure of the class is paralleling the formal structure that has been organized by the teachers. Furthermore, the peer groups in the primary school classroom seem, sometimes unbeknown to the teacher, to be based on relationships made outside the school, at home or in the local neighbourhood. The fact that many children who are in the same class also live close to each other, perhaps regularly going each day from their homes to school together in a group, provides the opportunity for building relatively permanent relationships. Thus, by eleven, when children pass to secondary school, their peer groups seem to have become larger, especially in the case of boys, more permanent and based on one sex only. John is never a friend of Jenny's, but has been a friend of Ian's for a long time.

(iii) *The Secondary Stage.* So far no differentiation has been made amongst the peer groups that have been considered, but recent work by Sugarman[1] makes clear that certainly by the secondary stage different types of peer groups exist within the school. In this study Sugarman interviewed a sample of eighty boys in the fourth form who were drawn from a grammar, two modern and a comprehensive school in the London area. No evidence was found even in the grammar school to show that prestige was given for academic success. Groups formed around different activities to which status was given within each category of group. The peer groups found amongst these adolescent boys could be divided into three categories. There were, firstly, those based on playing games in the school playground. In these groups the norms centred on the rules of the games and on being a 'good sport'. The sanctions used against deviants were, for example, rough play, refusing to pass the ball to them, or even leaving them out of the teams. Secondly, there were those groups who just talked. Topics were very varied, but sport and television were common subjects and some groups focused on such specific interests as motor cycles or pop music. Evidence will be

[1] B. Sugarman, 'Social Norms in Teenage Boys' Peer Groups', *Human Relations*, February 1968, espec. pp. 54–5.

cited in the next chapter to show that sometimes each peer group may specialize by favouring one type of music or one pop star, and sanctions are used to ensure that all members are followers of the speciality of their chosen peer group. In general, however, these groups of talkers tend to generate very specific systems of norms and sanctions that relate to their own particular interests. Thirdly, there were groups of 'hard boys'. Status was gained, as Hargreaves also found in a Lancashire secondary modern school amongst boys of this same age in the study that was noted in the last chapter, by being successful in fights.

These findings reported by Sugarman make it seem likely that peer groups in secondary schools centre on interests and hobbies which by this stage of adolescence are starting to be relatively specialized. How true this generalization is for groups outside the school is uncertain, mainly because, as Sugarman himself has shown in other work relating to the same study, teenagers in general have a high level of commitment to a mass youth culture based on pop music, fashion, dancing and coffee bars. Furthermore, the higher the commitment to the teenage role, the lower seems to be an adolescent's commitment to the role of pupil that is associated with the school.[1] Whilst at secondary school, John might be in a group with Ian that was based on a common interest that was probably totally unconnected with school, and out of school he and John might well meet Jenny and another girl to play some part in the teenage scene. In sum, the very fact that children grow older has clear implications for their behaviour in peer groups. For example, as they become more confident of their ability to choose friends, their groups become more permanent and more structured. In addition, as their interests become more stable, groups in school seem to become differentiated, specialist, and less centred on the school, although outside the school the power of the teenage culture may well have a homogenizing effect. However, clearly the changing nature of the sex roles is a powerful latent influence and must be given further consideration.

[1] B. Sugarman, 'Youth Culture, Academic Achievement and Conformity in School', *British Journal of Sociology*, June 1967.

2. Sex

As boys and girls grow towards adult status, their sex roles increasingly govern the nature and activities of their peer groups. In earlier years Blyth's results indicate that in the primary stage girls form smaller and less structured groups than boys do. In the USA, Coleman (1961) has reported similar findings for the secondary stage, since girls in high schools were members of small cliques more often than boys. They also seemed to have more intense friendships than did the boys. In addition, girls in the American high school conformed more readily to school and local norms than did boys.

It is when examining groups outside school that a crucial difference between the sexes appears. Boys and girls by the late primary stage have developed different leisure patterns that relate closely to their sex roles. Thus, boys are coming to centre their interests on sports and mechanical things, whilst girls are switching to sewing, knitting and cooking. Even where both sexes are interested in the same area, differences may emerge. Thus in unpublished evidence gathered in Aberdeen, twelve-year-old boys and girls were both keen on sport, but for boys this meant football and for girls swimming. The criteria for entry to the peer groups of each sex would, therefore, seem to be different. Furthermore, boys and girls use the groups of which they are members in different ways. In a study carried out in Sydney in the mid-1950s boys took an 'active delight in companionship'; they put the stress on being with their friends. Girls, however, wanted to be with their friends in order to tell each other about themselves. They talked of 'my dresses' or 'my school work'.[1] When the two sexes joined together in mixed groups, Dunphy noted that it was a boy who took the role of instrumental leader. Likewise in Bethnal Green, girls are 'picked up' or 'dated'; the boys must be seen to take the initiative. In general, as is only to be expected, peer groups reflect the social scene in which they exist, so that they are influenced throughout adolescence by the gradual development of the sex roles. More particularly, mixed groups reflect the inferior status of women compared with men in contemporary Western society.

[1] W. F. Connell, E. P. Francis and E. Skilbeck, *Growing up in an Australian City*, Melbourne, 1957.

3. *Social Class*

The influence of the latent role of social class on peer group structure and activities seems to have been little studied as such, though hypotheses about its effects are made. Thus, for example, Eggleston has shown that in various types of comprehensive school adolescents of both middle- and working-class backgrounds, but especially the former, stay on longer than at secondary modern schools, and has attributed this to the influence of peer groups rather than to the teachers concerned. The pupils more clearly see the advantages of the mainly middle-class habit of staying on and discuss this amongst themselves with the result that the 'sympathetic leaving' characteristic of the modern school is translated into sympathetic staying on in the comprehensive school. Eggleston therefore suggests structuring schools by, for example, providing common rooms so that the influence of peer groups may work more easily.[1]

Outside the school the power of the youth culture is such that since adolescents of differing social classes appear in some respects to have very similar interests,[2] peer groups will have rather similar activities when one considers the teenage scene, though perhaps in rather different settings because of the greater resources available to middle-class, compared with working-class, teenagers. Douglas did, however, find quite considerable differences in the hobbies of the adolescents in his sample. Thus, 36 per cent of upper middle-class boys as opposed to 16 per cent of those from the lower working class had academic hobbies; the situation for girls was very similar. Again, 28 per cent of upper middle-class boys, but 52 per cent of lower working-class boys were interested only in sports; the results for girls did not show a difference by social class.[3] However, many hobbies are practised as individuals or with close friends rather than in peer groups.

Just as much expected behaviour may differ by social class, so may misbehaviour, and the very different social situations of the social classes do seem to allow differing types of delinquency.

[1] S. J. Eggleston, 'Some Environmental Correlates of Extended Secondary Education in England', *Comparative Education*, March 1967, pp. 95–6.

[2] See, for example, *Enquiry I: Young School Leavers* (Schools Council), London, 1968, Ch. 3, espec. pp. 173–7.

[3] J. W. B. Douglas, J. M. Ross and H. R. Simpson, *op. cit.*, p. 102.

Willmott indicates that stealing and pilfering are quite usual activities in Bethnal Green, a working-class area, though adolescents are fully aware that this behaviour is seen to be wrong by those with authority. Middle-class adolescent delinquency seems, in contrast, to centre on drugs which tend to be expensive, and, perhaps, crimes associated with such political activities as 'sit-ins' or 'demonstrations'.

By the stage of adolescence it may well be that the social class of aspiration rather than that of origin largely influences behaviour. Willmott divides his sample into three groups: the 'middle class', the 'working class' and the 'rebels'. Each group had very different attitudes, learnt at home and at school, which governed their response to their environment and particularly the sort of life to which they aspired. Members of each category seemed to have a different style of leisure activity. Those with middle-class aspirations had a best friend who more often lived outside Bethnal Green, visited the West End more often and expected to marry later than those in the other two categories. The 'rebels' had low occupational aspirations, related more closely to the local area, and were more approving than the other adolescents of fighting.

Though the ways in which social class as such influences peer groups has not yet been studied in detail, by drawing on related studies we can see that there does appear to be some effect and that possibly we should give more attention as adolescents grow nearer to adulthood to the social class to which they aspire rather than that from which they are drawn.

D. The Power of the Peer Group

At the end of the last chapter the question had to be posed of whether the school or the family was the more powerful agency of socialization. Few findings from research were available to answer that problem. In the same way we must now consider the power of the peer group in relation to, firstly, the school and, secondly, the family. There are no sophisticated studies of a statistical nature to help us come to an exact answer. There is, however, in each case, some relevant and illuminating research that at least allows us to make a reasoned judgement.

1. *The School*

The very famous study of the American high school by Coleman (1961) has shown a situation where the system of peer groups almost dominates the school. In the sample of ten high schools that he investigated there were four sub-cultures named by Coleman, namely the fun, the academic, the vocational and the delinquent sub-cultures. The names largely explain the characteristics of each. The majority of pupils were members of the first culture, which was based on their participation through peer groups in the wide range of extracurricular facilities available at the American high school, and in the many leisure time activities outside school hours that were arranged whilst at school. The pupils came to school mainly to meet their friends and to arrange future fun at parties or on dates in the evenings or at weekends rather than to participate in academic or vocationally relevant learning. All this activity was closely related to peer groups of one kind or another, though this was less the case in country areas where adolescents had not so clearly broken away from parental control than in the urban high schools. The school had not been established with this aim in mind, nor did the teachers see this as either the purpose for which they were employed or the result of their daily teaching. But for the pupils the school was a place where one went to participate in groups dedicated to fun. These adolescents had imported the youth culture of the peer group into the school and it had largely taken the place of the official academic or vocational cultures.

These rather extreme findings must, however, be set against the British evidence already cited in the last chapter from the studies carried out by Hargreaves and King. In each case the schools that they studied were partially successful in that they either transmitted some of their values to some of their pupils or else supported and reinforced the values of the families from which some of their pupils came. In the latter case, even those who left the grammar school early did gain some academic success at 'O' level, presumably an achievement that the teachers wished for their pupils. In the former case, the boys in the 'A' stream of the secondary modern school behaved and studied largely as the staff wished, even though those in the 'D' stream were apparently little influenced in the direction in which the school hoped.

The examples so far quoted relate to the secondary age range and it is clear that the peer group is more influential amongst older children. Furthermore, in general most attention has been given in the research so far carried out to those peer groups that are opposed to the values of the school. Little attention has been given to those that must exist that are neutral, neither helping nor hindering the school, or that reinforce the lessons that the school is trying to transmit. Since we have seen that whether or not the school is successful in its aims is much dependent upon the family background of the pupils concerned, we may suspect that the type of peer group that an adolescent joins and how much it influences him for or against the school will also largely be rooted in his family circumstances.

2. The Family

According to Musgrove (1966) the family is so powerful a social influence that the school can avail little. Indeed almost the only way in which the school could succeed in its aims would be for the child to be removed from the family and entrusted totally to the school. There is a less strong version of the thesis that the family is all powerful which claims that despite the immense power of the youth culture and the peer group the family as a social institution ultimately reasserts itself (R. Hoggart, 1956). The argument runs this way. At adolescence children, particularly amongst the working class, move away from their families and come under the influence of the youth culture, especially within the peer groups of which they are members, for the reasons and with the consequences outlined earlier in this chapter. There follows a period aptly named by Klein as 'the splash',[1] when the adolescent or young adult is freer of what may be termed primary social responsibilities than he was before or ever will be again. This freedom ends possibly with marriage, but certainly with the birth of a first child, by which time the young adult has completed the socially essential move from his family of origin to his own family of procreation. The constraints of building a new home and family are such that young parents are compelled because of shortage of both money and spare time to leave the constantly changing peer culture and to submit to the timeless and relatively

[1] V. Klein, Samples from English Cultures, Vol. I, London, 1965, pp. 193–6.

unchanging demands of the roles implicit in membership of a family. In this way behaviour associated with the youth culture and expected of the peer group is replaced by the behaviour traditionally expected of young adults and parents in the social class and region concerned.

Even when the period of 'the splash' is considered more closely, Musgrove (1966) has provided evidence that seems to make the revolt of adolescents against parents something of a myth. He administered a sentence completion test on the expectations and the satisfactions gained in the home of a sample of 250 young persons aged fourteen to eighteen, who were members of youth clubs in the northeast of England and were of mixed IQ and social class. Both expectations and satisfactions were categorized as either instrumental, that is relating to the completion of tasks, or expressive, that is concerned with the emotions. 77·2 per cent of expectations and 72·3 per cent of satisfactions were found to be expressive. These young people did, however, put some important instrumental demands upon their families. For example, they felt that moral training, character development, some social skills and some forms of intellectual enlightenment should rightly be in the hands of their parents. Boys had a higher proportion of instrumental expectations and satisfactions than had girls. In some of the detailed categories of expectations and satisfactions the situation was not so clear cut. Thus demands for emotional security were largely met, but those for freedom and self-satisfaction less so. Though we do not know how the sample rated the importance of the various expectations and satisfactions, it seems that their hopes of their homes were largely satisfied. As Willmott noted, home was home till you married. Few, certainly of the working class, moved away to flats or digs, though this sample were out on four of the seven evenings of each week, and when they were in, television was the focus of family activity.

Elsewhere, Musgrove (1964) examined the relationship between adults and teenagers. In various samples drawn from adults and from boys and girls, aged between eleven and fifteen, in the Midlands he found that hostility towards adults was highest amongst boys at fifteen and girls at fourteen, but was apparently not so high in England as in the USA. However, adults expressed greater disapproval of adolescents than did adolescents of adults, though the adolescents were aged only up to fifteen whereas the adults were asked to comment on 'teenagers' in general. Yet, there is a real possibility that parents may wrongly perceive the views of their teenage children about their families and themselves. Apparently despite the power of, and indeed necessity for, the contemporary peer group, the family may still influence adolescents more than their parents feel or know, though one would want much more evidence upon which to build such a judgement with certainty.

E. Conclusion

Peer groups clearly play a definite part in the socialization process, but where a powerful youth culture supported by commercial interests exists, sanctions seem to be so strong for the adolescent to conform that the peer group can become a vehicle for teaching behavioural expectations that go against the aims of the family and the school. Yet there is evidence that contemporary adults wrongly perceive the opinions of adolescents who themselves may have more use for and satisfaction in their families than their parents think to be the case. After 'the splash' the responsibilities of marriage and parenthood seem to constrain former teenagers to take the traditional roles associated with the family much as their parents did before them, and much of the ability to do so was learnt previously in the peer groups of which they were members during childhood and adolescence.

BIBLIOGRAPHY

W. A. L. Blyth, 'The Sociometric Study of Children's Groups in English Schools', *British Journal of Educational Studies*, May 1960.

J. S. Coleman, *The Adolescent Society*, New York, 1961.

D. C. Dunphy, *Cliques, Crowds and Gangs*, Melbourne, 1969.

S. N. Eisenstadt, *From Generation to Generation*, London, 1956.

R. Hoggart, *The Uses of Literacy*, London, 1956 (Pelican).

F. Musgrove, *Youth and the Social Order*, London, 1964.

F. Musgrove, *The Family, Education and Society*, London, 1966.

P. Willmott, *Adolescent Boys of East London*, London, 1966 (Pelican).

7

Children and the Mass Media

The nature of mass communications is seen by some as determined purely by their technical characteristics, for instance, their dependence upon certain electronic developments or upon their ability to reach all groups in a population uniformly. This is not an incorrect, but an incomplete, view. In this chapter some brief attention will be paid to the technical differences of the various media, but the main focus will be upon 'mass', not upon 'media'. The mass may be seen as a national audience that can be described as heterogeneous, anonymous, spatially separate and unorganized, but it can also be divided into local audiences, which consist of groups of individuals organized by norms that, amongst other things, govern how they view the so-called mass media.[1]

There has been much research done in the field of mass communications by psychologists, but little sociological work has been carried out on the influence of mass media, especially in Britain (D. McQuail, 1969). Recently, however, a growing concern about how television affects children has brought about an increase in British research on this medium. The focus here will be on what part the media, especially television, play in the socialization of children. This way of phrasing the aim of the chapter allows the examination of both how children are affected and what use they make of the media. To order the findings that are reported, we shall bear in mind the question that the political scientist, Lasswell, asked in the late 1940s: 'Who says What in Which Channel to Whom with What Effect?'

[1] E. Friedson, 'Communications Research and the Concept of the Mass', *American Sociological Review*, June 1953.

A. Role Models

The imitation of a role model by a child entails an influence by someone in a certain direction. Therefore, by considering what role models are offered by and chosen from the media an answer to Lasswell's 'Who?' and 'What?' is implied. The mass media of television, film and comics offer to contemporary children a great variety of role models who offer styles of life to children and with whom they may identify. In a study made in 1967 in Aberdeen, in character still rather a traditional city, children of twelve were asked in relation to various media, 'If you were not yourself, who would you like to be for a week or so, now?' When asked about persons in television, 81 per cent of the boys and 48 per cent of the girls made a choice, and in connection with film and radio the figures were respectively for boys 70 and 42 and for girls 45 and 13 per cent.[1] Most of these children were choosing role models from amongst the offerings made by the media. What influences govern how such choices are made?

1. *Parental Influences*

In Aberdeen the proportion of mothers who claimed to forbid the watching of any specific television programmes by their children aged about twelve was found to be 47 per cent. The proportion who encouraged the watching of any programme amongst their sons and daughters was 40 per cent. These figures were to all intents and purposes the same for both boys and girls, and in addition there were very slight differences between the social classes. There are no comparable findings against which these may be judged, but the apparent degree of formal control by parents over the use of this medium seems low. Furthermore, except for a slight tendency for those children who claimed to watch television 'not much at all' to have mothers making the same claim on behalf of themselves and their husbands, there was no tendency for children to follow their parents' example either in the amount that they claimed to watch or in the types of programme that they liked or disliked. Thus these parents also seemed to exercise very little informal control over their

[1] P. W. Musgrave and G. R. B. Reid, 'Some Measures of Children's Values', *Social Sciences Information*, February 1971.

children's viewing habits.[1] These results parallel those reported much earlier by Himmelweit, Oppenheim and Vince (1958), who carried out a large-scale survey in London and four other large English cities in the mid 1950s, using samples of children aged ten to eleven, and thirteen to fourteen, in order to discover what effects television had on children. Few parents, and this also applied to those parents who were teachers, claimed to direct their children's viewing.

This lack of control seems to be set in a situation which, contrary to many popular views, is characterized by a conscious choice of programmes and between channels. About half the families surveyed in Aberdeen claimed to be choosing what they viewed rather than watching regardless of what was on. It would seem from evidence gathered in Ottawa that the position occupied in the family is an important determinant of who chooses what is viewed. Parents were more often successful in viewing what they wanted when their choice differed from that of their children, but children gained their choices more often in larger families and where they were adolescent rather than younger. In addition, families only viewed together when they had a common interest in a programme.[2] Such results support neither the myth of whole families unthinkingly watching whatever is offered, nor the view that parents govern the viewing habits of their children.

2. Cultural Influences

If parents do not have a direct influence on the tastes of their children for the media, perhaps teachers may. Unfortunately there is little evidence on this point. However, the hypothesis may at least be advanced that cultural norms, which are largely learnt in the family, will have some effect. In a relevant study done in the 1950s in the USA, Zajonc tried to induce children, aged nine to thirteen, to identify with a hero in the American culture who was not rewarded. He played two radio scripts to them about a trip to Mars on a space ship. In one, the leader, 'Buddy', was approachable and friendly,

---

[1] P. W. Musgrave, 'How Children Use Television', *New Society*, 20 February 1969.

[2] B. Ward, 'Television Viewing and Family Choice Differences', *Public Opinion Quarterly*, Spring 1968.

whilst in the other 'Rocky' was more distant and authoritarian. Both were successful after crises. Though some of the children identified with 'Rocky', perhaps only temporarily, the majority identified with 'Buddy', the type of leader that was approved by the culture.[1] Yet success is clearly a powerful source of identification in many cultures and this raises the question of whether children will identify with, for instance, a successful criminal. Certainly in many films, broadcasts and stories in comics there is no positive teaching that crime does not pay, but apparently many children know the culturally determined rewards and punishments that have been applied to them in the past, and seem to apply the standards implied to the choice of heroes with whom they identify. Thus, when considering television, cinema and radio, boys in Aberdeen more often chose sportsmen or aggressive heroes as role models, whilst though some girls also chose aggressive heroes, they tended consistently more often than the boys to choose pop stars.[2] The cultural norms that seem to be at work here are those connected with sex roles as defined by peer groups and the youth culture.

3. Group Membership

Powerful sanctions operate on adolescents from the peer groups of which they are, or hope to be, members in support of the various forms of behaviour approved by these groups, whether this relates to, for example, dress or television programmes or moral behaviour. In Aberdeen children of twelve claimed to watch programmes characteristically different from their parents. The children, already apparently influenced by the predominant youth culture, favoured programmes about pop music and aggressive heroes, whilst their parents preferred plays and serials.

One way of discovering how much influence membership of a group has on a child's consumption of the media is to compare children who are members of groups with those who are more isolated from their peers. Himmelweit divided her samples into three

[1] R. J. Zajonc, 'Some Effects of Space Serials', *Public Opinion Quarterly*, Winter 1954.

[2] P. W. Musgrave and G. R. B. Reid, *op. cit.* This interpretation is also supported by J. D. Halloran, R. L. Brown and D. C. Chaney, *Television and Delinquency*, Leicester, 1970, p. 165.

equal parts according to how much television they watched. The third that watched most, and it contained approximately equal numbers of boys and girls, were termed 'TV addicts'. In this group there was a predominance of insecure children who had difficulties making friends and consumed all media heavily. There appeared to be a feed-back mechanism at work. The already existing insecurity led to addiction and, thence, to less outside contacts, which in turn increased insecurity and further withdrawal. At the very least, the media had a greater chance of influencing these children. Work in the USA by Riley and Flowerman supports this view about isolates. They found that those who were isolates differed in their habits concerning media and in the uses to which they put various media. Adolescents who did not associate closely with their peers interpreted any programme that they saw in a different way from those of their peers who saw it. Furthermore, these isolated children tended to be more adult in their tastes than those who were members of a peer group.[1]

In the last chapter we noted that there were different types of peer groups which displayed different norms. The expectation would therefore be that different peer groups might have different styles of using media. Thus, Hargreaves reported that in the secondary modern school in Lancashire that he studied the higher streams read more and were more often members of organized youth clubs compared with those in the lower streams, who tended to watch television more, go to more films, prefer long-haired pop groups and to be members of unorganized clubs. One American study has shown that for acceptance in the youth culture some degree of conformity to the usage of media by the group to which one aspires is a necessity. Sanctions are used to ensure that the members of any group assent to the norms implicit in membership. Thus a manner of using the media is implied in becoming a member of a group and the media are intricately tied up with experiences undergone at the hands of various groups within which socialization occurs. Each group in a sense determines the content which must be learnt, and to which sanctions will be applied.

The different types of media used by the adolescents in this

[1] M. R. Riley and S. H. Flowerman, 'Group Relations as a Variable in Communication Research', *American Sociological Review*, April 1951.

American sample could be grouped into two categories. The first covered media that were relatively closely concerned with their own day-to-day experience, for example, programmes of pop music, and the second related to material that was not so closely linked with their everyday experience, for instance, the news. This latter type of programme was more used by the isolates than by those in groups, whereas the first category was more often watched by those in peer groups who were, therefore, well integrated into the youth culture. In other words, specialized tastes in the media function as symbols of status attached to particular positions in adolescent society and hence can be seen as influential points of reference for those who aspire to such positions. Furthermore, this principle is not only applicable at this general level, but applies to specific groups, since individual groups seemed to use different pop stars or styles of music as their focus. All those who wanted to be members of a group had to comply in following the norms of that particular group.[1]

There is, however, one point that is worth making and that is often forgotten in the almost universally critical remarks that are made about the influence of the media on children. Despite the easy availability of the media to contemporary children there continues to exist a culture of childhood that has changed but little within living memory and seems in the main untouched by the media. This exists amongst groups of young children and is made up of games, songs often of a robustly profane nature, rhymes and riddles.[2] Children, urban more so than rural, have a wide knowledge of this folk lore of childhood, which clearly is transmitted to them by other children rather than by their parents, many of whom would have felt much of it to be vulgar. Here there seems to exist an underground culture of childhood, located in peer groups of pre-school and primary aged children, into which our children are socialized despite family, school and media.

In one way the part that the media play in the life of the peer group may increase the conflict between an adolescent and his family. Today immense efforts are made by advertisers to increase the de-

---

[1] J. W. C. Johnstone, *Social Structure and Patterns of Mass Media Consumption*, unpublished Ph.D. thesis, Chicago, 1961.

[2] I. and P. Opie, *The Lore and Language of Schoolchildren*, London, 1959; for Australia see I. A. H. Turner, *Cinderella Dressed in Yella*, Melbourne, 1969.

mand for many consumer goods. Because their financial resources are limited, teenagers are unable to consume as conspicuously as they are encouraged to do by commercial advertisements in all the media, but they are often exposed to strong pressures as members of their families to behave in a more realistic manner. Conversation in the peer groups could, therefore, have a positive effect in directing attention to role models whose imitation could be beyond the means of a young person, whilst the family is trying to damp down unrealistic material aspirations.

In brief, the 'who' and the 'what' of Lasswell's question can be conceptualized in terms of the role models which the various mass media provide and with which children may identify, or may even imitate. Though the broad cultural norms learnt at home have some influence on the models that are taken the main constraint that determines which models are adopted, particularly in adolescence, seems to be the norms of the peer groups to which any adolescent aspires. King showed in his study of a grammar school that teachers have strong, though largely unfulfilled, views about which programmes their pupils should watch and what they should read. This is possibly particularly the case with teachers of English and music, who often hope to influence the use by their pupils of the media. Clearly, any teachers attempting to change the habits of children in this respect cannot afford to forget the nature of the social setting in which their pupils are, and which has been shown here to be a strong influence on the use by adolescents of the mass media.

B. Channels

In his question quoted at the start of this chapter Lasswell drew attention to the existence of channels through which messages pass to various recipients. The messages with which we are here concerned may be the transmission of the values and attitudes implied in identifying with a role model, or of a straightforward piece of information. In relation to the mass media channels lead to persons and, therefore, at this point we shall simultaneously consider the words 'to whom' in Lasswell's question. Here channels will be considered in three ways. Firstly, and most simply, there are the various forms of mass media. Secondly, messages often pass indirectly from the sender to the receiver in a step-like manner through various intermediaries; this process of transmission is not wholly mechanical, but influential intermediaries intervene to direct the pathway of the message through the social system to its destination. Finally, a similar emphasis can be put upon the social nature of the channels, but aggregates with differing characteristics may be stressed; the perception of messages varies for those playing certain important social roles, for example, those connected with age, sex, intelligence and social class.

1. *The Various Media*

The various media each have their own technical characteristics. These may, however, be divided into two main categories, those that depend upon print and those that do not. In the latter group are included film and the media of radio and television. These two electronic media are nearly always available for direct reception in the home and, in addition, television has great visual appeal. Film has something of the same characteristics, but to view it one must leave the home. The printed mass media differ in the reliance that they put upon the visual with books giving least and comics most space to pictures.

In addition to technical differences each medium has certain norms that are peculiar to it and which must be learnt. An obvious example is the use of bubbles containing speech in comics. A more complex case is that of the Westerns originally shown on film, but now common on television. The convention is such that the shooting of the bad man, usually after an exciting hunt, is expected and devotees do not see it as a violent or disturbing incident, whereas, as Himmelweit showed, certain other violence, such as fighting on the floor, can cause anxiety in children. In Westerns, anxiety diminishes as the conventions are learnt, and one wonders if a similar process is now at work to lessen amongst children the anxiety that adults perceive them to feel when viewing programmes about aggressive heroes. In all media, children must learn what has been called *adult discount*.[1] Through experience the young gradually become able to see plots as a whole so that they are more able to predict or anticipate what is to

[1] E. Friedson, 'Adult Discount: An Aspect of Children's Changing Taste', *Child Development*, March 1953.

come, thereby reducing the possibility of anxiety occasioned by seeing the unexpected. Again, they grow used to distinguishing between dramatic experience and reality so that they can remain aloof from what they are watching or reading with the result that less anxiety is created.

Because of its visual attractiveness, television competes strongly with other media. Himmelweit found that after the introduction of television, children initially read less, especially in the cases of boys and those with a low IQ. After a few years of experience of television the amount of reading returned to its original level, though the lower level of reading in the case of comics became permanent. New interests also seemed to have developed in the area of non-fiction. The comics and television, though one is in the print and the other in the non-print category, were both apparently visual enough in character to gratify similar interests in children, whereas books to a great extent competed with television. There is little research on children's reading of books, but it appears that girls read more than boys, who in their turn read more non-fiction and adventure stories than girls, the latter preferring animal stories.[1]

Media are clearly in competition with one another for a restricted period of leisure time, though there is one exception to this generalization. Because radio has the specific characteristic that it can be used as a background to other activities, the specialist provision of music apt for this purpose has been developed as a major function, though short news bulletins and sports commentaries provide other uses to which it may be put. Clearly, the different media, largely because of technical characteristics, are used in different ways by children, and hence different types of message are passed through each medium.

2. The Two-Step Flow

The route of any message from a medium to its reception is frequently influenced by the suggestion of someone in the recipient's social circle. Katz and Lazarsfeld (1955) discovered, in an influential study carried out in the USA in the early 1950s, that in any community there appears to be a number of specialized leaders of opinion who

[1] See e.g. E. Lawrence, 'Children's Tastes in Reading', *National Froebel Federation Bulletin*, April 1964.

have much personal influence over the direction that messages from the media flow in any local community. These leaders are found at a quite specific local level amongst small groups of acquaintances. In their study, if individuals wished to discover what film was good, what new book to read or what fashion to wear, they knew in each particular case whom to consult amongst their friends and on each topic there was a specialist leader of opinion in that field.

An opinion leader can serve as the initiator of ideas, as when by chance or design a leader in the local fashion field wears some garment in a slightly different manner from formerly; or he may diffuse an idea culled from outside the circle within which he is a leader, as when 'the reader' in a teenage group recommends a new comic to his peers; or, finally, he may sanction the use of a medium, as when a teacher asks his class to watch a play on television so that he may use it in an English lesson. Next to nothing is known from research about the manner in which this process of 'the two-step flow' operates amongst children, but from observation one would predict that there will be specialized leaders of opinion in each medium amongst children in much the same way as Katz and Lazarsfeld found was the case amongst adults. This would seem to be particularly likely amongst adolescents who grant high status to those who are up-to-date in the rapidly changing teenage world.

3. *Intervening Roles*
The main focus will be put on the important primary roles that children bring to the settings in which they are using the mass media. These roles can be said to intervene between the medium and potential recipients, thereby influencing which messages are received.
(i) *Age*. In a study made in the USA and Canada that was in many respects a replication of Himmelweit's earlier work, Schramm, Lyle and Parker (1961) asked about the number of hours per day that children in the age range from seven to seventeen watched television. The peak was around thirteen, but the time given to this activity was higher in the USA than in England. Himmelweit found the average in her English sample was around two hours per day. However, there is an important point to notice in the way that age influences the pattern of usage of the media. Although television now

T S E—E

tends to be the most regularly used medium throughout childhood and adolescence, the other media may be substituted for one another according to the age being considered. Thus, obviously adult programmes will be watched more often as children grow older, but also by the age of about fourteen television is apparently less of an attraction, because of the need to meet friends away from home, and this is a particularly strong need when the adolescent begins to go out with partners of the opposite sex. For this reason, at adolescence the cinema takes over in some respects from television. It should be noted that, though children go to the cinema at an earlier age, they do so to seek entertainment, whereas by adolescence they are using the same medium, the film, to provide an opportunity for courting. Both the emphasis given to and the uses of any medium can change with children's age.

(ii) *Sex*. Himmelweit showed that girls react to many forms of mass communication in a different way to boys. Their role in our society implies a greater interest in people, dress and social settings, so that they tend to form a more responsive audience for many programmes and in particular seem more disturbed by those plays for adults that are marked by anxiety. Himmelweit suggested that this may be due to the comparative absence on television of positive role models with whom girls can identify. Heroines tend to have an unhappy lot. This view is supported by evidence from the sample of twelve-year-olds in Aberdeen. The boys almost never chose a role model of the opposite sex, whereas about a third of those girls who named a role model on television or film made cross-sex choices.[1] The proportion of girls making cross-sex choices for radio was about twice as high as for the other two media, possibly due to the greater availability of such models as male disc jockeys on the radio.

Though Himmelweit found that adult crime serials were as popular with girls as boys, there are data, both from Aberdeen and from work done in the Midlands, to show that girls tend to prefer programmes about pop music and pop stars rather than those concerned with aggressive heroes. There is similar evidence from the USA relating to the reading of comics. In a study of fifth and sixth grade children carried out in Boston (Mass.) boys were found to be more exposed to comics and seemed to favour aggressive heroes more

[1] P. W. Musgrave and G. R. B. Reid, *op. cit.*

than girls.[1] The sex role, into which children are socialized very soon in their lives, seems to exercise an early and a powerful influence on the selection of messages from the media by children.

(iii) *Intelligence*. Intelligence has rarely been taken into account in studies of the uses and effects of the media. In Aberdeen differences between the two sexes and even between the social classes were more pronounced than those between intelligence levels. However, this may have been due to the particular topics studied, since Himmelweit noted very definite differences of usage in her sample between levels of intelligence as measured by IQ tests and these variations remained even when allowances were made for the different educational experiences undergone by children of a similar level of IQ in grammar or modern schools. For example, less intelligent children tended to view more, yet the differences between the groups with an IQ over 115 and those with an IQ between 100 and 114 were more marked than those between this latter group and the children whose IQ was below 100. In this situation it is not surprising that, in a detailed study of one primary school, there was a rise in the percentage of children choosing figures from television as being the famous figure that they would like to be as one passed from the 'A' to the 'C' stream.[2] Himmelweit suggested that it is a mistake to over-generalize about the effect of intelligence since the mental age at which children are most responsive may vary from topic to topic. For example, the maximum increase attributable to watching television in the field of general knowledge occurred for children who had a mental age of ten and below. It could be that children of different mental ages view each medium and the various areas of interest affected by the media in a somewhat different way.

(iv) *Social Class*. In the case of children aged ten to eleven, Himmelweit found differences between the social classes in the amount of viewing that was done; children from the working class viewed more than those from the middle class. In Aberdeen such a variation did not exist for twelve-year-olds, and in Himmelweit's sample the

---

[1] J. D. Halloran, R. L. Brown and D. C. Chaney, *op. cit.*; L. Bailyn, 'Mass Media and Children: A Study of Exposure Habits and Cognitive Effects', *Psychological Monographs*, 1959.

[2] B. Jackson, *Streaming: An Educational System in Miniature*, London, 1964, p. 69.

differences had disappeared by thirteen to fourteen. Seemingly the control exercised by middle-class families grows less close, more particularly in relation to television, by the time of adolescence. From research done by Wilensky (1964) in the USA the following proposition about the effects of social class can be advanced, that certain cultural norms that vary with social class influence the way the media are used. In other words, attention must be given not to the aggregates called social classes, but to the underlying nature of social class differences. A specific example concerns attitudes to education and more particularly the age at which children should cease full-time education. This is higher for those in, or for those aspiring to, the middle class. Thus, those who go to college or university in the USA seem to have a different view of television, radio and books from those with a lower educational aspiration and attainment. Their style of life includes a component governing their use of leisure, and hence, of how they use and feel about the media.

If education influences styles of leisure in this way, social class of destination and, in the case of children, of aspiration may be, particularly by adolescence, as important a determinant of the usage of media as social class of origin. Thus in a study of adolescents aged fourteen to sixteen in three Leicestershire secondary schools, the ways in which pop music was used suggested that 'involvement in the teen culture (was) more a function of where youngsters are headed in the social structure than where they have come from in terms of parental status'.[1] Wilensky noted that even a good average level of education appears to do little to cultivate a taste in reading and in the media very different from that of the majority. What counts is whether one completes college and especially whether one goes through one of a few favoured colleges. In his sample of 1,354 Wilensky found only 19 'media purists', of whom 16 were professors and 3 prosperous company lawyers. They used no television and read only highbrow papers, magazines or books. From this example it seems clear that a style of using the media is associated, not so much with social class aggregates, as with a pattern of life

[1] R. L. Brown and M. O'Leary, 'Pop Music in an English Secondary School System', *American Behavioural Scientist*, January/February 1970, p. 411.

implicit in certain types of job and the educational provision needed for them.

Similar cultural influences were seen to be operating on the working class in an English study of the uses of television by delinquents. In this research three groups were compared, consisting respectively of delinquents, a matched sample of non-delinquents and a sample of the lower middle class drawn from the same areas in the Midlands as the other two groups. In the majority of the comparisons it was the third group that stood out as different from the sample of delinquents and the controls, both of which were essentially working class in character. The similarities in their uses of television could best be understood by remembering that in the working-class culture, amongst other things, an emphasis is put upon masculinity, toughness and excitement, so that the stress, particularly by boys, on aggressive heroes may be seen in part as the gratification of working-class cultural norms.[1]

In considering the influence of social class, once again the conclusion must be that whenever examining the uses and effects of the media the social setting must be taken into account. Various channels exist, whether one conceptualizes these as the technically determined channels provided by the different forms of the media, or the socially determined pathways provided by opinion leaders, or the latent roles played when a potential audience is exposed to the media. Though the former way of thinking about media is important, yet it is the latter, where the emphasis is put on social channels to different recipients, that is the real sociological contribution to assessing how children, or any other age group, are reacting to the mass media.

C. Effects

The final part of Lasswell's question asked: 'to what effect?' Here we shall first look at some uses to which media are put before describing some of the effects.

1. *Uses*

Hoggart (1957) asked what are the uses to which literacy is put in an age when almost everyone out of primary school can read. Prior to

[1] J. D. Halloran, R. L. Brown and D. C. Chaney, *op. cit.*, espec. pp. 176–7.

this century, and certainly before the industrial revolution, few apart from the ruling elite and the clergy were able to read. This small group, similarly educated, had common standards of what was a good or a bad book. Today almost anyone can buy cheap books, magazines or papers, and there are many standards of moral excellence, so that in Hoggart's terms literacy is used to support 'the newer mass art', much of which consists of 'spicy magazines' and 'sex and violence novels'.

The control of the mass communications industry is almost entirely in the hands of adults so that a picture of youth drawn largely by adults is made available to the young. This picture is available to serve many culturally determined uses and the same manifestation, a song or a television show, may be used by teenagers as entertainment or for excitement, to supply the opportunity to withdraw for a few moments from a busy social life or to provide the chance to identify with a role model who has been given high status by a peer group. Some films, comics or television serials gratify socially induced wants such as the need to feel male or tough; others provide information on the teenage scene, for example, fashion hints or this week's hit tunes. Some media of the non-fiction type may be used for educational purposes. Furthermore, any one item may be used for varying purposes. Thus in Aberdeen, 'The News' was used by some twelve-year-old children as a source of information, but by a very few to gratify a need for excitement aroused by the sight of violence.

The last use to be mentioned here is possibly the most important for adolescents. All the media provide a coin of exchange or a common range of topics about which the young may talk and around which they may form the peer groups that have been shown to play so crucial a part in the process of socialization. In Aberdeen 62·7 per cent of the groups with which the children went around talked 'sometimes' about television, 14·4 per cent 'a lot' and 22·9 per cent 'hardly ever'.

2. *Effects*
There do seem to be several effects which can definitely be attributed to the media which are social rather than purely psychological in nature. More particularly the media seem able to influence the stereo-

types that children hold. Such mental constructs about others vary culturally and are important in governing how we feel and behave towards such whole categories of others as, for example, negroes, Jews and foreigners. As long ago as 1940 Orwell pointed out how grotesque were the pictures of foreigners that were presented in boys' weeklies. The Chinese were always shy or the French were loquacious and gesticulated.[1] In Himmelweit's research, however, the attitudes of the children towards foreigners were influenced by watching television. After being exposed to television for a year the children made more objective and fewer evaluative statements about foreigners, and they became less insular in their view of their own country. It would therefore seem that the views of other countries, carefully presented by the BBC, did influence the views held and in particular made them less rigid because television had given the children a wider view of reality, a process that invariably weakens stereotypes. This effect of 'opening windows' also widened the knowledge the children had about adult occupations so that they knew more of the nature of jobs and also of the ways in which status is given to various occupations. In other words this medium was assisting in the economic and the political socialization of children.

Some media present a more restricted view of the world which may, therefore, be expected to produce or reinforce stereotypes. Thus many books, magazines and comics give to children a rather more limited view of social and economic reality than is perhaps defensible. Orwell noted that those who read the typical school story for boys are being offered 'the conviction that the major problems of our times do not exist'. Wars, unemployment and poverty are never mentioned. The reader is possibly being socialized into support for the political status quo. In another sphere a somewhat similar process may be seen to be at work. Bailyn was able to show that the boys in her sample, who were, as already reported, much attracted to comics and, particularly, to a diet of aggressive heroes, were affected as a result in that they used stereotyped views in judging people. Apparently the stereotyped modes of thought in the stories that they read were in some measure learnt and influenced their behaviour. It would therefore seem that at the social psychological level the effects

[1] G. Orwell, 'Boys' Weeklies', in *Selected Essays*, London, 1957 (Penguin).

of media are largely dependent upon the number of alternatives that are offered to those whom the message reaches.

D. Conclusion

Communications, whether mass or individual, travel over pathways which, though to some extent technically determined, are best seen in terms of social relationships. Whenever the nature of influence of one of the mass media is being considered the nature of the social setting must be examined and two tools of analysis will yield vital clues to effect. Firstly, the concept of role model is important, particularly when considering adolescents in peer groups, since sanctions will in all likelihood be applied to members or to those aspiring to membership so that deviants are discouraged. Secondly, latent roles are brought to the situation in which the message is received so that the whole audience does not perceive or use any one message in the same way. Such primary roles as those connected with social class, age or sex intervene, with the result that the same objective reality is experienced in various socially patterned ways by those who often appear objectively alike, but unconsciously think differently.

BIBLIOGRAPHY

H. T. Himmelweit, A. N. Oppenheim and P. Vince, *Television and the Child*, London, 1958.

R. Hoggart, *The Uses of Literacy*, London, 1957 (Pelican).

E. Katz and P. F. Lazarsfeld, *Personal Influence*, Glencoe, 1955.

D. McQuail, *Towards a Sociology of Mass Communications*, Oxford, 1969.

W. Schramm, J. Lyle and E. B. Parker, *Television in the Lives of Our Children*, Stanford, 1961.

H. L. Wilensky, 'Mass Society and Mass Culture: Interdependence or Independence', *American Sociological Review*, April 1964.

PART II

The Sociology of the School

8

The Teacher in a Profession

An immense amount of work has been done in several fields of the sociology of education. As we have seen, sociologists have given much thought, for instance, to the relationships between the social class system and education, and also to the effect of social environment on school attainment. If one field has suffered comparative neglect, it is the sociology of teaching. Waller (1932) wrote the major text on this subject, but, though it is full of insight and in many ways still relevant, he wrote over thirty years ago and almost entirely about teaching in the USA. In the second part of this book we shall look at the same field and shall start by examining the teacher's position as a member of a profession, and pass to an analysis of the teacher in the school. After a chapter on the curriculum the part will conclude with two chapters considering respectively social interaction in the classroom and the role of the teacher.

In the present chapter we must first establish what sociologists mean when they speak of a 'profession'. In doing this we shall try to answer the question of whether there is 'a teaching profession'; this will demand reference to the historical growth of teaching as an occupation since the early nineteenth century (A. Tropp, 1957). Finally, we shall look at the determinants of the status of the individual teacher within his 'profession'.

A. The Teaching Profession?

There is a group of occupations which the general public usually refer to as the professions. In the nineteenth century doctors, lawyers and the clergy were included in this category. During the last hundred years there has been a 'flight into professionalism' (R. Lewis and A. Maude, 1952). In the main this has been a result of the rising proportion of occupations that have required a high standard of education. Many of these newer occupations have aspired to professional status. This tendency can be seen in the Census returns. In the 1901 Census 1·12 per cent of occupied males were classified as belonging to the major professions; by 1951 the figure had risen to 2·36 per cent. Though comparisons across successive censuses are difficult, this trend appears to have continued in more recent years. Over the same period the so-called lesser professions rose from 0·50 per cent to 2·23 per cent of occupied males and the teaching profession from 0·30 per cent to 0·57 per cent. Teaching rose less proportionately than either the major or lesser professions.

About 5 per cent of occupied males are, therefore, classified as members of professions. This is a large proportion of the labour force, and it forms an important group in view of the responsible nature of the work undertaken. Is this group of occupations merely a statistical category? Or has the term 'profession' entered modern usage because it proved a useful analytical tool to nineteenth-century social historians? Or are the professions what Durkheim called 'a social fact', namely a social phenomenon with a firm foundation that careful examination will reveal?

The practice of the professions that were recognized as such in the last century is based on a close personal relationship between the practitioner and his client (T. H. Marshall, 1950). The layman who is sick consults his doctor because he is ignorant of the nature of his illness, whilst the doctor is assumed to know how to cure it. In the same way the lawyer can help his clients because of his knowledge of the complexities of the law. Therefore, the professional situation is characterized by the expert practitioner in consultation with the ignorant client who has absolute trust in the advice tendered to him. The practitioner does not use his knowledge except to benefit his clients. This basic situation is that upon which the social fact of 'the professions' rests, and we must judge the more recent claimants to the title, including teaching, against this yardstick. Dependent upon the essential nature of this relationship there are common to all professions a number of characteristics. We shall examine these and in each case we shall see whether teachers as an occupational group have in the past shown, or do today display, these particular characteristics. In this way we shall be able to come to a conclusion as to whether teaching is a profession or not. It must be said in advance that this is a controversial question and there is no clear-cut answer.

1. *Knowledge*

The ignorance of the client is fundamental to the need to consult the practitioner. Therefore a member of any of those occupations that are normally called professional must have a command over a very definite field of knowledge, much of which will be particular to one profession. There would seem to be an 'optimal base of knowledge' for any profession. If the knowledge needed is too broad, the field can be split up and new jobs will be created. If, on the other hand, it is too narrow, too many can learn the knowledge easily, and the ignorance that forces the layman to approach the practitioner will largely disappear.[1] The mastery of such a core of relevant knowledge requires high intelligence and some training. Law and medicine provide clear examples, since considerable training is necessary and in both cases the nature and the complexity of the knowledge demands a high level of intelligence. There is even a certain mystique about the practice of professions. Here the church provides an example. In this context teaching is relevant, since it is often claimed that training is not enough to make a good teacher; there is some other undefinable quality that marks out the real teacher.

Under modern conditions the mass media and advertising have shown that they can sometimes teach better than many teachers. In the schools children have for some time now learnt from the radio and films. More recently, any claim to a mystique of teaching has been further undermined by the introduction of programmed textbooks and teaching machines. Teaching grows to be less of an art and more of a science as research reveals more about the process of learning and the best way to communicate information. Yet it is still true that to practise as a teacher assumes a core of specialized knowledge and that a relatively high level of intelligence is needed to be a teacher.

2. *Control of Entry*

The knowledge and training essential for any profession can be specified so that control of entry to the profession is possible. The

[1] H. L. Wilensky, 'The Professionalization of Everyone?', *American Journal of Sociology*, September 1964, pp. 148-9.

medical profession was the first to achieve control of entry in its modern form. In 1858 the Medical Act established the General Medical Council, whose main function is to keep a register of practitioners and to make certain that only those fit to practise are on this register. The academic qualification and length of training necessary for admission to the register are laid down in detail. This ensures that all medical practitioners are professionally qualified and thereby guarantees to the general public that professional advice is sound. The newer professions have established similar systems. For example, certain examinations and practical training lead to membership of the Institute of Mechanical Engineers and thereby to the status of a qualified professional engineer.

The struggle by the teachers to establish a similar register has been a long one.[1] Though a system of registration over which serving teachers have a large measure of control was inaugurated in Scotland in 1966 when the General Teaching Council for Scotland was established, so far teachers in England have been unsuccessful in their attempts to obtain similar machinery. In 1912 a Teachers' Registration Council was established, but it lapsed in 1949. It was never possible throughout this period to make the Register of significance, since unregistered teachers were permitted to practise. In the 1900s anyone who was over eighteen, had been vaccinated and was satisfactory in the eyes of a member of Her Majesty's Inspectorate (an HMI), was allowed by Article 68 of the Regulations to teach. Unqualified teachers are still permitted to teach for short periods under certain regulations of the Department. Furthermore, any graduate, at least in England and Wales, until recently could claim the status of qualified teacher regardless of whether he had any training in teaching or not, though this loophole whereby the profession may be entered by those without training will have been entirely closed by 1974. That untrained teachers may still practise may be due to the shortage of teachers, but their continued existence makes very clear that control of entry to the occupation of teaching has been lax compared with the medical and most other professions, old and new.

In addition, except in the limited example of Scotland mentioned above, teachers are not themselves responsible for control of entry,

[1] G. Baron, 'The Teachers' Registration Movement', *British Journal of Educational Studies*, May 1954.

since the system is operated by the Department through administrative regulations. The Department can both grant and withdraw the teacher's certificate. However, the teachers have had sufficient power through their professional associations, and more particularly the National Union of Teachers (NUT), to prevent the quality of the 'teaching profession' from falling through the appointment of a large number of untrained assistants. Many have suggested this latter course as one way to meet the desperate need for teachers. But to a sociologist much of the discussion over qualifications that takes place in the present shortage of teachers appears to be the defence of an assumed professional status.

In the inter-war years A. M. Carr-Saunders and P. A. Wilson wrote a well-known book on the professions. They saw 'the application of an intellectual technique to the ordinary business of life, acquired as the result of prolonged and specialized training, as the chief distinguishing characteristic of the professions'.[1] Because of this emphasis they considered formal qualifications to be of prime importance to the future development of professionalism. Qualifications must have a major place in any analysis of the professions since they guarantee competence, but in the case of teaching control of entry has to some extent been divorced from the question of formal qualifications. Unqualified practitioners, including the untrained graduates, can practise as teachers. Moreover it is in those subjects where graduate teachers are in shortest supply, namely in mathematics and the sciences, that young graduates appear to have entered the schools, very often without any training. Yet research in the teaching of these subjects shows that here, perhaps more than anywhere else, training is necessary in order to teach competently.

3. Code of Professional Conduct

A professional man must not only be of proved competence, but he must be trustworthy. The client assumes that his ignorance will not be exploited and that the practitioner is of a good character. We usually judge personality by behaviour or by what others tell us of a man. In the case of the professions we can rarely know the practitioner well and must refer to others to gain knowledge of his personality. Written references are commonly used as a means of

[1] Quoted in G. Baron, op. cit., p. 49.

guaranteeing a man's character. Teachers usually cannot apply for posts without supplying some references of their character. Many questions of fairness are raised by this system which is certainly less objective than most formal examinations.

The client trusts the practitioner to behave in a well-defined way. The older professions have ethical codes of long standing. There is the Hippocratic oath for the doctors, the inviolability of the confessional for the priest, the devotion of the lawyer to his clients' interests. In some cases the code can conflict with the interests of the State or of other citizens. A clear example is the case of the lawyer who is defending a murderer. The fundamentally personal nature of the relationship between client and practitioner is at the root of professional morality. A code of conduct guarantees that the doctor does not misuse the trust that his patient puts in him. The prohibition of the advertising of professional services prevents practitioners from behaving unethically with regard to others in the same profession and from influencing the public's judgement of their capabilities and suitability. Were we not considering the claim of teaching to be a profession, we might pause here to examine whether or not advertising is a profession.

Some of the teachers' associations have published codes to govern the behaviour of their members in relation to their clients – the children, to outsiders – the parents, and to their colleagues. One of the most important ideas implicit in the ethical codes of all professions is that the work is a thing of importance in itself. It has been said that the professional man does not work in order to be paid, but is paid in order that he may work. Yet, ironically, since we must trust a professional man, we feel that he must be of high status and this implies that he must be paid well. However, we tend to assume that a member of the professions will have a high sense of vocation. A doctor will turn out in the middle of the night to help a sick person; a lawyer will take work home at night, if necessary, without a thought of charging overtime; a clergyman will not refuse to preach because his pay is low. One of the most difficult questions of all for teachers has always been whether they ought to strike. This is more than a moral issue. It has sociological importance. Teachers have a calling to help their clients, the children. A strike would damage the children's interest and would, therefore, be seen by the general public

as unprofessional conduct, contravening the ethical code expected
in any profession. Despite their relatively low earnings, teachers have
rarely struck.

4. *Freedom to Practise the Profession*

There are sanctions on the actions of any profession. An ethical
code controls behaviour and only suitably qualified persons may call
themselves practitioners. In return for these restrictions the profession expects absolute freedom to practise its calling as the
members think fit. We assume that the doctor is competent and of
good character; he in his turn assumes that we shall permit him to
advise his patient in the way that he feels best and that we shall not
interfere with his practice. There is a tension in this position, since
where the State gives protection it may also wish to interfere.

Under modern conditions the State is coming to employ more and
more professional men. Some of the newer professions are wholly
employed by the State, for example, the colliery managers. In some
cases almost all the members of a profession work for the State;
examples are the doctors and the teachers. Very few professions are
totally outside State employment; instances might be the actors and
the journalists. Two dangers stem from this tendency. Firstly,
professional men often find themselves subject to laymen as they do
their work. Gone is the absolute authority implicit in the phrase
'Doctor's orders'; the Medical Officer of Health is perhaps more a
salaried adviser than a professional practitioner. In addition, once
the State has decided that it wants a job done, it can lay down the
necessary qualifications and conditions of service. Ironically the
professions as a whole, and particularly the teachers, have helped
this process of increasing dependence to come about. When a group
employed in one occupation has made a bid for professional status,
the members have put great stress on formal educational qualifications and thereby on longer education. Since the State now pays for
much of this extra education, it has naturally felt that it has the right
to a greater control of the use of such education. In the case of
teaching, the State pays for the greatest part of the education
provided in this country. It therefore wishes to exercise some
control over educational expenditure. Though the HMI has several
functions, at the heart of his work is the need to prevent the wasteful

use of public money. This entails inspecting the work of teachers. In this respect there are few other occupations which are in the same position as teaching. An HMI can walk into a classroom and criticize a teacher's work at any time. Certainly doctors and lawyers, even when employed by the State, are not subject to such very direct interference.

One of the main problems of the professions today is how to maintain their right to practise as they think best, although the contemporary tendency is for a larger proportion of their members to be employed by the State. When the majority of professional men were in private practice, the private practitioner set the standard for those who were employed elsewhere. The fewer there are in private practice, the less influence they can have, although there may be a time-lag before the State assumes major or complete control. When the State employs the whole of any profession, it can call the tune, and there is an arguable case that the profession in this situation has ceased to be a profession and has become a body of expert officials.

The teachers have a difficult position to hold. Very few of their number are privately employed and therefore interference could be easy. Furthermore the very nature of their work raises difficult questions of principle. The case of whether known Communists should be allowed to teach children in Britain illustrates the problem. Since 1950 there has been a ban on the employment of Communists as headteachers in Middlesex. On the one hand there is a strong argument that in this case the local authority is guarding the children from a probable source of propaganda; yet on the other this interference is preventing the absolutely free practice of the calling. These alternatives are implicit in any control of professions that are assumed to be free, even though the aim of intervention is that of safeguarding the general public. The work of the professional associations entails a constant watch that the freedom to practise the calling is not eroded by State intervention.

5. *Professional Organizations*

We have already seen that the professions have formed associations to whom they have delegated some important functions. It is usual, for example, for the professional association to control the register of practitioners. Professional associations are, therefore, normally in a monopoly position and could use their power of control of entry to raise the educational threshold of membership. This course would lower the supply of qualified practitioners and tend to increase the level of remuneration to those in the profession. The US medical profession has been accused of behaving in this way.[1] This was the policy of the trade unions with regard to apprentices. An association that follows such a course endangers the position of the profession, because it is fundamental that professional men are not seeking their own selfish or material ends. The profession is a vocation and has a duty to its clients. A trade union acts out of self-interest. A professional association works for advancement of the profession only so that it may more completely fulfil its social duty.

The association helps to build the framework within which its members practise. It provides the sanctions so that members undertake their obligations and responsibilities to society. Thus, in essence, it is disciplinary. The association ensures that its new members are able to provide the best possible service to their clients. When a practitioner fails in his obligations by acting in an incompetent or unethical way, that is unprofessionally, the association guards the public by withdrawing the right to practise from that member. The General Medical Council and the Law Society are responsible for both admitting members to and striking them off their respective registers.

Associations cannot call strikes in the way that trade unions do. The NUT has never called a national strike. In recent years there has from time to time been great pressure to do so over the question of salaries, but professional duty towards the children has overcome the desire to use unprofessional conduct. In the early part of the century the NUT did organize strikes on a local basis, mainly with the aim of gaining a national salary structure and uniform conditions of service. In 1907 teachers were withdrawn from schools in West Ham, and in 1914 the NUT forced the closure of more than sixty schools in Herefordshire. More recently in 1970 a series of rolling strikes, area following area, was organized. The clash of interests here is very difficult to resolve. The NUT, as representative of teachers, can maintain that without a higher salary scale recruits to the occupation

[1] M. Friedman and S. Kuznets, *Income from Independent Professional Practice*, New York, 1945.

will not be well enough qualified to do the job required. Yet, as has been indicated, the strike undoubtedly is unprofessional in that it harms the interests of the children.

The NUT, like other associations, takes as one of its most important functions political action of another type (R. A. Manzer, 1970). It carefully watches the professional interests of teachers in Parliament at question time and during the passage of any major legislation that has even a remote connection with education. There has been a series of famous teacher Members of Parliament. Two of the best known have been Yoxall, who had an influence on the 1902 Education Act, and Chuter Ede, who was Parliamentary Secretary to the President of the Board of Education, during the passing of the 1944 Education Act. Such political action is legitimate for a professional association in that it is not based on any selfish motive but helps to provide a more adequate framework within which the profession can serve its clients.

There is some danger in activity, particularly of a political nature, by professional associations, since the image that the public has of the profession may be changed by such action. The NUT followed a very forceful policy between 1870 and 1895. At the beginning of this period the school teacher was seen as a docile, lower middle-class, useful citizen; by 1895 many thought him to be a politically minded, ambitious pusher. A professional association that wishes to assist its members has to avoid appearing to follow self-interest. Once the public thinks that the profession is behaving in a selfish way, the trust between the profession and its clients may have been broken. Even policies that will ensure a more efficient fulfilment of that trust will be misconstrued by the general public.

On the whole, since 1945 the NUT has followed high professional standards in its activities. In one particular instance between 1950 and 1952 it set the very highest example possible. The local authority in County Durham tried to impose a 'closed shop' on all the teachers whom it employed; all had to belong to one union. The NUT, despite obvious advantages to itself, successfully opposed the authority on grounds of professional freedom. During the period 1954–5, however, the NUT was pressed by many of its members to follow a policy of militancy in a fight with the Government over changes in the statutory superannuation scheme that were disadvantageous to teachers.

In this struggle the NUT acted more like a trade union, though actual strike action was avoided.[1] Yet the NUT has largely retained the image of a professional association, and this is clearly symbolized in the fact that only in 1970, its centennial year, did the NUT join the Labour-oriented Trades Union Congress. Such a move would have political connotations unwelcome to most professional bodies.

6. Conditions of Service

A field in which professional associations have always been very active is that covering conditions of service. They have been eager to secure adequate pensions, good tenure of office, the chance of promotion and a minimum of extraneous duties for their members. This has been more especially true of those professions whose members are employed by the State or industry rather than in private practice, since by control of conditions of service the State may interfere with the freedom of a profession to practise its calling.

The teachers' associations, especially the NUT, have paid considerable attention to conditions of service since their foundation. This has been so for two main reasons. Firstly, conditions were very bad for teachers in the early and mid nineteenth century, and this reflected the low status of teachers. Secondly, the associations wanted to raise the status of their members and saw that by gaining adequate conditions they were promoting respectability. They hoped that in time this would lead to higher status. The battle for adequate pensions has been waged since 1846, and Fisher's Superannuation Act in 1918 was a landmark in the struggle, since it founded a scheme of pensions backed by the State. Security of tenure was gained by 1902, although dismissal is still not in the hands of teachers themselves but under the control of the State or its representatives; this is very different from the position in the old professions, where a court of one's peers strikes one off the register. One of the ways in which teachers fought for adequate promotion possibilities was by requesting the admission of elementary teachers to the inspectorate; this was achieved by the late nineteenth century.

A major problem for teachers has always been the demand that they carry out duties extraneous to teaching. In the middle of the last

[1] N. N. Roy, 'Membership Participation in the NUT', *British Journal of Industrial Relations*, July 1964.

century many teachers knew that they would only be appointed if, for example, they played the church organ on Sundays. As late as 1891 the NUT found that 400 out 1,200 of the teachers in four areas were in the position that their appointment depended on their doing extraneous duties. The nature of these duties has changed considerably. The growth of what may be called welfare services in the schools has led to the need for teachers to collect dinner money and supervise meals. Many teachers regard such tasks as unprofessional. The achieving of a satisfactory position with regard to conditions of service gives stability and respectability to a profession. Yet it is true to say that for a member of the old professions in private practice, the problem did not arise. The new concern with conditions of service is due to the greater proportion of professionals who are not in private practice and to the increased number of occupations of a rather different nature from the old professions that are now considered to be professions.

7. *Recognition by the Public*

At the beginning of this examination of what is meant by the term 'profession' we found that there was a factor common to the old professions. This was the nature of the relationship between practitioner and client. Yet by the end of the last paragraph we are admitting that the principle of the self-fulfilling prophecy may work in the case of professions. Thus, the majority of teachers consider themselves to be members of a profession; on the whole the public and the authorities treat them as a profession. Therefore, teaching is a profession. Is this true? Does professionalism merely depend upon a consensus of opinion?

The occupation of teaching is based on a personal relationship between, on the one hand, children who are lacking in knowledge and their parents who, even if they actually have this specialized knowledge, do not know how to impart it, and, on the other, a teacher, who is usually trained and who is guaranteed to be of good character. Despite the possibility of inspection the teacher is trusted to have almost complete freedom in his classroom to practise his vocation. As in all the professions the exact balance between the teacher's duty to children and parents and his own interest is difficult to assess. The main differences between the teacher and the typical professional are two. The teacher practises on more than one client simultaneously; however, this can be claimed to be a difference of degree rather than of kind. Secondly, the teachers have far less control over their own occupation; in this respect the State seems to exercise its powers of control according to the best professional standards.

Thus far the teacher can on the whole claim to be a member of a profession.[1] Yet historically teachers have had a status rather lower than those occupations admitted to be professions. Therefore much of the work done by their associations has been much more akin to that done by trade unions than that of professional associations. Typical of such work were the strikes to ensure uniform conditions of service referred to above. By the 1970s the status of teaching has risen. This may be due to the work of the professional associations or to the fact that education has come to have a higher status in Britain, but certainly teaching is now often included in those occupations called professions. Many of the other new professions are comparable with teaching in that they are not of the 'pure' nineteenth-century type, since so many of their members are employed by the State in one capacity or another. For the most part these new professions stick to the standards of conduct implicit in the personal relationship fundamental to the 'pure' professions. This is also the case for teaching.

So far the case for considering teaching to be a profession has been built on a definite functional relationship between clients and practitioners. Recently an attempt has been made to outline a natural history of professionalism.[2] The development of eighteen American professions was analysed, and on the whole each seemed to pass through an identical series of stages. First, the occupation must have become a full-time job, as teaching had become in Britain well before 1800. Next, a training system must be established; this took place after 1839 for elementary teachers, though its development for graduates is not entirely complete even now. Thirdly, a professional association is founded, as occurred in Britain in the case of elementary teachers in the 1870s and of secondary teachers around the turn of the century. In some professions these associations achieved legal

[1] For a somewhat different summing up see The Editor's article, *The Yearbook of Education*, London, 1953, pp. 27–30.
[2] H. L. Wilensky, *op. cit.*, pp. 142–6.

recognition, but this does not appear to be an integral part of the process of becoming a profession. Finally, a code of ethics is evolved; this also has taken place in the case of teaching in Britain. Teaching would seem to have passed through all the stages deemed necessary in the American situation for developing into a profession. This reinforces the conclusion already reached that there is an arguable case for saying that there is a teaching profession. This case is mainly based on the theoretical grounds that a particular relationship exists between teachers and taught, but has been reinforced by indicating briefly that in its history teaching has evolved in much the same way as the more widely recognized professions have done.

There is one final point. Who are the members of the teaching profession? Should all those employed today in the field of education be considered as members of the profession? Those administering education are in a very different sociological relationship, since they are far removed from the profession's clients, the children. The administrators are much nearer to experts and hence should be excluded. There are also teachers who are in a professional situation in other educational institutions, for example, the universities. Their position is hard to assess until we have examined what determines the status of individual teachers within the profession as a whole. The differences in status between teachers may be so great that teaching may not be a unitary profession.

B. The Status of the Individual Teacher

A recent High Master of Manchester Grammar School was created a life peer. Headteachers of primary schools who appear in the Honours Lists are awarded the MBE. This is one indication of the very wide range of status that exists within the occupation of teaching. We shall here consider four main determinants of the status of individual teachers (The Editors, *The Yearbook*, 1953).

1. *Sex*
In the nineteenth century there was no doubt that women had a lower status than men in the world of teaching. The struggle for emancipation for women and the subsequent fight for equal pay for women in many occupations affected the position of women teachers.

In the years since the war women teachers have been granted equal pay, so that today there is the same salary scale for both sexes in teaching. But, since there are more men in the more highly paid posts of headteacher or of head of department, the average earnings of women teachers are lower than in the case of men.

This is a common situation throughout the labour market and has a real basis in the fact that few women today expect to follow a career unbroken by motherhood. They therefore in effect lose their position on the scale of seniority and normally expect to forfeit their chances of promotion. In recent years the position has been complicated by the growing number of part-time married women teachers whose status appears to be considered lower than full-time married teachers.[1] Women teachers may be on the same salary scale as men, but they do not seem to have the same status in the schools.

2. *The Status and Age of the Pupils Taught*

There is an immense range of status of schools from independent schools such as Eton to maintained schools in slum areas. The status of the pupils attending these schools covers an equally wide range and to a great extent the status of the pupils affects the status of those who teach them. Up till 1944 this difference was enshrined in two terms in common usage – 'the teacher' and 'the schoolmaster'. The latter was applied to those who taught in grammar or private schools, whilst the former was given to the lower status elementary school. The schoolmaster was usually a graduate of a university, whilst the teacher had been to a training college. A degree has always had a higher status than the teacher's certificate. As late as 1949, when the term 'elementary' had officially been abolished, those running the London School of Economics survey of social mobility found that 'elementary teacher' was the term that the general public most readily understood when considering teachers. The sample ranked the elementary teacher as having equal socio-economic status with a news reporter, a commercial traveller, and a jobbing master builder, and of higher status than an insurance agent, but of lower status than a Nonconformist minister.[2]

[1] M. Collins, *Women Graduates and the Teaching Profession*, Manchester, 1964, p. 52.
[2] D. V. Glass (ed.), *Social Mobility in Britain*, London, 1954, p. 34.

Since the 1944 Act we can speak of primary and secondary teachers. It is doubtful whether the general public can or does distinguish amongst teachers in general. The only differentiation seems to be that they still use the term 'schoolmaster' in the case of those who teach in grammar and private schools. However, a group of 178 students, training for the Post-graduate Certificate of Education at an English provincial university, were asked in the late 1960s to rate teachers in various types of school in two ways. They first indicated how they perceived the general public would rank these teachers and secondly, how they themselves would do so. The order that they attributed to the general public was as follows: teachers in independent schools, maintained grammar schools, comprehensive schools, secondary modern schools and, lastly, those in primary schools. They themselves both saw far less difference in status between the various types of teacher than they considered the general public to do and also rearranged the order of the first three cases in the following way: teachers in maintained grammar schools, comprehensive schools, and independent schools.[1] W. Taylor (1963) clearly showed that a difference in status between the two main types of secondary school does exist, although the growing numbers of comprehensive schools may end this situation. In Taylor's view the grammar school has higher status than the secondary modern school and this difference is based on the fact that the modern school recruits its pupils from low-status parents and channels them into jobs that are of low status. This difference in status between the schools is reflected in the average earnings of those who teach in them, since teachers in the modern schools earn less than those in the grammar schools.

Despite the common salary scale, such differences occur not only between those teaching pupils of different status, but also between those teaching children of different ages. Those who teach the younger children in the primary schools earn less on average than those in secondary schools. This seems to be a measure of a difference in status, which is partly connected with two other facts. There are far more women than men teaching in the primary schools. In 1969, out of the 155,588 teachers in these schools 115,830 (or 74·4

[1] G. Bernbaum, G. Noble and M. T. Whiteside, 'Intra-Occupational Prestige-Differentiation in Teaching', *Europaea Paedagogica*, 1969, p. 49.

per cent were women. Furthermore, only 4·5 per cent of all teachers (3·5 per cent of women) in primary schools were graduates.[1]

Such internal differences in status are important, since they may act to prevent structural change in the educational system. Some teachers realize that they cannot claim individual status from the profession as a whole; they therefore cling to the status of the institution to which they belong. Today grammar school teachers may, at least unconsciously, oppose the change to a comprehensive system of secondary education because they believe that this will lower their own status.

3. *Subject Taught*

In the nineteenth century the place given to science in the public schools was very low and those who taught science were often considered to be of a lower status than those who taught the classics. Today the situation has changed radically. There is still, however, an academic pecking order in some universities, with classics and the pure sciences high, whilst the social sciences, especially education, and applied science are put low. For example, in one small study in the Midlands, where teachers ranked those teaching certain special subjects by prestige, they put sixth-form mathematics teachers higher than modern language teachers, both of whom were rated considerably higher than teachers of religious education, commercial subjects, woodwork, domestic science, or physical education.[2]

To some extent qualifications have come to be tied up with the status of subjects. In primary schools teachers tend to be general practitioners, most of whom have the same qualification, the teacher's certificate, and therefore status cannot be accorded by the subject taught. But in secondary schools specialists are the rule. The growth in the number of graduates in the old elementary schools did help to raise the status of these schools. Graduates are not uncommon in the secondary modern school today; in 1969 17·8 per cent of men and 13·5 per cent of women teachers in such schools were graduates, and this may have made the modern school more acceptable to many.[3]

[1] *Statistics of Education, 1969*, Vol. IV, *Teachers*, London, HMSO, 1971, p. 18.

[2] F. Musgrove and P. H. Taylor, *Society and the Teacher's Role*, London, 1969, pp. 74–6.

[3] *Statistics of Education, 1969*.

But there are some subjects in which graduates are almost unknown. The clearest examples are handwork and physical education in the case of both boys and girls. Despite the important part played by games in British schools the PE teacher seems not to have the same status as other teachers, and this is particularly true in the grammar school where he is often one of the few non-graduates.[1]

4. *The Social Origin of the Teacher*

In the last century teaching was a common route for upward mobility. In a sample of 8,516 teachers taken in 1955 J. E. Floud and W. Scott (1956) found that almost half were descended from working-class grandfathers whose sons showed a more than average likelihood of rising up the social scale when compared with the rest of their class. Perhaps rather oddly, six or seven times as many as might be expected were descended from grandfathers who were farmers. However, trends in recruitment since the war seem to indicate that this pull on working-class children to enter teaching is no longer effective. Whether due to the greater security provided by industrial employment today, or because of changes in salary differentials, teaching is no longer so attractive an occupation and proportionally more middle-class youths are entering teaching.

If this trend continues, there will be a slow change in the social background of teachers. In a fairly representative study of teachers carried out in the mid 1960s, 24·8 per cent were children of fathers in managerial executive or professional work and 26·3 per cent of fathers in administrative or clerical jobs. Thus over half the sample came from 'homes with the pattern of "white-collar work", implying middle class status'.[2] During the last century very many teachers came from a lower social class than was usually associated with the old professions. This rubbed off on the status of the occupations as a whole. Hence they often aspired to higher status. Today the status of teaching and the social background of teachers appear to have risen

---

[1] See Charmion Cannon, 'Some Variations on the Teacher's Role', *Education for Teaching*, May 1964, espec. pp. 32–6, for the role of the PE teacher in girls' selective secondary schools (also in P. W. Musgrave (ed.), *Sociology, History and Education*, London, 1970).

[2] E. P. Duggan and W. A. C. Stewart, 'The Choice of Work Area of Teachers', *Sociological Review Monograph No. 15*, February 1970, p. 54.

and teachers are on the whole on a par with the new professions. There is no longer the same need to aspire to professional status. Though this may be true of the profession as a whole, circumstances may be different for given individuals.

The proportions of teachers from various social classes do vary by type of school. The position in the case of men in grant-earning schools in 1955 was as follows:

Father's Occupation when Teacher left School	Primary	Modern	Technical	Maintained Grammar	Direct-Grant Grammar
	%	%	%	%	%
Professional, administrative	6·0	7·5	6·0	12·5	19·8
Intermediate	48·3	45·9	51·0	55·1	61·5
Manual	45·7	46·6	43·0	32·4	18·6

Source: J. E. Floud and W. Scott, p. 540.

The trend in the case of women was much the same. The proportions of teachers from working-class homes were higher where the status of the school was lower and, conversely, the proportions of teachers with parents of higher social status rose as one went from the lower to the higher status schools.

This pattern matches what we should expect from our discussion on the relationship between the status and age of pupils and the status of their teachers. The differing status of these schools is much more likely to be a result of the age and status of the pupils in the schools than the social origins of the teachers concerned. In a society that has a relatively high rate of social mobility the social status of any occupational group tends to be given to all its members whatever their social origins. This is the more likely where geographical mobility is high, since in most cases no one will know the kin of any individual and status will be given according to the socio-economic position that is achieved. Many teachers move to obtain new posts and this may be an additional force in obscuring the influence of social origins on the status of the individual teacher.

C. Conclusion

In the first part of this chapter we saw that there are grounds for calling teaching a profession, but we now see that there is a range of status amongst teachers. There is a similar range within the medical and legal professions. We may compare the surgeon or specialist with the general medical practitioner and notice that there is a difference in status. Despite this both are members of the medical profession. Teaching then is not disqualified on these grounds. There are differences in status, but teachers are sufficiently near in status to be grouped as a profession with perhaps the exception already noted of the difficult case of those who teach in universities. We may finally speak, as we have so far on the whole avoided doing, of 'the teaching profession'.

Historically the profession was born in 1833 when the State intervened to raise the standards of training amongst elementary teachers, who soon founded associations to watch their professional interest, more particularly after the 1870 Education Act. In 1902 the State stepped in to organize secondary education; at about this time some secondary teachers formed their own association. The aim of the 1944 Act was a unified educational system. Symptomatic of the failure of this aim is the fact that the teaching profession is still not a unified one, since the teachers in selective secondary schools tend to stand apart from the rest.

There may be a sociological argument for speaking of the teaching profession. The case is based on the relationship between teacher and taught. Teachers are, however, in danger of becoming a group of experts employed by the State rather than a profession. This is a danger common to the majority of the professions today, but as the last paragraph indicated, teaching is, and for the last one hundred and fifty years has been, extremely dependent upon the State. If teachers wish to remain professionals they must hold fast to the code of conduct implicit in any professional relationship. Professional status implies a contract to serve society over and above any specific duty to client or employer in return for the privileges and protections given by society to the profession. Private practitioners in all professions set the standard. Private schools may set teachers the best example of their code of behaviour. Teaching will not remain a profession if teachers only work from nine to four or if, without extreme provocation, they go on strike.

BIBLIOGRAPHY

The Editors, 'The Social Position of Teachers', in *The Yearbook of Education*, London, 1953.

J. E. Floud and W. Scott, 'Recruitment to Teaching in England and Wales', 1956, in A. H. Halsey, J. E. Floud and C. A. Anderson, *Education, Economy and Society*, New York, 1961.

R. Lewis and A. Maude, *Professional People*, London, 1952.

R. A. Manzer, *Teachers and Politics*, Manchester, 1970.

T. H. Marshall, 'The Recent History of Professionalism in Relation to Social Structure and Social Policy', in *Citizenship and Social Class*, London, 1950.

W. Taylor, *The Secondary Modern School*, London, 1963 (espec. Chs. 3 and 4).

A. Tropp, *The Schoolteachers*, London, 1957.

W. Waller, *The Sociology of Teaching*, New York, 1932 (reprinted 1961).

9

The Teacher in the School

We can consider any teacher in a school to be at the centre of a web of forces that act upon him, some more strongly than others, but all influencing his professional behaviour. These forces may come from outside the school, but can nevertheless have a big effect on the quality of his work. This type of force will be termed external; examples are the influence of the State, the governing body of the school and the parents of the pupils. Other forces can be called internal since they originate within the school, as, for example, the influence of the head of the school, the other members of the staff, and the children themselves. A third group of forces are those that affect the teacher from outside the school, but over which he himself can exert some control. An example of this reciprocal type of force is the examination system. We shall examine each of these three groups in turn later in this chapter.

The educational system is a complex of institutions, some of which are old and some new (G. Baron, 1965). When once an institution has been established, values and patterns of behaviour develop autonomously within it. Teachers do their work in such living institutions, each of which is different, but the majority of which have certain important common features. If the latter can be isolated, we shall distinguish one major influence on the teacher in the school. Those aspects of the schools in any country that are common to all are the outward signs of that nation's idea of what a school shall be. In Britain these common features indicate the British idea of a school.[1] This idea will define much of a teacher's work. In this chapter we shall first examine what the British idea of a school is and then consider how the three groups of forces described above

[1] The next section owes much to Professor G. Baron of the Institute of Education, University of London.

play upon the teacher as he teaches his class within a British school.

A. The British Idea of a School

The range of school types in Britain is immense. On the one hand there is the public school and on the other the primary school. There are also historical differences between the school systems of the constituent countries of Britain though they are today of less importance than they were even fifty years ago. It seems almost impossible to say that there is one idea of a school in Britain. The position taken here is that the following four assumptions underlie most British people's idea of what a school is:

(1) A school should have independence and individuality.
(2) A school should be small enough to have a common purpose and be under one head.
(3) A school should mould character, and
(4) should therefore transmit a definite set of values.

Each of these assumptions will be examined in turn.

1. *Independence and Individuality*

The care given to ensure that all schools have the independence necessary to develop their own individuality can best be seen in the attention paid in legislation to the establishment of governing bodies for schools. During the latter part of the nineteenth century the independent schools felt the need to defend themselves, more particularly by founding professional associations, against the possibility of State intervention. At the time of the 1902 Education Act those who had political power and those who advised them were men reared in this tradition of independence, and they therefore felt that they should write specific provision into the Act that was to found the new maintained grammar school. So as to guarantee a degree of autonomy all secondary schools by statute had to have a board of governors. In the 1944 Act similar arrangements were made and the new primary schools were given boards of managers. These provisions, certainly at secondary level, have ensured the wide diversity of internal organization and curriculum in British schools that is

T S E—F

remarkable to any foreigner who examines our educational system. Another sign of the same desire for individuality and independence is that nine different examining bodies organize the General Certificate of Education. In Britain the educational unit tends to be the school, whilst the administrative unit is the local authority. This is not always so clearly the case in other countries, nor need it logically be so. Paradoxically, one common feature of British schools is that they all may be different.

2. A Community that is Small and under one Head

(i) *The Community*. Education need not necessarily take place in a community that is set apart. One of the oldest of European educational institutions is the apprenticeship system, whereby individuals are educated and trained not in a school but at their place of work. Similarly, in higher technical education there has been a growth since 1945 in the number of so-called 'sandwich courses' in which the student undertakes a part of the course in an educational institution and part in the factory. However, the influence of the British boarding school has been great in this respect as in others. During the nineteenth century these schools grew by recruiting their pupils from a wide geographical area. This tended to limit their contacts with the immediate locality. More recently, many of these schools have moved somewhat in the other direction and have encouraged their pupils to go out into the community around the school to undertake social service in various forms. Yet the emphasis remains the same; the school, either consciously or unconsciously, is the educative community. This leads to a stress on communal activities. Meals together and school games have a higher importance than, for example, in Germany or France.

(ii) *Size*. To most British parents and teachers a school must be small so that each individual child may be known well by his teachers. It has often been said that no school should be so big that the Head does not know each child as an individual. The claim that large schools would be more economic to run has usually given way in the interests of the individual child. The fact that some of the most famous British boarding and day schools have a thousand or more pupils is conveniently overlooked. These schools have developed the house system so as to guarantee that despite their large size someone is responsible for knowing each child well enough to watch his growth. Many have opposed the development of comprehensive schools on the ground that they are too big to cater for the child as an individual. Invariably these new schools have bowed to the British tradition and have organized elaborate house systems in order to gain the advantages of the small school whilst remaining large.

(iii) *The Headmaster* (G. Baron, 1956). In the mid-nineteenth century the headmasters of the public schools who felt that they must fight for their independence often did so by stressing their own authority. In addition to this the *laissez-faire* economic ideas of the time helped to ensure that interference was rare. By 1909 a famous headmaster, Sir Cyril Norwood of Harrow, could write that the headmaster in this country was 'an autocrat of autocrats'. Between 1828 and 1842 Thomas Arnold of Rugby had built the model that was to be imitated by most later heads. He was the leader of a community and was also a clergyman, and from this the idea evolved easily that the head had a pastoral care for his pupils.[1] Such a headmaster would do all in his power to identify his pupils with the aim of the school as determined by himself. All these characteristics of the British idea of a headmaster as it developed in the late nineteenth century tended to force schools to be small. The shepherd's flock could not be too large if he were to tend them properly. Yet it must not be thought that this was an inevitable result. Even by 1850 the position of the headmaster was not as stable as it came to be. In schools in both England and Scotland it was not unusual for the masters to take turns to act as head. The organizational problem of how to run a school larger than was normal at the start of the last century had still not been solved.

Today a similar problem faces the comprehensive school. The tradition of what a British head should be is opposed to an administrative non-teaching headmaster, to what an American head of a large high school once called 'a four-ulcer man doing an eight-ulcer job'. The Arnold tradition passed into the State secondary system after 1902, since so many of the first heads of the new maintained grammar schools were educated and had taught in public schools. From grammar schools this idea of a head has passed into the other

[1] Matthew Arnold's poem 'Rugby Chapel' (1857) can be read as a gloss on this sentence.

types of secondary school and also into the primary schools. Everywhere the head is thought of as a man with power who often has great control over the appointment of staff and who certainly expects to be allowed to mould his school as he wishes.

3. *Character Training*

It follows from the British idea of a head that a school must care for all aspects of the child's development, for his character as well as his academic attainments. In Europe the formation of character is left to the home, the church and the youth organizations. In the USA the school tries to adapt the child to the community's, and not its own, idea of good character. But in Britain the school tends to lay down the way in which children are to behave and it holds itself responsible for enforcing this code. The school also takes a protective attitude towards the effects of the rest of the environment on the child; for example, the school must defend the children against the damage that the mass media may do. Therefore, the school concerns itself with how its pupils spend their leisure time and organizes games and societies in order to inculcate the approved virtues and interests. Again, this is not normal in European schools.

4. *Values*

This stress on the formation of character assumes an agreed standard of values by which personality may be evaluated. In fact the teacher in Britain has become an agent by which the attempt is made to transmit the typical middle-class values.[1] Since the educational system did not grow from the community, but was imposed from above, it was the values of those in positions of higher status that were considered, usually unconsciously, as worth inculcating. No moral judgement is here being passed on this set of values, but the result has been that many teachers see the schools as a rescue operation to save the children from their parents and their social class.

Schools in Britain vary enormously, but these four assumptions are common to the majority. Comparison with other countries shows that such assumptions are not universal. In the future mass literacy may bring change, but at the moment this is the idea of a school that

[1] See especially the study mentioned in Ch. 5 by R. King, *Values and Involvement in a Grammar School*, London, 1969.

influences the way in which administrators, teachers and parents see schools and therefore this idea governs much of what a teacher considers he ought to do as he practises his vocation.

B. The Forces at Work on the Teacher

1. *External Forces*

(i) *The State*. In this country the finance of education comes from two main sources. The Treasury provides funds through the Department of Education and Science; initially this money has come from national taxation. In addition, certain local authorities find further money from rates. Since both national and local authorities jointly hold the purse-strings, both are in a position to influence the schools and thereby the teacher.

(a) *The Department of Education and Science*. About 55 per cent of the funds for current expenditure on education is supplied by the central Government through the Department. The largest part of capital expenditure is financed centrally. Thus the Department is in the position of being able to lay down the regulations that govern how this money is spent. As was indicated in the last chapter it is a major part of the Inspectorate's work to see that the regulations are observed. The influence of these regulations is far-reaching, since they cover staffing ratios, the dimensions of classrooms, the scale of equipment for laboratories and gymnasia, and a multitude of minor features that matter much to the practising teacher. The sheer detail is immense, but, unless a new school meets the present standards of the Department, expenditure will not be authorized and, if old buildings are not up to present standards, criticism may be expected. This system governs the immediate material surroundings within which the teacher carries out his work.

The financing of British education was organized purposely so that both the central Government and the local authorities played a major part. The intention was that local interests should come to bear in a democratic manner on the provision of the local educational system (G. Baron and A. Tropp, 1961). But this seemingly admirable aim has within it the possibility of conflict, since there is always the chance that the two financing authorities may wish to pursue opposite or different policies. Since both Government and local council are democratically elected, their respective majorities may represent different political parties. In Britain since 1945 local government, particularly in the large cities, has often been dominated by the Labour Party, whilst the Conservatives for much of this period have formed the central Government. Since the 1950s the educational policies of the two parties have grown more unlike. There is, therefore, the chance of head-on collision. An example may be given; in 1955 the Manchester Council wished to establish two new comprehensive schools in line with the policy of its Labour-dominated council. The Ministry (as it was then called) refused permission, since Conservative policy was only to allow expenditure on such schools on certain conditions that did not apply in this particular case. The conflict went to the point that the Ministry threatened to withdraw Manchester's financial grant, a step that would have brought the city's school system to a halt. This sanction forced Manchester to abandon its scheme.

This is a very striking case of what is always possible, but rarely happens. The Department has greater power than the local authorities to push through its own policy and is able to prevent local schemes with which it does not agree. Hence its power over the teacher in the school is greater than is often realized. However, the Government's power is not absolute, and once again the case of the comprehensive school is relevant.[1] In 1945 the Ministry, in its pamphlet *The Nation's Schools*, indicated that its policy was a tripartite secondary system of grammar, technical and modern schools. During 1946 the local authorities began to submit their development schemes to meet the requirements of the 1944 Act, and the Government realized that local feeling demanded a change in policy towards the provision of more comprehensive schools. In 1947 the pamphlet, *The New Secondary Education*, took notice of this and envisaged a greater variety of types of secondary school. Despite the power of the State, democratic pressures, in education as in other fields of Government expenditure, can bring change to Government policy. To the individual teacher, however, the possibility of his influencing policy seems so remote that the Department remains a powerful, if indirect, external force.

[1] See D. Rubinstein and B. Simon, *The Evolution of the Comprehensive School: 1926–1966*, London, 1969.

(b) *The Local Authority*. The local authority both acts as the channel for expenditure of State funds and finances education from its own rates. It therefore stands between the Department and the school, appearing to the teacher to be the main direct external force that influences his work. Though the whole council is responsible for all local government, there are committees responsible for each major field of expenditure. The Education Committee consists of democratically elected members – councillors or aldermen, members co-opted to this committee, and paid officials of the council, such as the Director of Education – who give advice as experts on the matters under discussion.

The political complexion of the council will normally decide the composition of this committee and, as local politics have become more a party matter, so policies on education have tended to be judged on national political, rather than local educational, criteria. However, the position of the Director of Education can be very influential. He is a former teacher and in close touch with his teachers in the schools. In theory he may be purely an expert who tenders his advice, but often because he alone has the necessary knowledge amongst a committee mainly consisting of laymen, he has great power. Major policy decisions may stem from his advice. Thus the Cambridgeshire Village College system owes its existence to Henry Morris, the pre-war Director for that area.[1]

There are few studies of the forces at work when local education authorities make decisions about the systems that they control. In one recent study of the manner in which Corby made plans to reorganize secondary provision in that area, there seemed to be a number of groups that influenced the ultimate decision. The local headteachers exercised some power and local branches of more than one professional association expressed views that affected the outcome, although the NUT carried more weight than the smaller associations. Yet these latter groups had more influence than might have been expected because of the presence of a few very active members. The final report of the authority's Chief Education Officer, which had the support of the NUT, carried the day. Yet in this rural area issues on the local council were not decided along party political lines so that

[1] For the case of Reading see J. Brand in D. Peschek and J. Brand, *Policies and Politics in Secondary Education*, London, 1966.

an administrator giving what was ostensibly technical advice that had the backing of the majority of teachers would wield much power. Local political conditions must always be taken into account when considering both how a local education authority will operate and also how much power the Director of Education may have over decisions. Thus where councillors are not subservient to their expert advisers, the Director of Education and his staff, they may be more aware of such other local interests as parents or a locally powerful religious denomination. This was the case in the 1950s in Middlesex where middle-class Roman Catholic parents were able, through members of council who pushed their case, to preserve their right to free places in local fee paying schools.[1]

Local authorities have great power over their schools and the teachers within them. Often teachers are appointed to the authority rather than to the individual school. But the power of the local authority varies according to the type of school. The authority has most influence on fully maintained schools, since it provides either directly from rates or indirectly from the Treasury the whole of the finance needed to run such schools. In addition there are the various types of voluntary schools – the aided, the controlled and the special agreement schools. The factor that differentiates these three school types is the amount of State finance received in each case. The more money given to the school, the greater influence the local authority can claim over it. This control is symbolized in the proportion of the governors or managers that the local authority may nominate to the school's governing body. The more finance the authority finds, the more governors it appoints and hence the more power it can exercise over the workings of the school. This will affect the appointment of the head and staff, and to some extent the activities of the teachers in the school. The intention of this complicated system is to safeguard the interests of the mainly religious bodies who since the nineteenth century have provided so many British schools.

The schools that are least influenced by local authorities are the

[1] For Corby see S. J. Eggleston, 'Going Comprehensive', *New Society*, 22 December 1961; and for Middlesex, R. Saran, 'Decision-Making by a Local Education Authority', *Public Administration*, Winter 1967. For studies of Darlington and Gateshead see R. Batley, O. O'Brien and H. Parris, *Going Comprehensive*, London, 1971.

direct-grant schools, whose finance comes directly from the Department, but who by law have to provide some places for children coming from maintained schools. The local authorities have some interest in these schools since they pay the fees of a substantial proportion of the children in such schools, and therefore they will wish to ensure that ratepayers' money is not spent on poor education. However, direct-grant schools are in many ways more akin to the independent schools which must now be considered.

(c) *Independent Schools*. There are a substantial number of schools that are independent of the Department. They may be run on a profit-making basis or as charitable foundations. These schools include the famous public schools, the so-called 'progressive' schools, and many privately run kindergartens. By Part III of the 1944 Act, which came into operation in 1957, all independent schools must apply for registration by the Department. They are liable to inspection and must on the whole conform to the Department's regulations. These regulations are not rigorously imposed. If they were, the experiments of progressive schools might be curbed, but the philosophy of the 1944 Act is that, although parents should be permitted to choose their children's school, the State should safeguard the public by preventing the setting up of poor schools.

Since the independent schools are liable to inspection, they must be influenced by the regulations that set the Department's standards. However, in many respects, especially in the case of the public schools, standards are higher than in maintained schools. The strongest influence on the teacher will be either the proprietor or the governing body of the school. Teachers in these schools need rarely worry about the influence of the Department or any local authority.

(ii) *Governing Bodies*. As has already been indicated, since the 1944 Act all maintained schools by law are supposed to have some form of governing body, though the Education Act for Scotland does not carry a similar clause. In fact it is only in the last few years that much has come to be known about what these boards do or even to what extent or in what form they exist. It seems that though by law boards of governors or managers ought to exist, this is not always the case, and that the types of board and method of recruiting their members vary greatly from place to place.[1] Secondary schools seem to have

[1] See D. A. Howell, 'The Management of Primary Schools', Appendix 13,

governing bodies more often than primary schools. In some local authorities especially, but not always, in county boroughs where the population is dense, boards of governors or managers frequently have minimal powers in systems that are strong and run by highly centralized bureaucracies. Under these circumstances schools may be grouped under one governing body, the membership of which is restricted closely to members of the local council and of the Education Committee. Here little lay influence can be brought to bear on decisions about the schools. In other areas, especially in the counties where population is scattered, each school has its own board of governors or managers to whom more responsibility is given. Here, particularly at the secondary level, members of boards play a large part in appointing senior staff and especially in choosing a new head, a decision that is always crucial for the future development of their school; their advice also carries weight in financial matters. Members of these boards are drawn in varying proportions from three main sources. Firstly, there are the political nominees to whom reference has already been made, many of whom may change with political fortunes. Secondly, since the religious bodies still play so large a part in English education, there are clergymen or nominees of denominations, perhaps watching the interests of a major local denomination or of the sect that originally founded the school concerned. Lastly, sometimes there are representatives of the parents and sometimes former pupils of the school. In general, governors recruited from all these sources may tend to be rather conservative, and wary of educational change.

The governing bodies of the independent schools, originally the model for the system adopted in the State schools, are extremely influential and provide a strong and continuing influence. Headmasters may come and go, but the governing body remains, though its membership slowly changes. It is the guardian of the school's traditions. In many schools and also in, for example, some colleges of education, a legal trust lays down what interests shall be represented on the governing body and thereby perpetuates the intention of the

Children and their Primary Schools (Plowden), Vol. II, London, HMSO, 1967; and G. Baron and D. A. Howell, 'School Management and Government', Research Studies No. 6, *R.C. on Local Government in England*, London, HMSO, 1968.

institution's founder. Many independent schools have religious foundations, and provisions of this nature ensure that the school continues in the spirit in which it was started. The governors guard their trust in two main ways. They personally appoint the head-master, choosing, as far as they can, the man who seems best fitted to continue the tradition entrusted to their keeping. They also control the financial affairs of the school. Since the school finds all its own funds and none come from the State, the governing body has a big influence on the life of the school. Decisions concerning changes to the fabric of the school, such as a new laboratory or gymnasium, are ultimately in their hands.

In maintained schools the governing bodies are much less power-ful, since they are not in a position of financial independence. They can play a part in choosing the head and can watch the interests of the school in local affairs. Governors have been known to fight for their school's survival when the local authority wished to close it down. On the whole, these boards of managers or of governors function in a rather paradoxical manner to link their schools to the local community and education authority whilst simultaneously going some way to ensure their independence *vis-à-vis* the local authority and parents.

(iii) *Parents.* Parents can influence a teacher indirectly through their children, but here we are thinking of their direct influence. In a small village or town the teacher may well live in or near to the school. Most of the parents of the children that he teaches will meet him in the street and can easily talk to him about the school and their children. In the contemporary large urban area this is not often the case. Teachers do not want to live in the middle of a slum area or even in a city. They prefer to travel long distances to their schools. Under these conditions, that are typical for the majority of schools, relations between parents and teachers must be structured. It is because of this that in some schools today Parent–Teacher Associa-tions have been established.

Teachers and parents alike are dedicated to the interests of the children. In theory, therefore, disagreement is impossible. In prac-tice, however, it is very likely since in this country the parents' wishes are usually held to be subordinate to the teacher's idea of what is good for the child. The teacher assumes that he knows better than the parent, and thus few heads in this country have established any form of parents' association, since this would allow the parents a direct influence on the running of their schools (M. D. Young and P. McGeeny, 1968).

The contact between parents and teachers is closest with younger children. This may be exemplified if one calls to mind the picture of parents clustered about the doors of an infant school around 3.30 p.m. during term-time; the junior school next door has a much smaller group. In secondary schools far less contact is observed; in grammar schools fear or shyness may prevent visits by parents, particularly amongst parents who did not themselves attend such schools.[1] But at any age the chance of conflict between parents and teacher is great. Values may differ between the middle-class teacher and the working-class parent or methods have changed since father was at school. Yet there is usually no machinery to resolve these differences.

In the case of the independent schools the position appears simple. The parent is a customer who is buying education for his child. If he ceases to be satisfied with the service provided, he may withdraw his custom. In fact, though organized ways in which parents may approach the school are rare, there is a long tradition that the head-master or the housemaster is in close touch with the parents of his pupils.

In the USA the situation is very different. When a new school is established, the local parents can have a very strong influence on the type of school built and on the choosing of the headteacher. One author goes so far as to write of the American school as 'belonging' to parents and family. Social pressure is great enough to ensure that a high proportion of American parents belong to Parent–Teacher Associations. In one area 40 per cent of middle-class parents were members, though the working-class proportion was somewhat lower. But a study in England revealed that only 3 per cent of all the parents in a comparable area were members. In the large sample of primary schools studied for the Plowden Report, 17 per cent had Parent–Teacher Associations, though over 60 per cent arranged meetings for educational or social purposes with parents.[2]

[1] B. Jackson and D. Marsden, *Education and the Working Class*, London, 1962 (Pelican), pp. 205–9.
[2] H. E. Bracey, *Neighbours*, London, 1964, pp. 125–9; *Children in their*

The relationship between parents and teachers in Britain is summed up by the feeling so often expressed in staffrooms that 'we could do so much better a job if only the parents would not interfere'. The contact that is necessary at the infant stage, because the child is young, can create a partnership between parent and teacher in the education of the child. But the teacher of the older children will rarely meet their parents unless there is an organized channel for this purpose. In this country Parent–Teacher Associations are rare, though any increase in the real interest of the general public in education might bring about a change. It seems odd that 'the office', the symbol of the State and the local authority, should have so much more influence on a teacher than the parents of the children that he teaches.

2. *Internal Forces*

(i) *The Headteacher.* The forces which play upon the teacher's position from outside the school are in the main impersonal or corporate. We have only so far mentioned the influence of one individual, the Director of Education. But as soon as we turn to those within the school who influence the teacher we are in the world of individuals, all of whom have their own characteristics. The first person to be considered in any school is the head. In Britain the tradition is that the head is all powerful in his school. Once appointed he has very great freedom to influence the development of the school for which he is responsible.[1] For instance, he decides the outlines of the curriculum and the broad allocation of time to each subject. This decision in itself deeply affects the work of all his staff.

Teachers tend to speak of 'strong' and 'weak' heads, as though the former determines the ethos of the school, whilst under the latter things just drift. This may be so, but many of the 'weak' heads intend to act in this way in order to create a spirit of tolerance and democracy. If they achieve this, it is as much due to their influence as any

---

Primary Schools (Plowden), Vol. II, London, HMSO, 1967, p. 223. See also W. H. Whyte, *The Organisation Man*, London, 1957 (Penguin), Ch. 28, for an account of parents' influence over the establishing of a new school in the USA.

[1] See W. R. Niblett, 'Administrators and Independence', *British Journal of Educational Studies*, November 1958.

effect of a 'strong' head. The point that must be appreciated is that whatever the personality of the head he can act to establish the atmosphere that embodies his values whatever they are, and this will affect his teachers. Or, if he is inefficient, he will do nothing and in this case the teachers will be influenced in that they will have to exert the leadership that has not been given by the official leader.

One of the main ways by which a head maintains or creates the ethos of a school is in his choice of staff. In as much as he makes or influences appointments he can try to pick teachers who appear to meet his needs, though he may be limited by shortages of particular types of teachers. The limiting case of the public school shows very clearly how the head goes about choosing his staff. If the school stresses games, he will want to find 'Blues' for his vacancies; if, however, the school has an academic tradition, the head will look for 'Firsts'. The average headteacher has an average policy and so there is a big range of indeterminacy within which his choice of staff may fall. The average teacher will suit him.

Bad choices are possible. The head may choose wrongly or the teacher may allow himself, consciously or unconsciously, to be appointed to a post for which he is not suitable. In these cases the teacher may realize the mistake and move to another post. The head, however, can influence him to apply elsewhere by hints or by making his life unpleasant. In such moves, as in all changes in school staffing, the question of references is relevant. One of the most powerful, if hidden, sanctions by which a head can maintain a conformity to his wishes amongst his staff is the fact that the majority of applications for posts elsewhere must be backed by a written reference from him. If this reference is not forthcoming, questions will be asked as to why the applicant left his last post. This is no doubt an extreme example, but it is in just such cases that we can see how much influence the head can ultimately have over his staff.

(ii) *The Staff.* Once the teacher is in his classroom with his children he has very great freedom in Britain. How and what he teaches is very largely his own affair, though he may receive suggestions from visiting inspectors. His classroom is his own territory, rarely, if ever, visited by his colleagues. Yet he cannot be entirely independent of the rest of the school staff. In most secondary schools there will be a head of department who is responsible for the work in a major area of the curriculum. He will influence, even if only by consultation, the subject matter that is taught. He may be responsible for spending the department's allowance for books or equipment and in this way influence what or how the teachers in his department can teach. In primary schools teachers will have to cooperate with those in the classes a year ahead or behind their own so that continuity is ensured for the children who are passing through the school. All these relationships involve individual personalities.

In all schools there are some activities that cut right across the normal work of the school. Duty lists for school dinners or for the playground must be fixed, and this demands cooperation amongst the staff. Some teachers organize out-of-school games or clubs, the timing of which may force consultation amongst the whole staff. There are great personal problems involved in the need to do things about which some teachers may be keen, others apathetic and to which some may even be opposed. A teacher's work depends for its success not only on his skill with children, but on the way in which he handles his relationships with his colleagues. Philosophical issues of means and ends are involved here. On the one hand there is the scheming, but charming teacher who is out for his own interests; on the other there is the teacher who furthers the interest of the children for whom he is responsible by cooperation with other teachers. It is to the latter way of handling personal relationships that attention is here being drawn.[1]

(iii) *The Children.* In Chapter 11 the way that the teacher and his pupils interact in the classroom will be examined at some length. Here the intention is merely to establish the point that the children can influence the way the teacher runs his class. This is not merely a question of the poor disciplinarian whose class takes over. It will be remembered that in the discussion of the sub-cultures within a school Coleman's work in the USA was quoted. The fun culture in the high school attracted many adolescents away from the values and ways of behaviour that the teachers wished to instil in these pupils. Similarly, in Britain there are many teachers in secondary modern schools who know that their approach to the fourth-year leavers, aged around fifteen, is partly influenced by these children and is not

[1] A useful text here is Josephine Klein, *Working with Groups*, London, 1961.

entirely controlled by themselves. In girls' grammar schools the dress that may be worn by sixth formers is often not controlled by the school and may be of a type that does not meet the full approval of the teachers.

There is a clear example of this process in higher education. The ideal of the university that the newer British universities on the whole tried to imitate was that of a group of teachers and learners meeting together to pursue a life of scholarship and discussion. Today many university students study from nine to five and return daily to the suburban life from which they came. No residential facilities or organized societies will change their habits. The university and its teachers must alter, and not the students.[1] It would appear that this power of the pupils to influence the teacher is a matter of age. In the primary school children are still very much under the influence of their parents and lack sufficient knowledge or confidence to challenge their teachers. But the older the pupils, the more they can become an independent force determining the actions of their teachers.

3. *Reciprocal Forces*

There are channels through which influence can be brought to bear on the teacher, but through which he in his turn can bring pressure on those who are trying to change or determine his course of action. This final section will deal briefly with three such channels.

(i) *Syllabuses*. The broad outline of what a school will teach is decided by its head, but within this framework heads of departments and class teachers have a wide choice. Often, however, the teacher has to prepare his pupils for an external examination. In this case he may feel himself to be very much at the mercy of the examining body that sets his syllabus. Yet teachers can influence examining bodies, since there is machinery available to ensure that the teacher's voice may be heard. Professional associations annually collect comments on GCE papers from the schools and, if there are any complaints, bring their influence to bear on those setting the papers. A panel of university and school teachers set the examinations, though university members predominate; a larger, but similar, panel mark the scripts, though in this case school teachers form the majority. Therefore,

---

[1] See B. R. Wilson, 'The Needs of Students', in M. Reeves (ed.), *Eighteen Plus*, London, 1965.

teachers have some chance of influencing the setting and marking of this examination, though their attitudes may coincide with those from the universities, since most were educated there. Finally, few teachers apparently realize that, if they want it, examining bodies will arrange to set special papers for individual schools. The teacher who feels really strongly can almost completely control the syllabus and examination papers of his pupils, though the examining board must approve the standards of these special papers.

This picture of the GCE may seem idealistic, but it is in part a description of existing machinery that is little used. The organization of the CSE puts the onus of running the examination very largely upon the teachers. The boards in each local area that are responsible for drawing up syllabuses and setting examination papers are made up almost entirely of teachers. Only after pressure from their association were lecturers from training colleges invited to sit as observers on the panels responsible for the examination papers in the various subjects. Here the secondary school teacher has the fullest opportunity to teach a syllabus set entirely in accordance with the wishes of himself and his colleagues. He can, if he wants, escape the influence of those examining bodies who have so long been accused of hampering the school's work.

Since the establishment of the Schools Council in 1964, much energy has been put into the development of new curricula by many specialists including inspectors, lecturers from colleges or departments of education and teachers. A complicated structure of committees, usually based around existing school subjects, has been set up to enable teachers to test and criticize suggested curricula during their development and use. More particularly teachers' centres have been established in many areas so that teachers may participate effectively in this process. Their aim is that 'as many teachers as possible' should help 'to define . . . objectives (which) will probably reflect, as far as is humanly possible, the contemporary needs both of the pupils themselves and the community as a whole'.[1] By such means teachers are able to feed back influential advice to a new category of specialists, the experts on the curriculum.

One syllabus is less open to influence from the schools than most, namely that in religious instruction. Voluntary schools have the free-

[1] *The New Curriculum* (Schools Council), London, 1967, p. 12.

dom of teaching religion according to their trust deeds; syllabuses
will meet the needs of the denominations that are responsible for each
particular school. But by the 1944 Act maintained schools must
follow an agreed syllabus. This is drawn up by the representatives
of local religious interests, of teachers and of the local authority.
Agreed syllabuses are rarely revised, and some local authorities have
adopted the syllabus of another authority. In all these cases the
teacher has far less influence than in other school subjects, and his
freedom to teach as he wishes is diminished in a way that offends the
English tradition. This position is the price of the compromise
between the various denominations and the State that was needed to
ensure the passage of the 1944 Act.

(ii) *The General Public.* Public opinion influences the school and
hence the teacher by the normal democratic process. The policies of
the various political parties, both nationally and locally, are brought
to bear on the provision of education in the same way as on the
supplying of the other services maintained by the State. But teachers
in their turn can influence the parties and the public. This is done
in several ways, though the place of the professional associations is
important. Local branches watch local educational problems, whilst
at the national level headquarters is in close touch with the Department and also lobbies Members of Parliament. In the case of deciding
pay these associations are also represented on the committees that
propose the various salary scales.

Manzer (1970) has suggested that there is 'an education sub-
government' and that power over the decisions made is dispersed
widely amongst the members of this system, different members
having more or less power according to the nature of the decision to
be made. The principal members in England are the Department of
Education and Science, the local education authorities and the
teachers' organizations, which in the latter case largely means the
largest and most powerful of these bodies, namely the NUT. On
certain specific issues religious bodies and economic organizations
may also be included. Over the years conventions of consultation and
negotiation have been evolved within this system, and those who take
part regularly in this sub-government have a clear interest in preserving it and thereby retaining power in their hands. However,
social changes such as growing radicalism amongst some groups

within teachers' associations do threaten the present system. In the years since 1945 the professional associations have been more able to influence decisions made in technical matters and had much power, for example, over the nature of the decisions made concerning the establishment of the Certificate of Secondary Education and of the Schools Council. In matters with wider political implications they have had less power, partly because of divisions within their own ranks and partly because of the very powerful tradition that professionals should not use such weapons as the strike. Thus the associations have been less successful in influencing decisions concerning salaries and pensions, issues relating directly to the central political question of how the financial resources available to the government of the day should be divided between the various sectors of expenditure.

Professional associations operate in all sections of the educational system. Thus, the NUT guards the interests of teachers in the schools; there are associations of teachers in training colleges and universities that fulfil the same functions for their members. These bodies use many methods, as do their local branches. The officers and secretaries of professional associations make radio and television broadcasts in order to work on public opinion. They form delegations to call upon the Minister or Members of Parliament so as to influence administration or legislation. Letters may be written to national and local newspapers on specific issues as they arise. Lastly, perhaps rarely, but certainly to great effect, teachers' associations submit evidence to committees or Royal Commissions. The democratic dialogue is no less real in education than in any other field, and teachers can in this way influence the way the educational system is run.

(iii) *The Central Advisory Councils.* One of the major political institutions that Britain has invented is the office of the Leader of the Opposition, who is paid by the State to stand by to form a Government if the present majority party loses the support of the country. In the field of education a rather similar institution has been created. The 1944 Act laid down that there should be two permanent Central Advisory Councils, one for England and the other for Wales; the ancestry of these bodies dates back to the 1902 Education Act. Similar machinery exists for Scotland. Representatives of a wide range of educational institutions and also informed outsiders are

members of these Councils. The Minister remits to them topics that are central to the educational problems of the time. The Councils deliberate for as long as they feel necessary, examine any witnesses or evidence that they feel fitting, and issue a report. The Government pays all the expenses. In the past the Councils have always interpreted their function as being to make constructive criticisms of the educational system in the light of the best contemporary knowledge, and they have tended to be progressive rather than *avant-garde*. Here is an institution that ensures that criticism is built into the educational system. There is a demand for ideas to come into the open, to influence opinion and to assist the Government of the day to form policy. Teachers are represented on them; they, as individuals and through their associations, can and do change the course of the Councils' reports by their evidence.

4. *Conclusion*

All teachers are members of institutions and do their work of helping children within an administrative framework. Very often they feel lost and incapable of determining the direction in which the educational system as a whole is moving. Teachers can only hope to influence this system if they have some knowledge of the administrative machinery within which they are operating and of its historical background at national and local level. Only in this way can they know the forces at work that have brought the system to its present position. If they understand the strengths and weaknesses of today's situation as created by the past, they have a greater chance of changing things in the direction that they feel necessary. In a country where evolutionary change is the rule, a successful revolutionary must work for his purpose in this way. The external forces that were described earlier in this present chapter form the more permanent forces at work within the contemporary educational system; they provide the elements of stability and the framework within which manœuvre can take place.

The teacher must deal with many people as he plays his role of teacher. R. K. Merton has referred to the complement of roles organized round any particular role as its *role-set*.[1] In this chapter we have studied many of the roles that impinge on the teacher both from

[1] R. K. Merton, 'The Role-Set: Problems in Sociological Theory',

outside and from within the school; in other words we have examined the role-set of the teacher. The exact nature of the complementary roles has often been influenced by their historical development. It was partly for this reason that a brief historical account of the British idea of a school was necessary.

One of the problems of any role-set is how the central role, here the teacher, manages to play his role effectively when influenced by so many other roles that often act upon him in contrary directions. The position of the teacher in Britain is eased in several ways. The law creates a number of checks and balances to control some of the influences on the teacher. The composition of governing bodies and their position between the local authority and the teacher is one example. Another is the way that the local authority exists as a buffer between the Department and the school. The traditions that the school is independent and that the teacher is king in his own class-room help further to lessen the influence of the role-set, since in both cases the actions of the teacher are insulated from the outside world. Membership of a professional association enables the teacher to face the role-set from a position of greater strength and no longer as a mere individual. Finally, the teacher, and more particularly the head, takes steps to abridge the role-set by failing to establish adequate channels of communication with parents. It is in such ways that a teacher can cope with the pressures put upon his position in a school.

Role-sets consist of individuals who have different personalities. The incidence of any one type of person, strong or weak, is largely unpredictable, but it is through the personal relationships between individuals of very different characters that change can come within the educational system, as in any other institutional framework. Teachers, who wish to follow their vocation of teaching children in some way that is even slightly different from the generally agreed methods, must know how to work with their colleagues to gain their legitimate end. To do this successfully they must study the forces at play on their position that come both from outside and from within the school, and they must know what channels they can use to influence those who make the decisions that govern the educational system.

British Journal of Sociology, June 1956. This extremely important article uses the role of the teacher as an example on several occasions.

BIBLIOGRAPHY

G. Baron, *Society, Schools and Progress in England*, London, 1965.

G. Baron, 'Some Aspects of the Headmaster Tradition', *University of Leeds Institute of Education, Researches and Studies*, June 1956 (also in P. W. Musgrave (ed.), *Sociology, History and Education*, London, 1970).

G. Baron and A. Tropp, 'Teachers in England and America', 1961, in A. H. Halsey, J. E. Floud and C. A. Anderson, *Education, Economy and Society*, New York, 1961.

G. Manzer, *Teachers and Politics*, London, 1970.

M. D. Young and P. McGeeney, *Learning Begins at Home: a Study of a Junior School and its Parents*, London, 1968.

IO

The Curriculum

In the first part of this book we examined the process of socialization and gave particular attention to the part that the school played in the process of creating social reality in the child. Central to this process in the school is the *curriculum*, which may be defined as 'those learning experiences or succession of such learning experiences that are purposefully organised by such formal educational agents as schools. Such experiences may or may not take place within the educational organisation that plans them' (P. W. Musgrave, 1970). From one viewpoint the curriculum sums up the effects of the wider social system outside upon the school and from another viewpoint it represents the effect that the school hopes to have upon its pupils (D. K. Wheeler, 1967). Therefore, in this chapter we shall initially analyse the way social influences affect the curriculum, and secondly, after a brief examination of the curriculum itself, we shall consider the curriculum as a determinant of the behaviour expected of teachers and pupils in the school, and hence, at least in part, of the social reality born in the pupils.

A. Society and the Curriculum

1. *The Nature of Knowledge*

Since Durkheim wrote *The Division of Labour* in 1893, one important way of categorizing societies has been by the degree of complexity in their role structure. Modern societies have a very complicated structure of positions and roles. Hence the distribution of knowledge is very different from that found in less developed societies. Under contemporary conditions there is an increase of knowledge, specific to particular social positions. Today, for example, surgeons, specialists, general practitioners, pharmacists, matrons, sisters and nurses, in each case often practising a particular specialism, have replaced the barbers of our own society three or four hundred years ago or the witch-doctors in other societies. Knowledge with a wide relevance becomes relatively less important, so that in modern societies universally meaningful propositions apply to much narrower ranges of common experience than in less complex societies. This important generalization is clearly seen to be the case in relation to academic disciplines where, for example, laws in science or findings in history are only relevant to one subject, but it also applies to norms governing social behaviour which are found to cover such special sub-cultures as social classes, members of a profession, or even the old boys of a school. This extension of the generalization to norms of social behaviour is obviously of relevance to what is included in a school's extracurricular activities, and, since such activities have been shown to have such importance to the British idea of a school, they must be included in any consideration of the curriculum as it has here been defined.

At any one time the known stock of knowledge is divided up according to agreed definitions of what each subject should include. Likewise each subject is organized by more or less universally agreed theories using accepted concepts so that it is possible to speak of the normal version of any discipline (J. Ziman, 1968). These 'normal sciences'[1] are the contemporary outcome of a process of definition, often with a long history, whereby scholars, respected within their own fields, determine what that subject shall be. They write articles or textbooks, adding or organizing knowledge; they edit journals, examine theses, and comment to publishers on the desirability of accepting manuscripts. In all these ways they certificate new knowledge as acceptable or condemn it as heresy. In addition they choose new members of staff in universities, thereby controlling what sort of person shall continue the particular academic enterprise. A somewhat similar process would seem to be at work in relation to normal behaviour in that there are experts who decide what behaviour is deviant or permissible. Important experts here would appear to be judges, clergymen, community leaders, and under modern conditions leaders of the entertainment industry, who decide what and how

[1] T. S. Kuhn, *The Structure of Scientific Revolutions*, Chicago, 1962.

much or little we shall wear and what sort of behaviour is allowable for young or old.

The point to note is that in complex societies there must evolve social positions which carry the power to decide what shall be seen as normal knowledge and normal behaviour. In both cases, but perhaps more clearly in the latter, those who fill these positions have 'the power to *produce* reality'.[1] They manage the social pool of knowledge, determining how much and which specific knowledge shall be available to various categories of persons in that society.

2. *The Stock of Knowledge and Behavioural Patterns*

Within any society important different aspects of knowledge may be discerned by using various sociological concepts to analyse the existing stock of knowledge. Here three will be considered: culture, structure and personality.

(i) *Culture*. There is a heritage of values which underpins the present organization of any society and which those in power will, whether consciously or not, and whether by force or not, try to pass on to the next generation. The pattern of values will be the result of the challenges of past history and present circumstances. Thus, in Britain, schools teach children about the long evolution of representative democracy, partly to preserve that version of democratic government. The concept of culture also covers a body of 'recipe knowledge' that is needed for everyday social living and interaction, including, for instance, the norms that govern etiquette and dress. Such knowledge is transmitted through the sets of rules and conventions, often peculiar to individual institutions, that are made in any school. Such rules can be seen as one way of directing learning experiences and hence as a latent influence on the curriculum. Another form of recipe knowledge is the set of stereotypes that enables us to categorize others so that we know how to behave towards them. Children, especially at primary school, learn how to recognize the occupants of various occupational roles. They come to recognize teachers, inspectors, foreigners and so on, and learn what patterns of behaviour they are expected to show towards them. Many of these stereotypes and much recipe knowledge is learnt at home;

[1] P. L. Berger and T. Luckmann, *The Social Construction of Reality*, London, 1967, p. 137.

this is particularly the case for middle-class children for whom the home provides a much fuller version of what has been called 'the hidden curriculum'.[1]

(ii) *Structure*. Societies can be seen as patterns of positions and role expectations. These expectations are mutual and therefore knowledge must be 'structured in terms of relevances'.[2] Colloquially we may say that in any society who ought to know what about whom is also socially defined. For example, curricula for training persons for such specialized positions as those of doctor, mathematics teacher or plumber can be seen as social prescriptions of the knowledge required to fill the expectations of others with whom doctors, teachers or plumbers will interact. Furthermore, in any society there will be social definitions governing the part to be played in the whole process by each of the agents of socialization. Thus, in different societies the curriculum of the school will differ according to the tasks given to the family or the church. As already noted, in many Continental countries much of the so-called extracurricular content of a British school is defined as the task of these two agents of socialization.

(iii) *Personality*. The way in which any individual has integrated the roles that he plays can be seen as basic to his personality. In some degree each culture specifies a different type of personality, which governs styles of perception and of thought. The organization of patterns of thought is particularly relevant to academic curricula.

Each discipline orders its material according to theories and concepts so that those who learn it perceive a specific version of reality. The same event or problem considered from the viewpoint of diverse disciplines will probably seem different. Thus, a physicist will view a metallurgical problem differently from a chemist, and a doctor may not prescribe the same cure for alcoholism as will a psychiatrist. Normal sciences, however, change as alternative theories are suggested and are ultimately upheld as more fruitful or as leading to truer views of reality. In this way in the 1930s Keynes changed our view of the economy by relating full employment to the effective demand for goods and services; a little later F. R. Leavis, an academic teacher of English, altered the way that many think about the mass

[1] See F. L. Strodtbeck in C. W. Bunnicutt (ed.), *Urban Education and Cultural Deprivation*, Syracuse, 1964.

[2] P. L. Berger and T. Luckmann, *op. cit.*, p. 58.

media and advertisements by applying to the social environment the same concept, namely discrimination, that he used in criticizing English novels; and finally, more recently, the biochemists who discovered the function of DNA transformed our perception of what life is.

These changes in normal sciences ultimately affect school curricula, though the rate at which new styles of thought spread through a culture is very slow, because there are many whose personal styles were formed as a result of learning the old theories and who find change difficult to achieve. Change also comes as old disciplines split up, creating new specialisms that contend for a place in the curricula of schools. Thus, out of the subject of history there have differentiated economic and social versions of the one original discipline, both of which compete for school time. Perhaps the one most accurate index of the complexity of any culture is the dictionary of the spoken language concerned, which lists the emphases and indicates the patterns of what has to be transmitted as school curricula. Thus, the Eskimo language has several words where English uses 'snow', whilst certainly till recently English had many words relating to motor vehicles where the Arabs had but one, whereas they had a whole complex of words built around the one English word 'camel'. Clearly the styles of thought relating to cultures and disciplinary subcultures are linguistic codes akin to those that Bernstein associated with the sub-cultures of social class and raise similar problems of understanding and translation.

3. Decisions about the Curriculum

At any one time there are social definitions of what education shall be. Today, many of these are enshrined in the academic subject of education which has itself only become an accepted subject in Britain in the last fifty years or so. In fact, this book may be seen as an example of one such definition, in that one contemporary version of the normal science of the sociology of education is set out here. There are ruling definitions of all the normal sciences and normal patterns of behaviour that are relevant to the school curriculum. From these definitions can be found what is considered worthy of rational study and what is seen as metaphysical. Furthermore, social definitions exist of who shall be permitted to learn various types of knowledge. In Britain for a long time the view has been held that only a few should stay at school beyond fifteen and that even fewer should go on to university, whereas in the USA a much greater proportion has been allowed to go on to each level of education. Within subjects there are agreed standards, seen as examinable, that determine who may go forward or be seen as qualified at a given level. There are also agreed definitions, largely based on the present versions of the normal sciences of psychology and of education, concerning who shall be known as mentally or physically handicapped and therefore not be permitted to follow the usual educational pathway.

In each academic field there is a group that has the power to control what the curriculum shall be. This is very clearly seen in the case of those professional disciplines such as medicine and law where there is a statutory mechanism that controls entry qualifications. Here, as in most similar cases, there is a very close relationship between those in the universities and the members of the profession concerned. Likewise, professional engineers, chartered accountants and bankers play a large part in controlling the nature of the syllabuses that those who wish to qualify as practitioners in these professions must successfully complete. At lower levels examinations which greatly influence schools and the writers of textbooks are much affected by those in the universities in two ways. Academics are concerned about the standards of those who wish to enter upon higher education and also govern what is currently seen as normal science. There are, however, no formal examinations of normal behaviour and, as noted above, the relevant mechanism of control is less easy to pinpoint.

This system of defined structures of knowledge is very complex, but, as the division of labour in industry becomes more specialized, so more quasi-professions and more posts requiring technical expertise that seems easily testable are likely to evolve. The problem then arises of keeping these curricula up-to-date. The members of the bodies that certify professionals, technologists and technicians are usually aware of technical and economic changes that demand different curricula and attempt to keep their prescriptions related to contemporary techniques. The problem is more difficult in the case of the school curriculum, partly because the economic measure of profit and loss does not apply as directly as in technical education, but partly also because the school is dealing with more elementary and basic theories which change less often than does their application to specific techniques.

The curricula of schools become obsolete for a number of reasons. Most obviously, the normal science may change in a revolutionary way so that even in the early stages the school curriculum must be redefined. Discoveries made in physics since the war have had such an effect. Normally these changes are transmitted to the schools through such channels as the relevant association of subject teachers, through the recruitment of staff who have recently been trained at universities, or through the interaction of university teachers with school teachers on the committees that decide curricula and supervise examinations. Secondly, there are the changes brought about because of the way the social institutions that interlock with education alter through time. Thus, there has been a lessening of the salience of religion for education and a rise in the importance of the economy, so that less time is now given to religious instruction and more to science and mathematics than a century ago. The influence here seems to have worked in an indirect manner through a redefinition in the minds of citizens, parents and teachers, of what education is. Sometimes the effect of the changing salience of an institution interlocking with education works more directly and more quickly. The so-called 'Return to Learning' in the USA during the late 1950s seems to have been due to a sudden realization that national security depended upon the military forces and the industries supplying them, both of which put a high emphasis on scientific skills and knowledge. Thus, although curricula in English, history and foreign languages were reformed, the first moves came in physics and mathematics (W. K. Richmond, 1971). Thirdly, autonomous change occurs within the educational system itself. Research, which was always a built-in agent for change in science, has now begun to affect the relatively new subject of education. The results are seen particularly clearly in the recently evolved new methods of teaching certain subjects. The teaching of mathematics, science and modern languages, all noteworthy for the possibility of their use in the economy, has been revolutionized and teachers have themselves spread the knowledge of the new ways of organizing experiences whereby children may learn more effectively. In addition, as we saw in the last chapter, the Schools Council and other bodies interested in curricular development have played a part.

The work of the Schools Council can be justified by the need to adapt the curriculum to change generated elsewhere in the social structure. There are, however, those who follow another ideological position, namely that, rather than supporting the status quo, those in schools should teach a curriculum that has the aim of changing society.[1] In some societies there is one prevailing ideology that governs what shall be taught. This is the case in the USSR or China. In other societies, the making of decisions is less centralized and there is more chance that the existence of different ideologies may be reflected in the curricula of different schools. This is possibly true of Britain, though in some senses there is a lowest common ideological denominator that tends to guarantee some agreement over large areas of what is to be taught. There is always the chance that this alliance of ideologies may be changed because of the work of deviant educators who try to redefine the curriculum and the relevant teaching methods. In Britain, a succession of such progressive educators as Susan Isaacs, A. S. Neill and Kurt Hahn have acted in this way to alter somewhat our view of the curriculum and, more particularly, that of the primary school (R. Skidelsky, 1969).

Since just after 1900 those responsible for the central administration of education in Britain have pursued a policy of allowing schools and teachers more freedom to decide what shall be taught, though in many ways this initiative has been offset by the growing emphasis put upon examinations. Teachers seem, however, to have continued to be governed by the existing curricula or textbooks and not to have taken the freedom offered to them.[2] The committees concerned with examinations have continued to exercise power. Those members drawn from the schools would seem to have been recruited from more experienced, hence older, teachers, who may possibly be more conservative. Likewise, those responsible for making the school rules governing normal behaviour have been drawn from the older generation. Thus, even when the opportunity to decide both the method of

---

[1] P. W. Musgrave, 'Two Contemporary Curricular Ideologies', in R. J. W. Selleck (ed.), *Melbourne Studies in Education*, Melbourne, 1972.

[2] For a particular example of this see P. W. Musgrave, *Technical Change, the Labour Force and Education*, Oxford, 1967, pp. 147–8.

and the content for examinations, as is the case in the Certificate of Secondary Education, Mode Three, is given to teachers, their attitudes may prevent them from taking the freedom offered to them. There are pressures upon teachers that could account for this and for their seeming lack of initiative in instigating courses in which there are no examinations. Firstly, textbooks and curricular material already often exist, which predisposes teachers in a given direction. Secondly, the teacher who is trying to innovate may be hampered by lack of resources with which to buy new teaching materials. Indeed, one much used way of bringing about curricular change is for the group initiating the new curriculum to use financial resources as a lever. Thus, new materials may be given to a school, if they are used according to the wishes of the innovator.[1]

B. The Curriculum

So far we have been examining the social forces at work on the curriculum which govern the ways in which disciplines emerge as social systems. These disciplines are taught to teachers in universities or colleges and they in their turn decide what parts of the subject matter and the organizing theories or concepts shall be taught to their pupils. There is, therefore, a long series of links between the research worker at the edge of contemporary knowledge and the teacher in a primary school. An additional factor which must be taken into account in this process whereby a normal science is filtered into a curriculum is that teachers rarely determine the goals of their schools which are culturally defined. In this way, control over what is actually taught is divided between those within and those who are outside the educational system.

The goals given to schools as a result of social and political processes are represented in definitions of what education shall be. These may most easily be found spelt out in broad terms in statements, oral or written, by educationists or political leaders. Thus, in 1861 the Newcastle Commission on the State of Popular Education in England defined elementary education in terms of the ability to read 'a common narrative', to write 'a letter that shall be both legible

[1] B. R. Clark, 'Inter-organisation Patterns in Education', *Administration Science Quarterly*, September 1965.

and intelligible' and to know 'enough of ciphering to make out, or test the correctness of a common shop bill', together with a little geography and the ability 'to follow the allusions and the arguments of a plain Saxon sermon' – in other words a Christian version of 'the three Rs' for boys and girls up to the age of ten or twelve.[1] This definition was worked out by the experts of the (then) Education Department as the Revised Code of 1867 which laid down in detail just what children of each age level were expected to know.

Today the uncertainty over who controls the curriculum is greater than in the last century. Particularly in Britain, but also elsewhere, interventions in decisions about the curriculum are seen as wrong because the freedom of the teacher is now given great weight. Yet simultaneously there is a contrary influence. New specialisms are arising within education itself as a result of which a new specialist, the curriculum expert, is now found. His output of advice on curricular matters and of packaged kits tend to remove from the teacher the very freedom to which he is so committed. This tendency may even be increased by educational conspicuous consumption which drives one school to use the latest curricular device, even when not fully persuaded of its value, because a neighbouring school is doing so.

The existing disciplines are usually translated into school terms as textbooks and these are dependent for their quality on the existence of an established theoretical framework in the relevant normal science. Thus, for example, no textbook in metallurgy other than those merely describing machinery and techniques as opposed to analysing the nature of processes could be written much before the 1860s, by which time the relevant theories in chemistry and physics had been evolved.[2] It is the knowledge enshrined in such books as are prescribed by those in power that is tested in examinations. Research starts where the advanced level textbook ends. Therefore, the way in which textbooks emerge and change is crucial to the

[1] See P. W. Musgrave, 'A Model for the Analysis of the Development of the English Educational System from 1860', *Transactions of Sixth World Congress of Sociology*, Vol. IV, Milan, 1970 (in P. W. Musgrave (ed.), *Sociology, History and Education*, London, 1970).

[2] P. W. Musgrave, 'Metallurgy and the Department of Science and Art', *Technical Education Abstracts*, July 1909 (in P. W. Musgrave (ed.), *Sociology, History and Education*).

understanding of the manner in which curricula are decided, but the process has so far hardly been studied and, more particularly, next to nothing is known of the ways in which the commercial publishing companies encourage and sponsor authors, or of their policies concerning the retaining or withdrawing of profitable textbooks that represent out-of-date versions of a normal science.

Yet any textbook is capable of different interpretations, since it is filtered through the ideology of the teacher to reach his pupils. Thus, for example, during the first world war the teaching of Latin in Britain, then at war with Germany, could be justified in the following words: 'We must go to Rome for our lessons. To govern people who differ in race, language, temper and civilisation; to raise and distribute armies for their defence or subjection. . . . Latin then stands in our education partly on linguistic grounds, partly on the heroic character in its history, or the interest of its political and imperial problems, and on the capacities of its people for government.'[1] A few years later in Germany under the Nazis, children in the *Volksschulen* were working exercises in simple arithmetic in which a table gave the sum of money paid annually by the State for elementary and secondary education and for those in mental homes, in order to show that a person who was mentally ill was an expensive liability; the child was then told that there were 200,000 lunatics in Germany and he was required to estimate how much these cost the State each year, and how many marriage loans could be financed with this sum.[2] Even in a subject where values might be thought to play a small part, ideologies can be transmitted through textbooks.

In the last decade various versions of modern or social studies have come to be taught in schools and nowhere are there more chances for teachers to filter apparently similar curricular material through differing ideologies, thereby producing totally different lessons. With the coming of what may be termed the end of the age of deference, the nature of political authority has been a topic quite commonly recommended for consideration by pupils in the early teens. How-

---

[1] R. W. Livingstone, quoted in F. Campbell, 'Latin and the Elite Tradition in Education', *British Journal of Sociology*, September 1968 (also in P. W. Musgrave (ed.), *Sociology, History and Education*).

[2] R. H. Samuel and R. H. Thomas, *Education and Society in Modern Germany*, London, 1949, p. 87.

T S E—G

ever, it is extremely difficult, even for a teacher who has carefully examined his own stance, not to betray unconsciously what his own sympathies or position are on such matters, so that an effective teacher may mould the views of children at an impressionable age in a way that many in society might not wish.

C. The Curriculum and Society

This analysis has now begun to pass the middle point and to consider the effects of the curriculum on pupils. We have seen that there are socially determined definitions of what at any time education is seen to be. These definitions are translated into curricula that specify to the teacher in much or little detail what is expected of his pupils after they have undergone any course. Sociologically such details can be seen as prescriptions for specific segments of the role of the good pupil. They govern the nature of the reality that the school, or rather the teacher on its behalf, hopes to, and in some measure will, create in its pupils, and the order in which the process will occur.

Examinations are the mechanisms in which this process may most clearly be seen at work. The expected intellectual behaviour of a pupil who gains a distinction at some level of a course in mathematics, science or languages is capable of a high degree of prediction, whereas in relation to normal behaviour there is a wider range of tolerated behaviour, and, therefore, prediction is not so accurate for such roles as prefect or class captain. British schools traditionally provide a very wide range of learning experiences which occur in classroom and library, on the games field and school trips. The aim is to affect cognitive, emotional and aesthetic behaviour, indeed, to mould the nature of the child's whole personality. In schools where this wide curriculum is provided the process is usually referred to as 'education' and the outcome as integrated in any individual is somewhat unpredictable, whereas in those institutions such as technical or trade schools, whether organized by the educational system, industry or the armed services, where closely specified outcomes alone are the aim of the curriculum, the process is usually called 'training'.

The work of Brookover is relevant here. He has shown that pupils can develop self-concepts of their own ability that differ according to the academic subjects included in the curriculum and which influence how well children achieve in the relevant subjects. For example, he studied the self-concepts of ability in mathematics, social studies and English. Such self-concepts are influenced by the various socializing agents with whom the child interacts. Teachers, parents and school counsellors all play a part.[1] It would also appear that the status that the world outside the school gives to particular achievements influences the importance that children give to subjects in schools, regardless of most efforts to the contrary that teachers may make. Thus, in some schools, much attention is given to non-examinable subjects, but pupils tend to see these as less important than those subjects that the world rates highly by demanding success in an examination.

This is clearly one more example of the way in which latent roles are brought into the school. Many attributes that pupils have already learnt will influence the way in which they view the curriculum. Thus, whether or not they speak in restricted or elaborated code, to use Bernstein's terms referred to in Chapter 4, will constrain how well they do in academic subjects. In addition, motivation is important. This attribute, usually seen in psychological terms, is often connected with teaching methods, but the curriculum itself can also be structured to increase or lessen the pupils' motivation. Three elements of the curriculum as usually organized at present are important. Firstly, there is the possibility of a 'mismatching' of the scale of time within which the pupils think and that implicit in the curriculum, since so many, particularly working-class, children are unable to defer present gratification in the hope of future gain, whilst the benefits of many learning experiences, as now presented, can only be appreciated after advancing several stages further into a subject. Secondly, much curricular content is not seen as intrinsically rewarding; the academic emphasis in English, music and even in science, often compares in many children's minds unfavourably with the vividness of their comics, pop music and the programmes about science fiction seen on television. Thirdly, pupils regard teachers both as teachers and as judges who write reports and can pass or fail them in examinations; they are unable to prevent their hostility to the latter role from spreading to the former. One solution to such

[1] W. B. Brookover, S. Thomas and A. Paterson, 'Self-Concept of Ability and School Achievement', *Sociology of Education*, Spring 1964.

problems that has been suggested is the use of simulated games in academic work in order to motivate pupils on the assumption that they are attracted to games which also give quick rewards.[1] Whilst this may be seen basically as an innovation in teaching method, the analysis draws attention to the fact that the organization of the curriculum contributes in itself to the sanctions that a school has available to influence its part in the process of socialization.

There is great difficulty in practice, if not in theory, in separating the influence of the content of any curriculum and the methods used to teach it. Prescribed content tends to be given more emphasis in such traditional types of schools as most public and grammar schools than in the so-called progressive schools. In the latter, content covers a wider range of topics from which the pupil may choose and, though facts are still on the whole important, it is the processes involved in thinking upon which the main emphasis is put. Thus, the aim may be that ultimately the child shall be a questioning and creative being, though these qualities are difficult to prescribe in operational terms. Many contemporary curricula, including those where kits of materials are provided, have such aims. The Nuffield Science projects provide an example. The teacher is supplied with the resources to arrange a series of learning experiences, in which the pupils experience situations that give fairly immediate rewards, that seem related to everyday life, and that appear more under their own control than that of the teacher. Furthermore, any school that provides such experiences where the pupils must make more choices and where the learning of processes is important, would seem to meet contemporary social needs more aptly than a curriculum where the great degree of choice that must be exercised under contemporary conditions by everyone is overlooked.

The nature of the social reality created in schools grows more complex as the child becomes older and especially after he passes to the secondary school, where many more specialized positions with specific role expectations are made available to him. There are many more subjects to be learnt and a variety of clubs of which pupils may be members. Each type of school, or even each individual school, indicates a pattern of priorities amongst the various positions that are

[1] S. S. Boocock and J. S. Coleman, 'Games with Simulated Environments in Learning', *Sociology of Education*, Summer 1966.

available. Thus, games or physical fitness may be given a higher priority than academic success. For example, one small Scottish public school has as its motto, '*Spartam nactus es, hanc exorna*' ('You have gained Sparta, live up to it'), and not surprisingly during the first half of this century produced more internationals in the field of rugby football than any other British public school. Other British schools have given academic excellence the highest priority and over the years have gained a high number of open scholarships to Oxford and Cambridge. These emphases are backed by sanctions, so that the integration of the roles made available that takes place at the level of personality in their pupils differs from school to school. It is because of this that the claim, often in practice true, is made that the past and present pupils of certain schools can be fairly easily recognized. In this way the school recreates its own version of social reality at the cognitive, emotional and perceptual level.

The positions made available in any school as a result of the nature of the curriculum often, particularly where external examinations are given importance, form a number of pathways through the school, offering very different experiences. This situation is symbolized in the Arts, Science and Modern sides of many grammar schools. Choices that relate to intended future career have to be made and these inevitably rule out the possibility of other curricular experiences. Because of the standards at present required for entry to tertiary education, such choices are often irreversible and have to be made by pupils as young as thirteen or fourteen. The perhaps extreme example of entry to the English sixth form may be sited. Choice of any pattern of subjects to be taken at Ordinary level of the GCE at sixteen years of age is usually made two or three years beforehand, with the result that in the mid 1960s 6, or under certain circumstances 16, per cent only of those taking eight or more subjects had definitely kept all future options in higher education open, whilst for a further 39 per cent there was some flexibility possible, but only if extra work was done in the sixth form.[1]

Size of school has effects that have as yet been little investigated. The larger the school, the more specialization is possible amongst staff and pupils. However, contrary to expectations, such opportuni-

[1] *Enquiry into the Flow of Candidates in Science and Technology into Higher Education* (Dainton), London, HMSO, 1968, p. 167.

ties do not necessarily imply that all pupils in larger schools have a fuller curriculum than those in smaller schools. In a study of a number of high schools in Kansas it was found that, although small schools offered a narrower range of both academic and extracurricular experiences, yet the pupils in these schools both filled a larger number and undertook a wider range of such positions than their peers in the bigger schools with supposedly greater opportunities.[1] A richer availability of curricular experiences will not necessarily be used by pupils.

So far the analysis has been of the role of the pupil, but expectations in any position are mutual and the role of the teacher must, therefore, also be considered. The teacher manages the environment within which the pupil is to learn. Thus, a particular type of curriculum implies a particular set of expectations in the teacher. In curricula described broadly as progressive the teacher exercises less direct control than the traditional teacher, and this in itself means some redefinition of his role in comparison with the more usually held expectations for a teacher. It follows that any curricular change implies a change, great or small, in the role of the teacher. Such a change may stem from a number of sources. It may be due to an alteration in the agreed version of the normal science or a new pattern of normal behaviour may affect the extracurricular experiences that teachers offer. The process of changing teachers who already have fixed ideas of how they are expected to behave is one of adult resocialization, and to be successful must be undertaken in favourable conditions. One recently developed method is the establishment of teachers' centres where peer groups of practising teachers, all presumed to be motivated towards change, support each other's efforts to learn a new role. These teachers eventually bring back to their own schools new ideas that are accepted the more easily because those who have been changed have the status of experienced, practical teachers. Formerly the hope was that young teachers, fresh from college or university, would impart new ideas to the curriculum, but, though they may have some influence, their suggestions do not carry great weight since they are made by newcomers to the profession who are often seen as too theoretical and short of practical experience.

There are a number of social mechanisms that exist to preserve

[1] R. G. Barker and P. V. Gump, *Big School, Small School*, Stanford, 1964.

the status quo in the curriculum. Deviant teachers who try to innovate are sanctioned by the disapproval of their peers and even by their pupils. Thus, until recently, low priority was often given in the British public school to knowledge that had vocational relevance, whereas a high priority was put upon the cultivation of those qualities of personality that were associated with a choice of success in a professional career in which service to others, rather than great monetary reward, was possible. Many social norms, not the least of which was the amateur tradition so powerful in English society, worked to maintain curricula based on such principles. In addition external examinations are often perceived by teachers in such a way that they find great difficulty in deviating from prescribed academic curricula. Equally powerful sanctions control the normal behaviour of staff and pupils. Deviant staff can be dismissed in independent schools and eased out of their positions in any type of school by giving them difficult classes, heavy teaching loads or poor facilities. The parents of deviant pupils may be encouraged to withdraw their children at or soon after the minimum legal age for leaving school. Lastly, in all schools except Borstals, pupils may be expelled. We therefore have the paradoxical position that in institutions dedicated to changing persons, those who prove recalcitrant are removed from the system and its total failure is thereby rendered almost impossible. Yet in respect of all role expectations, whether academic or behavioural, there are ranges of the behaviour that will be tolerated. It is within these ranges that permissible academic and behavioural creativity occurs. Some slightly deviant behaviour is acceptable and if institutionalized forms one major source from which new versions of social reality enter the curriculum to be transmitted to future generations of pupils.

In this section the effect of the curriculum at the interpersonal level has been considered. Another focus would be to carry the analysis a step further in order to see the ways in which the curriculum affects the wider social structure. An example can be quoted that relates to the system of stratification. The modern form of the public school was developed in the nineteenth century largely in answer to the demands for a suitable education for the sons, and later the daughters, of the rising middle class. However, once these schools existed they undoubtedly worked to reinforce the existing system of social stratification. Thus, their curricula guaranteed that their pupils were gentlemen of the type defined as normal in the England of the time with a little Latin and less mathematics or science, but with the belief that they had been trained to take up positions as leaders in every walk of life throughout the Empire.[1] Many other examples of the effect of the curriculum at the structural level in relation, for example, to culture transmission, the polity and the economy, will be cited in the third part of this book, which is entirely concerned with the social consequences of the contemporary educational system.

D. Conclusion

The curriculum is deeply influenced by the structure of the society, the ideology of those with power and of those who teach and by the present state of normal sciences and behaviour. These constraints govern the nature of the distribution of the social stock of knowledge. In its turn the curriculum prescribes the academic and social behaviour of pupils and, in as much as the aims of those who organize it are successful, the social reality that they perceive will be recreated in those whom they teach. The fact that there are so many very different curricula in any society today would suggest that reality is being variously construed with differing effects on those who learn. For example, those who learn physics through a traditional course have been shown to view physical reality in a different manner from those using a more modern type of curriculum.[2] There is, however, little research on this topic, nor is there yet much sociological work at all in the field of the curriculum which is coming to be seen as one, if not the, central focus of the sociology of education.

[1] R. Wilkinson, 'The Gentleman Ideal and the Maintenance of a Political Elite', *Sociology of Education*, Fall 1963 (also in P. W. Musgrave (ed.), *Sociology, History and Education*).

[2] E. Brakken, 'Intellectual Factors in PSSC and Conventional High School Physics', *Journal of Research in Science Teaching*, March 1965.

BIBLIOGRAPHY

P. W. Musgrave, 'A Sociology of the Curriculum', in *Europaea Paedagogica*, 1970.

W. K. Richmond, *The School Curriculum*, London, 1971.

R. Skidelsky, *English Progressive Schools*, London, 1969 (Pelican).

D. K. Wheeler, *The Curriculum Process*, London, 1967.

J. Ziman, *Public Knowledge: The Social Dimension of Science*, Cambridge, 1968.

II

The Teacher in the Classroom

A major part of the school day for any teacher or pupil is spent teaching or learning that part of the curriculum that is taught in the classroom. The school class is a group that consists of a teacher and a varying number of children. Like any other social system the class can be divided into its constituent parts in order to see what function each part is playing in the whole. It should also be possible to see how the various parts interact with each other in fulfilling their functions. In this chapter we shall first examine the school class as a social system and secondly, we shall describe a technique, namely sociometry, that has been devised to study the interrelationships within such small groups as the school class.

A. The School Class as a Social System

The functions of the educational system are complex and will be fully considered in the next part. Briefly, however, the school assists the family in developing the intellect and personality of the growing child, and it helps to allocate the child when he has grown up to the most fitting niche in adult society. In any school the major part of these tasks is done in the classrooms. Talcott Parsons (1959) has advanced the thesis that the school class as now organized will always differentiate the children in it by their achievement. This, if true, will make the process of allocation much simpler. Parsons examined schools in the USA but his method of analysis can be applied to British schools and yields somewhat similar results.

The great majority of school classes have certain common conditions that govern their organization. It is usual today for all the children in any one school class to be of approximately the same age. This was not the case in Britain in the early nineteenth century, nor is it always so in the underdeveloped countries today. Often in addition the children are of the same social class. This is particularly the case for smaller schools with homogeneous catchment areas as is true for many primary schools. The children in the big secondary modern schools of large urban areas tend also to come from more or less the same, mainly the working, class. Independent schools mainly consist of middle-class children, and only two British school types can be guaranteed to contain a mixed social class composition, namely the selective grammar school and the non-selective comprehensive school. Thus in very many British classrooms the children are equalized for both age and social class.

Though there is a tendency nowadays to allow pupils more individual choice of activity than formerly, the teacher often gives a common undifferentiated task to the relatively homogeneous group that forms his class. This is obvious at secondary level, where all the children will do the same set of sums or the identical questions to test their comprehension of a passage of prose. Much the same pattern is true of the top forms of the junior school; even in the lower forms and in the infant school, for much of the time the teacher will split the class into small groups that will each have their own individual common task. When all the children are doing the same, comparison becomes easy, and, since variations in age and social class are often absent, the standard of performance in the work that all are doing seems to the children the obvious and main measuring rod of any differences between themselves.

This stress on academic achievement is somewhat offset in British schools by the tradition that the school shall play an important part in moulding the child's personality. Many teachers make a point of giving as much individual attention to the children in their class as possible. This both helps the children's academic achievement and enables the teacher to know the quirks of character of each individual child. Although this emphasis is true at all stages of education, it is particularly true in the infant school where academic education is not stressed so much. Yet the teacher who moulds character assesses his results in terms of good and bad. The children soon know the standards and can compare their own behaviour or 'moral achievement' in much the same way as they compare their academic results. There are also a number of progressive schools in which the emphasis is on cooperation rather than competition and on the development of personality rather than academic achievement. Yet, even in these schools, the children often work in small groups in much the same way as in the junior schools; attainment determines the membership of these groups and comparison of achievement is still possible. Therefore, despite these apparent exceptions, Parsons' analysis seems to hold. The organization of the contemporary school class is such that the children are bound to stress comparative achievement, whether it is moral or academic.

A closer examination of the school class will reveal that it is in addition performing other functions of a very different nature. Although it was set up to socialize and to allocate, it has autonomously come to do other things as well. An obvious way to see what is happening in the classroom is to divide the social system into its main parts, namely the teacher and the children, and to see how each undertakes the two main functions. Finally, we shall put the two parts together again as a school class and see how they interact. Throughout we must note what additional functions this social system as a whole fulfils.

1. *The Teacher*

In one respect the teacher is in a unique social position. He has been formed by the social system to which he returns to form others. He can very easily transmit the values that he has picked up himself as he passed through the educational system. The 'teacher' in a secondary modern school who went through a maintained grammar school and a college of education will have learnt a different set of values from the 'schoolmaster' in a public school who attended an independent school and Oxford or Cambridge. Despite such differences due to the inbreeding of values, all teachers have the two main functions described above in common, namely of teaching the three Rs and of moulding personality, although in the latter case the 'teacher' may aim for a different ideal from the 'schoolmaster'.

The stress on achievement is considerably strengthened because of the nature of the relationship of teacher and child. The teacher is an adult who is usually much older than his pupils and therefore appears as the judge of what they do. As the only adult amongst a group of children this seems almost inevitable, but the fact that most

British schools have highly developed assessment systems makes the emphasis on achievement certain. There are many complex arrangements that force the children to compare their achievements with those of their classmates. These are inherent in the types of sanctions used in schools. Even in infant schools ticks and stars on sums correctly done lead to comparisons. Beginning in the junior school, but especially at secondary level, marks on individual pieces of work, tests and examination results are publicly displayed in form lists so that all, often including parents, can see. The measurement of moral achievement also is often institutionalized. For example, one of the benefits of playing games is supposedly that it builds character. The winners of house matches gain points and at secondary level, sometimes even at younger ages, competitions between houses are common. Thus the children can compare their toughness and determination as well as their English and arithmetic.

As the British educational system was organized until recently, the emphasis on doing well in academic work increased on entry to the junior school and grew greater the nearer the children came to taking the eleven-plus examination that determined whether or not they were to go to a selective secondary school. Up till eleven years of age the majority of children came under this influence from the teacher or their parents or both, but after eleven there was a difference, since some would have been selected for grammar school and some would have failed at this hurdle. Those who went to the grammar school had been chosen for education for the elite. They had been 'sponsored' either for upward mobility or for remaining in their present middle-class position. Those who had gone to the secondary modern school had at an early age to adjust to failure in the competition for social status, since transfer to grammar school after eleven was rare. The teachers in the modern schools therefore played a part in helping the children to readjust their aspirations to a more realistic level.

The comprehensive school has been established to overcome these disadvantages inherent in the eleven-plus system. The aim is that in the comprehensive school a situation more akin to that in the US high school will be found, since here the final choice for the elite has not yet been made. The teacher can put emphasis on competition to achieve at school until at least the minimum legal leaving age. In this new type of secondary school the avenue to the elite is meant to be through achievement, rather than through sponsorship as in the former system of grammar and modern schools.[1] However, from what little is known of the way in which comprehensive schools are working this hope does not seem to have been fulfilled. The failure would seem to be due to the organization within the comprehensive school of streams that in a sense replicate the two types of school that the one school was meant to replace.[2] Thus, the mechanism of sponsorship still seems present in the upper streams of this new type of British school, though not perhaps in so severe a form since a larger proportion of former secondary modern pupils stay beyond the legal minimum leaving age, thereby achieving more than they would have done in the old system.

If the teacher is to fulfil his functions he must influence his class by providing the leadership that is usually referred to as discipline in discussion of this topic in schools. There are purely legal sanctions on the teacher to maintain discipline since a chaotic classroom cannot provide the education envisaged in the 1944 Act. There are several types of leadership and each ensures a different atmosphere in the classroom. The problem is to discover whether any one type will enable the teacher to do what he wants more efficiently.

In 1939–40 three American social psychologists undertook a famous series of experiments that is relevant at this point. This work was very sophisticated and can only be described in the briefest outline here. Lippitt, Lewin and White (R. Lippitt and R. K. White, 1940) arranged for three groups of adolescents to have three different types of leader for the activities that they undertook in a youth club. There were authoritarian leaders (the reader should throughout mentally substitute 'teacher' for 'leader' so that he may catch the full relevance of this experiment), who gave orders without reasons, accepted no questions as to aim or method, distributed blame or praise without any objective explanation, and remained aloof from their groups. There were *laissez-faire* leaders, who allowed their

---

[1] R. H. Turner, 'Sponsored and Contest Mobility in the School System', *American Sociological Review*, December 1960 (also in A. H. Halsey, J. E. Floud and C. A. Anderson, *Education, Economy and Society*, New York, 1961).

[2] J. Ford, *Social Class and the Comprehensive School*, London, 1969, espec. pp. 133–4.

groups to do what they wanted, made no suggestions and were neither critical nor helpful. These leaders were merely adults who were present. Finally, there were democratic leaders, who gave suggestions without forcing them on their groups, gave constructive and objective criticism and praise, did not interfere excessively, and tried to be positive without being masterful. Each type of leadership was found to create a totally different atmosphere in a group. Authoritarian leadership resulted in a lack of cooperation amongst the adolescents who stressed 'me' rather than 'us'; there was an air of either rebellion or repression. The *laissez-faire* leader's group were unable to work together, as they found no common aim and so merely drifted. The democratic group decided what was to be done, cooperated well and enjoyed what they did together. It would seem that a teacher who creates a democratic atmosphere by the leadership that he gives in Britain as in America can hope for good results and a happy class. Democracy can be viewed as an end in itself, but here it is seen to be a method of leadership in a classroom that results in the children imposing a discipline upon themselves so that they accomplish the work that their teacher feels necessary.

Another investigation that was carried out in the USA in the 1940s reinforces this conclusion.[1] It was found that teachers' behaviour in the classroom was dominated by two opposing aims. The desires to dominate and to achieve social integration were both present in all the teachers observed, but the relative amounts varied in each teacher even within any one day and also through a school term. However, the children reacted differently according to whether dominance or social integration was the predominant aim. Where social integration was the major element, the children were less restless, contributed more to the lesson and showed more initiative than where dominance was shown. The pattern of behaviour shown by the teachers did not seem to be influenced by different groups of children, since they were observed a year later with their new classes and exhibited the same patterns. There was little doubt that the teachers were influencing the children and not vice versa.

The importance of these findings has been indicated by work in Salford in 1951. Here Wiseman found that progressiveness in the

[1] Work of H. H. Anderson, quoted in K. M. Evans, *Sociometry and Education*, London, 1961, pp. 102–4.

teachers was a factor that could be separated out as a statistically significant influence on children's success in school. More especially, progressive teachers had considerable effect on the attainment of children in reading and writing.[1] Activity methods are seen by many teachers as a philosophy rather than as a means to more efficient education. A teacher's philosophy can influence the children's success at school, so it should be no surprise to find that teachers' attitudes can influence the achievement of the children whom they are teaching, even if only by adopting a curriculum or method that grasps the attention of their pupils.

2. *The School Class*

The school class, considered on its own apart from the teacher, may be seen as a group of equals or as a number of small peer groups. Teachers are often so immersed in fulfilling their functions of teaching the three Rs and of moulding character that they forget that membership in a peer group itself plays a large part in educating children. The process of education in such a group is unconscious but none the less real.

As has been indicated the family is too simple a social system to provide all the needs of the growing child. For many purposes the best way to view the socialization of the child is to consider the family and school and peer group as one social system. The child goes out from the family into the primary school where he is a member of a peer group, the school class. In this group he tests out the personality that he has learnt in the family and, if he cannot survive with that set of traits, he must modify his personality, adapting to meet the world at large outside his family. The child who bosses his young brother around at home learns to be bossed around at school as he undoubtedly will be in adult life. The new learning is achieved with the security of the family as a support upon which he may fall back.

The school class is one of several peer groups of which British children are members and which may include the Scout troop and the street gang, but it is the group to which the child must belong by law and in which he must participate very regularly for about ten years. Hence it is of great importance. In the school class the child

[1] S. Wiseman, *Education and Environment*, Manchester, 1964, pp. 158–61.

moves in a much more egalitarian group than in the family. The child must learn to move amongst his peers and gain non-adult approval. This is a preparation for mixing with others in the way in which he will commonly have to do as an adult. Very soon the selfish child must learn to adapt to the wishes of the rest of the class in the playground or else suffer unpopularity and rejection by his peers. The child must experiment with personal relationships. The friendship groups in the younger age ranges change rapidly as the children learn whom they can trust and in what way they must behave towards their contemporaries. Parents are used to a child coming home from school and saying 'John's not my friend any more' of the classmate who was his inseparable companion till yesterday. The school class is an important testing ground for experience and in it the child will be valued by his peers as a whole personality, not just on his school work or on his 'good' character as judged by the teacher's criteria.

All small groups such as the school class quickly create particular patterns and standards of behaviour to which their members must adapt. The group will provide models of behaviour either from its own membership or in the form of a hero, for example a cowboy or a spaceman, to which its members will look. An important additional function of the school class is that minority groups begin to be differentiated out from the group as a whole even as early as the junior school. Where academic streaming is practised, either between or within classes, children come to be seen in stereotyped terms as 'bright' ('A' streamers) or 'dim' ('C' streamers). This process often takes place despite attempts to disguise the nature of the streams by giving them names that supposedly hide their hierarchical nature. In addition, despite the efforts of the teacher and some enlightened parents, children as they mix at play with their peers come to realize that our culture on the whole treats Jews and those with darker skins in a somewhat different way from other people. Children will try to live up to these standards much more readily than those provided by the family or the teacher, since the authority or power within the peer group is of a very different and usually more acceptable nature.

Little is known about the type of sanctions used amongst children in their classrooms. Five categories of resource that could be used to influence peers were found to be important in one study in the USA.

These were expertness, seen by children either as 'smartness at school' or 'good ideas about how to make fun', strength or the ability to coerce others, social skills which enabled a child to be 'friendly' with others, the willingness to associate with his classmates in play, and, finally, a residual category containing such qualities as good looks. Though the use of such resources varied by age and sex, the more of them any child possessed, the greater influence could he wield in his group.[1]

In primary schools children tend to remain with the same group of peers for long periods and often right through the years till they go to secondary school, though in some, particularly inner-city, areas, high rates of geographical mobility are found which disturb this stability. We have seen in Chapter 6 how children gradually move from groups of both sexes into those containing one sex in which girls form smaller and closer cliques than the boys. Through this process the children are beginning to learn their sex roles. This process continues into secondary schooling and obviously far more chances for such learning to take place are provided in a coeducational school than in schools for only one sex.

At the age of about eleven, British children in the State system move to new schools and this can mean a reshuffle of friendship groups. For the children who go to selective schools that serve a large catchment area the school class mainly consists of children who were unknown to them in their junior schools. In one northern grammar school, Lacey (1966) has shown that more than half the pupils who entered in one year came from primary schools that sent six or less pupils, the average contingent being 3·5 boys per primary school. For some the range of peer groups is only determined by age, but for others social class can be an influence. The school class in the secondary modern school will tend more often to consist of a single social class, but the grammar school includes children from all social classes. The question can be asked as to whether friendship cliques in such schools are formed on the basis of social class. If the results of work done in the early 1950s in four London grammar schools is typical this would not appear to be the case in this type of school. But friendship groups do seem to be bound up with the socio-economic status of the family in the US high school and perhaps

[1] M. Gold, 'Power in the Classroom', *Sociometry*, March 1958.

also to a considerable degree in the English comprehensive school.[1]

The influence of the school class on vocational aspirations is important. A group who have either failed the eleven plus or never taken it and now find themselves considered out of the competitive race for high social status will together readjust their ideas about the jobs for which they wish to aim. The group who have passed into a selective secondary school feel that they have succeeded in that activity upon which the educational system puts greatest emphasis, namely academic achievement. The majority of this latter group will be from the middle class or aspire to it, often under the pressure of their parents. In this situation the whole school class will tend to reinforce each other in continuing to stress the academic work that they know will lead to a chance of success in later life. This tendency will be stronger, the greater is the proportion of middle-class children in the school class.[2]

In addition to its function with regard to academic achievement the school class provides adolescents with opportunities for socialization that do not occur within the family, but the peer group that is the school class may have effects contrary to those expected. The studies by Hargreaves and by Lacey, already cited, show the way in which pupils in both grammar and modern schools gradually polarize into those who are academically oriented and those who find themselves to be increasingly at odds with their school. This process may start because teachers differentiate the successful from the less successful so that school becomes a pleasant and rewarding experience to the former, who gain status from the recognition of their good work, whereas status is withdrawn from the latter. However, once such a tendency has begun, it seems to gain a momentum of its own and the members of the out-group seek status in a group with its own norms, which will differ according to the nature of the school and its social setting. In Hargreaves' secondary modern school, by the

[1] A. N. Oppenheim, 'Social Status and Clique Formation Among Grammar School Boys', *British Journal of Sociology*, September 1955; J. Ford, *op. cit.*, Ch. 5.

[2] Compare B. Jackson and D. Marsden's evidence for a high proportion of middle-class children (*Education and the Working Class*, London, 1962) with H. T. Himmelweit's description of the opposite case (in D. V. Glass (ed.), *Social Mobility in Britain*, London, 1954).

fourth form the out-group had developed near-delinquent norms, whereas in Lacey's grammar school the teenage culture was the focus of those who were unsuccessful according to the school's academic criteria. In addition, Coleman has shown how the American high school, which was set up to fulfil educational aims, has in some senses developed out of the control of its teachers to become a meeting place for the teenage culture. We can now see that in the school class, a peer group structured specially for educational purposes, social processes can operate that ultimately lead to conflict between pupils and teacher.

3. The Teacher and School Class as a System

Where there is not great discontinuity of values between the school class and the teacher, the classroom is a social system in itself that performs certain definite additional functions. The teacher is not merely manipulating the children by providing leadership, but by his very presence he affects the currents of feeling that flow between the members of the group and between the group and himself. To the children in the school class the teacher is a superior adult who is not a member of their families. Before going to school the relationships of most infants with adults have been of an expressive nature. The family have cared about happiness. The teacher, even of young children, puts stress on performance and the older the child grows the more true does this become. This is an important preparation for life as, when the child leaves school and starts a job, he will meet many who are in a superior position to himself and who will concentrate on his achievements, for instance at work, rather than on his personality as a whole. This process is made easier in the primary school because the teacher is normally a woman and can be seen by the child as like his mother. But the class teacher changes year by year and the child comes to see the difference between the position of teacher and the individual teacher who fills that position. The absence of this idea can be observed when children call their teacher 'Mummy', and its growth when, as sometimes occurs, a child is taught by his father and in the classroom addresses him as 'Daddy-Sir'.

The whole social system of teacher and school class adjusts through conflict. This is not just a question of children letting off emotional steam. It is most clearly seen when a teacher takes over a school class that is new to him. The children must learn his ways and the teacher must discover the characteristic manner of each child. Each must test the other to learn the limits of behaviour, but this conflict serves a useful function in that it leads not to a position of equilibrium, but to a point where tension is reduced to a minimum for this group. When this is achieved, teacher and children know what to expect of each other and the class as a whole can fulfil its functions as efficiently as possible.

As a rider to this it follows that since there must almost always be tension between the teacher and the children, the school class must usually be working below full efficiency. For example, the problem of social class learning will show itself early in the primary school and may hinder the academic achievement of some children, and the clash of the teacher's middle-class culture with the values of some of the class may depress the moral achievement of others. In this situation teachers are often hostile to the school and its values.[1] Such dysfunctional conflict can be very important in the secondary modern schools of slum areas. It is clear that, whereas the teacher and the school class will have more chance of reinforcing each other's ends in the selective grammar school where each tend to be working towards the same purpose, in the secondary modern school there is the possibility of the type of conflict that leads to a separate youth culture radically opposed to the school.

B. Sociometry

So far we have analysed what the functions of the teacher and the school class are but have not tried to see what are the exact inter-relationships within the class itself. If the teacher wishes to see the class objectively as it is and not subjectively as he thinks it is, there is available to him the technique of sociometry. This is a particular way of measuring social behaviour that leads to the study of the structure and development of groups. J. L. Moreno invented the method in Austria before 1914 whilst doing group therapy with children. Moreno developed his ideas further whilst organizing a

[1] For an account of such a school see J. Webb, 'The Sociology of a School', *British Journal of Sociology*, September 1962.

refugee camp in the 1914–18 war. In 1925 he went to the USA and gathered a group of disciples in New York. Together they did much research work. Moreno always held the view that his methods could be used to lower social tensions and make the world a happier place.

There is no doubt that the tools that Moreno and his co-workers devised can be used to provide an objective and quantitative picture of the relationships within such a group as the school class. The first step is to ask the members of the group individually a series of questions in which they have to choose with whom they would undertake some relevant task (G. Jahoda, 1962). For example, the teacher might ask each child in a junior class with whom he would like to sit to read or with whom he would like to go out to tea. The answers to these two particular questions would give some idea as to whom each would prefer as a workmate in the first case or as a friend in the second. The technique is easy to administer and might be of help to the teacher in two ways. He could in a rather academic way learn more about the children in his class, and thereby be helped in his handling of his class. Secondly, he could take specific action. In one experiment in a junior school a sociometric test showed that a class was split into two groups of boys who did not mix. The groups came from the same social class, but had different intelligence levels, leisure interests and home areas. The teacher did not suspect this cleavage because the children gave no trouble.[1] The teacher here could use this knowledge in order to reorganize the children's seating plan so that they had to mix with each other, if this was what he considered to be good for these children.

The answers to the questions given in sociometric tests can be plotted as a sociogram (K. M. Evans, 1961) that displays in schematic form the relationships within the group. Groups of three persons who choose each other will be represented as a triangle with its apexes joined by lines. Mutual friends who choose each other can easily be seen. A popular figure who is the choice of many will appear in the sociogram as the centre of a star, whilst those who are not chosen at all will be seen as isolates. Such a diagram will reveal to the teacher the social forces at work in his classroom at a moment of time in respect of the particular activity about which he has asked the

[1] W. A. L. Blyth, 'Sociometry, Prefects, and Peaceful Coexistence in a Junior School', *Sociological Review*, February 1958.

children. If he wishes to observe whether change is taking place, he can repeat the test after, say, three months.

One of the problems that sociograms can pose is what to do about isolates. To place the child in an existing group may make this child withdraw even further. To put a number of isolates together in one group may prove even worse, as the qualities that make them incompatible to the rest of the class may well make them unacceptable to each other. Teachers can, if they are not careful, create isolates by the way that they treat individual children; rejection by the teacher may cause his classmates to isolate this child.

There have been a number of general findings in English sociometric studies (W. A. L. Blyth, 1960). The tendency towards complete division between the sexes and the difference between groups of boys and girls have already been mentioned. In addition, the pattern of class changes through the academic year in one of two ways. Either a scatter of mutual choices leads to an aggregate of subgroups who eventually form a group with a single star or collective leadership at the centre, or there is an initial pattern at the start of the year that changes, but reverts to its original form by the end of the year. It would also seem that where regrouping of the class is undertaken after sociometric analysis, some slight improvement in social adjustment takes place without academic performance falling away, but in all such experimental work there is great difficulty in defining the criteria of measurement.

Sociometric studies have been made of teachers as well as of children.[1] In both the USA and Britain it has been found that different generations like and dislike very similar traits in teachers. For instance, they like a kindly, patient and firm teacher, but not one who is sarcastic, domineering and has favourites. If a teacher knows this and understands that he has a character trait that works to his disadvantage in the classroom, one would presume that by control he could rid himself of it. However, from work done in the USA it seems that teachers build up patterns of behaviour over the years which they use both in and out of the classroom. They can modify teaching techniques, but, in as much as their response to their pupils is governed by their personality, change is very difficult. Certainly the main lesson from such studies is that students must learn their

[1] See K. M. Evans, *op. cit.*, Chs. VIII and IX.

disadvantageous habits and traits before these become so deeply ingrained in their patterns of behaviour that change is difficult or almost impossible.

C. Conclusion

Sociometry is a method that a teacher can use in the classroom to see just what is happening amongst the children in his class. He may treat the results of sociometric analysis as a valuable addition to the knowledge upon which he bases his decisions concerning how he will

| Function | Age | Sub-system | | Teacher/ |
		Teacher = Leader	Class = Peer Group	Class = Conflict
Socialization	Primary	Testing moral attainment	Testing of personality in a group away from family	Contact with mainly one adult (woman) in an instrumental role
	Secondary	Testing moral attainment	Development of sex roles to opposite sex	Contact with several men filling the role of teacher
Allocation	Primary	Testing academic attainment	Experiment in values	Start of culture clash
	Secondary: Selective/ Top streams Comprehensive	Educating for sponsored mobility	Group stressing high aspirations	Parts of subsystem reinforcing each other
	Non-Selective/Low streams Comprehensive	Helping readjustment of aspirations	Group adjusting to failure	Definition of the gang (v. the school)

handle the whole class or individuals within his class. Moreno used the technique that he invented with the aim of promoting social harmony and social effectiveness. The teacher can use the same methods with caution as one means towards whatever ends he has in view.

Knowledge of the detailed structure of his class may obscure for the teacher the picture of what the whole social system of the class is doing to the children in it. These functions were analysed in the first part of this chapter. In outline they may be represented by the table opposite, in each space an example has been quoted to give an indication of what part that sub-system is playing.

BIBLIOGRAPHY

W. A. L. Blyth, 'The Sociometric Study of Children's Groups in English Schools', *British Journal of Educational Studies*, May 1960.

K. M. Evans, *Sociometry and Education*, London, 1961.

G. Jahoda, in G. Humphrey and M. Argyle (eds.), *Social Psychology through Experiment*, London, 1963, Ch. 6.

C. Lacey, 'Some Sociological Concomitants of Academic Streaming in a Grammar School', *British Journal of Sociology*, June 1966.

R. Lippitt and R. K. White, 'An Experimental Study of Leadership and Group Life' (1940), in G. E. Swanson, T. H. Newcomb and others, *Readings in Social Psychology* (rev. ed.), New York, 1952.

T. Parsons, 'The School Class as a Social System', *Harvard Education Review*, Fall 1959 (in A. H. Halsey, J. E. Floud and C. A. Anderson, *Education, Economy and Society*, New York, 1961).

The Role of the Teacher

So far in the second part of this book the position of the teacher has been examined from several viewpoints with the intention of building an adequate sociology of teaching. It is clear from Chapter 8 that the teacher is marginally a member of a profession; this defines the social status of his role as a teacher. In Chapter 9 the main forces that impinge upon the position that the teacher fills in the school were described; these forces can be conceptualized as working through the complex of complementary roles around any teacher that is termed his role-set. The examination of the curriculum in Chapter 10 indicated some central sectors of the role of the teacher, whilst a brief introduction to the sociology of the school was presented in Chapter 11. The aim of the final chapter of this part is to bring the second part together by examining more fully the role of the teacher (E. Hoyle, 1969) and then to see what the effect of filling this position is upon teachers.

A. The Role of the Teacher

'Role' is a two-way concept. Any role covers the set of values and expectations of a particular position in a social system from the point of view of both the occupant of the position and those with whom he interacts. Implicit in the idea of a role, therefore, is a self-image and a public image. The role of the teacher is organized around the functions that he fulfils – to be more specific, in the main around the transmission of that knowledge and those values that are defined as the curriculum of the particular school in which he is teaching. In different parts of the educational system the weight given to these and to other functions will vary. For this reason the role of the teacher in the infant school will not be the same as that of the secondary teacher. The results of research done in Britain on this topic have only recently begun to be available so that in this chapter often the findings of workers in other countries will be quoted, not as definitive, but as suggestive. Yet such evidence must be used with care since clearly the role of the teacher in a school system that is characterized by non-selective secondary schools as in the USA will differ in many ways from that of a teacher in a British grammar school.

There is a close connection between the self-image and the public image of any profession. A change in the self-image may affect the public image and hence the prestige of the occupation. This in turn may well influence the occupational choice of the next generation. This process is particularly important in the case of teaching, since the supply of new recruits to the profession has for many years now been below the demand for them. The way in which teachers view themselves will be reflected in the way that the public look at teachers. Furthermore, how teachers are seen by the public will help to determine how many young people take up teaching.

The possibility exists that there may be a difference between the public and the self-image of any occupation. As a result of a survey J. Kob (1963) has shown that this was the case for teachers in secondary schools in Hamburg. Here the public rated teachers higher in respect of social prestige than teachers voted themselves. Nothing is known of such comparative rankings in Britain.

1. *The Public Image of Teaching*

Most people have in their minds a number of imaginary pictures that cover what they consider to be the salient features of any occupational role. Walter Lippmann, the American journalist, christened such pictures *stereotypes*. If teachers are called to mind, several stereotypes exist. There is, for example, the stern and dignified teacher and there is also the gentle and self-effacing teacher (W. Waller, 1933). Much of our social intercourse is determined by the stereotype of the occupation with which we are at the moment in contact. When we meet our doctor or a clergyman in the street, the stereotype that we have of these occupations governs our behaviour towards that particular doctor or clergyman. Parents are often heard to say of their child's teacher, 'He's a typical teacher', or 'She's not at all like a teacher', and they will adjust their behaviour to this teacher according to the way in which he differs from their stereotype.

A very full investigation of the public image of the teacher has been made by the University of Missouri in Kansas City between 1958 and 1960.[1] This work showed that the most usual stereotype of the American teacher was centred around three points. The first and most important was the relationship between teacher and child; the teacher was expected to show no favouritism and to be interested, helpful and loving towards his pupils. The second focus was the manner in which he taught the children; he was expected to stress things, particularly of a verbal nature, to observe the children and to give them tasks to do. Finally, control was important and was seen in terms of order and quietness. The public considered the relationship between teacher and children to be much more important than the other two points. This emphasis on the emotional support of the child at the expense of his instruction is probably one of the main differences between the role of the teacher in Britain and the USA.

A thorough survey was made into the way in which the public expected teachers to behave. Teachers were expected to reflect the general moral values of the community in their behaviour and to set a good example by their high standard of conduct. They were expected to avoid all the interesting sins of our age. If they sinned at all, it was to be by omission rather than by commission. Teachers were seen as conformists and as rather neutral persons who do nothing out of the ordinary. In an investigation in Britain in the early part of the 1939-45 war the absence of an adventurous spirit was noted amongst teachers.[2] This might be expected amongst a conformist group. However, at that time the attitudes of teachers were governed by a very different set of social conditions from today and more particularly by the prolonged mass unemployment suffered by this country during the inter-war years. In such a time timidity at work is more understandable.

[1] B. J. Biddle, H. A. Rosencranz and E. F. Rankin, *General Characteristics of the School Teacher's Role*, Columbia, 1961, especially Vol. II, *Studies in the Role of the Public School Teacher*.

[2] W. B. Tudhope, 'Motives for the Choice of the Teaching Profession by Training College Students', *British Journal of Educational Psychology*, November 1944.

The American survey was made in the late 1950s since when widespread changes in social expectations have affected the role of teacher. Even then the wide extension of the teacher's role seemed to be coming to an end. Certainly up to 1939 the role of the teacher covered many aspects of his life away from school. He was always a teacher in the eyes of the public. Today in America and in Britain this is not so true. Men teachers need not always dress in a restrained manner, and women teachers may smoke and wear make-up. Yet one suspects that a full investigation of the role of teacher in Britain today would still reflect some of the tendencies found in the USA, ten or so years ago. The public image may not be so all-embracing as formerly, but the teacher is probably still expected by the majority of people to be a virtuous conformist.

One of the main social functions of the educational system is to assist in social selection, and therefore the teacher's role contains an element concerned with selection. He helps children towards the opportunities for which he feels that they are best fitted and he acts as a model of the behaviour in the status to which the children are aspiring or to which they are made to aspire. The British teacher stresses both moral and academic attainment in the classroom so that he becomes a model in the field of behaviour as well as in matters of the intellect.

The teacher has often been called 'a social stranger'. This is almost inevitable because of his position. Firstly, the teacher spends much of his life amongst children; to parents he is nearly always known only in connection with their children. His life is built around those things usually associated with childhood such as games, examinations and school rituals. In this respect the teacher is in many ways cut off from the world of adults. But he is also bound to be remote from children because he must keep discipline in his class and usually has at his command a whole arsenal of rewards and punishments. Secondly, the teacher is often culturally (in both senses of the word) apart from the community that he serves. If he lives in it, he is not of it, and if he travels daily to his school from a distance, geographical as well as cultural separation exists. This cultural aspect is important since it indicates that the role of the teacher is a mediating role; it acts as a bridge, linking present and future. The clergyman links sacred and secular, the psychiatrist sick and well, and the teacher taught and untaught.[1] Those who play mediating roles must try to stand in two worlds and hence tend to belong to neither.

One of the most striking pieces of British empirical research that is relevant at this point is the investigation that W. M. Williams carried out in Gosforth, Cumberland, during the early 1950s. In the course of this he asked those living in the area to rank each other according to social position. A hierarchy resulted that was akin to social class. There were upper and lower classes, but in between was an intermediate group, smaller than any of the sub-categories into which the two classes were divided. In this were placed those who were 'neither one thing nor the other' and it included the local schoolmaster and a retired teacher who lived locally. The comments of the other classes on the intermediate group make clear the isolation that is here under consideration. The upper working class spoke of 'school teachers and that sort' who were 'in between because of education'.[2]

This tendency to social isolation is reinforced by the fact that teachers are often transients. The Newsom Report showed that in England and Wales the proportion of teachers who were appointed to secondary modern school staffs in September 1958 and who were still in the same school three years later was 65 per cent for men and 58 per cent for women.[3] Although some movement may be expected this is a very high turnover of staff. Teachers come from outside the community. Children and parents know that they may not stay long. This is particularly true of all young teachers. Young women teachers are expected to marry early and leave school to look after a family. Young men teachers who wish for promotion are expected to have had experience in several schools. If movement is assumed to be normal, neither the teacher nor the community will be seen to sink much emotional capital in the other, and isolation will once again tend to be the result.

One of the signs of the isolation of the teaching profession has been the tendency to intermarriage. The proportion of trained

---

[1] K. D. Naegele, 'Clergymen, Teachers and Psychiatrists: A Study in Roles and Socialization', *Canadian Journal of Economics*, February 1956.

[2] W. M. Williams, *The Sociology of an English Village: Gosforth*, London, 1956, pp. 94–5 and 107–9.

[3] *Half Our Future* (Newsom), London, HMSO, 1963, p. 245.

women graduate teachers who married teachers remained at around a quarter between 1936 and 1954, but the proportion of certificated teachers who married teachers slowly diminished between 1936 and 1955 from 18 per cent to 14 per cent.[1] This decline and the possibly abridged nature of the role of the teacher described above may perhaps be taken as a measure of the somewhat less isolated nature of the college-trained teacher.

Despite the lack of British empirical work it would seem that several clear stereotypes of the teacher do exist. Though he is not perhaps so cut off from the world as he used to be, the teacher still tends to be a social stranger by virtue of his very position. He is thought of as a paragon and as a model to be imitated. As a representative of middle-class virtues the teacher is not expected to be too different in any way, and it may well be that as a result teachers tend to be conformists.

2. *The Self-Image of the Teacher*

(i) *Men of Knowledge.* Teachers may serve in 'learned schools' or in 'generally educative schools'.[2] In the first type of school social roles may be taught, but knowledge is stressed and in a theoretical or academic form. The British grammar school is obviously a relevant instance. In the generally educative schools the balance is reversed and the emphasis is rather on ensuring the maintenance of the social order, though the rise in the educational qualifications demanded by many employers has led to a greater stress on academic learning in these schools. The secondary modern school is relevant here. Teachers serving in these two types of school will tend to see themselves in very different ways. In the first case the teacher is a graduate and whilst at university he associated with scholars who were engaged in research. The grammar school teacher will wish to initiate his pupils into this world, whether he is teaching the arts or the sciences, and will tend to see himself as a junior colleague of the university lecturer. In the generally educative schools the stress will tend to fall on personality and behaviour; the teacher will see himself as more committed to the interests of the whole child.

[1] *Women and Teaching* (Kelsall), London, HMSO, 1963, pp. 24-5.
[2] F. Znaniecki, *The Social Role of the Man of Knowledge*, New York, 1940, pp. 153-7.

The age of the children taught will influence the view that the teacher has of himself. The younger the children the more diffuse is the teacher's role. Tasks are not usually specific in the primary school. The job of the primary teacher is concerned with both mathematics and morals. The teacher is committed to the child. Unlike many roles today his is not a neutral role. The doctor cares unemotionally for 'cases', the teacher with warmth and understanding for children, and often for a much longer period of time than the doctor.[1] It seems clear that there are two types of men of knowledge that match the two types of school. We shall return to this point later.

(ii) *Motive*. Essential to an understanding of how teachers view themselves is a knowledge of why they choose to teach rather than to follow some other occupation. Since the war three surveys have been made that throw some light on the motives of those taking up teaching in Britain. Two of these were carried out in Scotland. In 1951-2, at St Andrews and Dundee Training Centres, 296 students were asked to rank twenty motives that were most influential in their decision to teach. Fondness for children was ranked first, desire for a profession closely associated with one's favourite studies second, fondness for teaching third, security fourth and ideals fifth. However, within the overall pattern there were differences between the sexes and between graduates and non-graduates. Women and non-graduates both ranked fondness for children first, but men and graduates placed first the desire for a profession associated with their studies. Women and non-graduates put fondness for teaching second, whilst graduates and men placed it fourth and fifth respectively. Graduates put fondness for children second, but men ranked it eighth. Comparable results were reported from a study of 542 students in training that was carried out in Edinburgh. All the students, whether men or women, over or under twenty-one, on postgraduate or diploma courses, reported that they put 'reasons reflecting social concern and idealism' and their fondness for and interest in children very high amongst their motives for choosing teaching. However, amongst the younger women studying for diplomas this idealism was 'quite unconnected with the realities of teaching', whilst for all the other categories in

[1] B. R. Wilson, 'The Teacher's Role', *British Journal of Sociology*, March 1962, and K. D. Naegele, *op. cit.*, pp. 53-4.

the sample, idealism was 'associated with some concern about the realities of teaching'. Also, the older, non-graduate women, most of whom were mothers, put much more emphasis on their interest in, rather than their fondness for, children.

In 1961 a survey was made in sixteen universities in England and Wales of third-year women undergraduates who were questioned about their attitudes towards teaching. Forty-nine per cent of the sample put teaching either firmly or tentatively as their first choice of career, only 8 per cent of whom considered their choice as a reluctant acceptance of the inevitable. Of those with teaching as their first choice, 47 per cent stressed the holidays as an attractive feature of their chosen profession, 32 per cent work with the young, 22 per cent helping children progress, and 21 per cent mentioned the chance of continuing their academic work. Those who put teaching as their second choice on the whole stressed the intellectual element of the work rather than the contact with children. The study referred to above that was carried out in Edinburgh may also be compared to this English survey. Men who were graduates saw teaching as having good prospects, whilst all categories of women students rated attractive working conditions as a high priority. Women seemed to see teaching as a 'sensible expedient' and the older, mostly married, women apparently hoped to find teaching a less boring job than others that might be available to them.

A number of conclusions can be drawn from a comparison of these three studies. Most teachers, but especially women, seem to stress the motive of working with children. However, many graduates want to continue their intellectual interests. The men are more conscious of their occupational role as a career, whilst for the women their possible familial role assumes saliency. These impressions are reinforced by a small survey reported in 1962. In a sample of 131 teachers and 43 first-year students at training college, the graduates were oriented towards teaching their subjects, and those connected with colleges of education put stress on the child's need for understanding and sympathy rather than his need to be taught or to learn.[1]

[1] A. F. Skinner, 'Scotland. Part I. Professional Education', *The Yearbook of Education*, London, 1963; M. Collins, *Women Graduates and the Teaching Profession*, Manchester, 1964; B. Ashley, H. Cohen, D. McIntyre and

(iii) *Three Ideal Types*. A sociologist uses the term *ideal type* without any connotations of value. The term carries no moral overtones, but is a descriptive model which need not necessarily exist in its pure form in the real world, and which is constructed for analytical purposes as characteristic of the institution or particular social phenomenon under consideration. In this examination of the role of the teacher we have gone far enough to give two ideal types of the way in which teachers view themselves. There is the academic teacher and the child-centred teacher. Later it will be necessary to add a third, the missionary teacher.

The academic teacher is usually in a 'learned school' and is keen on his subject. He sees his role as centring on the stress on knowledge. He was trained at a university and feels himself to be a little lower in status than the majority of graduates who have entered other professions. He therefore tries to seek prestige by taking part in social activities outside the educational world such as the local dramatic society. In Gosforth the upper class thought that the presence of people like teachers in the village was 'handy when you have about a dozen village organizations to see to'.[1] The second type is the child-centred teacher who sees himself as teaching the child and not as teaching any particular subject. He therefore puts much more emphasis on the skills of teaching than on any subject matter. For this reason the child-centred teacher tends to be much more of a general practitioner.

The important question for the sociologist to answer is whether there are any particular determinants of these two types (J. Kob, 1958). Training is one of the most important factors to be examined. The teacher from a college of education has undergone a professional course that lays great emphasis on the psychological needs of the child. Concurrently he has studied one or more academic subjects. There is every chance that this academic knowledge will be related directly to the teaching of the child in the school. This is particularly the case since nearly all the college lecturers who teach academic

R. Slatter, 'A Sociological Analysis of Students, Reasons for becoming Teachers', *Sociological Review*, March 1970, espec. pp. 64–7; P. H. Taylor, 'Children's Evaluation of the Characteristics of a Good Teacher', *British Journal of Educational Psychology*, November 1962, p. 264.

[1] W. M. Williams, *op. cit.*, p. 107.

subjects to students will themselves have served as teachers for some period. There may be dangers of the inbreeding of methods and attitudes in an ethos that is usually markedly child-centred, but the final result in all probability will be that the young teacher is committed to teaching and to children rather than to any academic subject. The teacher who comes from university has spent three years doing academic work under teachers who rarely, if ever, have taught children. He then may, but need not necessarily, have a year's vocational training before he begins to teach, but his subject was studied apart from the need to teach it in schools, and any professional training will take place after the student has become attached to his specialism as a subject. The graduate teacher can be a graduate in exile in the schools, who teaches inefficiently what he knows and loves to children whom he does not really understand.

There is very little British evidence against which to test this ideal typical analysis. However, the one comparative study of the training of teachers in Britain and the USA contains some relevant material. What is surprising is that, although, as may be expected, the graduates scored higher than the students from colleges on an intelligence test and on all but one of the measures of academic achievement in specific subjects, the scores of the two groups on a measure of their attitudes towards various characteristics of teachers were surprisingly similar. There were nine parts to this scale. On four of these parts the scores of the graduates and college students were more or less identical, whilst on two parts, those concerning learning centredness and verbal understanding, the graduates scored higher, but in the remaining three parts concerning responsibility, methods of stimulation and classroom procedures, the students of the colleges had the higher scores. The impression that college students perhaps had a more professional and less academic attitude is, however, not entirely supported by the fact that on the tests of professional knowledge the graduates scored higher.[1] Perhaps the most crucial test of the effects of the two different methods by which most British teachers are trained would be to carry out a careful survey of a sample of both types, after they had been teaching for some ten years,

[1] G. E. Dickson et al., *The Characteristics of Teacher Education Students in the British Isles and the United States* (mimeographed), University of Toledo, 1965, pp. 126-8.

in order to measure their effectiveness in and adaptation to the role of the teacher.

The way that the teacher views himself as a result of his training may be reinforced by his social origins. Teachers in primary schools are mainly from colleges of education and a high proportion have come from working-class parents. In 1955 45·7 per cent of the men and 38·9 per cent of the women teachers were children of manual fathers, whilst in the grammar schools the figures were 32·4 per cent of men and 19·1 per cent of women.[1] The teacher from the college who is aspiring to higher status has firmly chosen teaching as a profession to which to rise and has either forgone or never had academic pretensions. He (in fact the majority of teachers in this category are women) sees himself as a teacher of children, not of subjects, and thus fits well into the ethos of the college of education. The graduate teacher tends more often to come of middle-class parents and clings to his own connection with the university. He stresses his own claims to the status of the majority of those with university degrees. This is especially the case for that fair proportion of graduates who take to teaching as a second choice and fully realize that thereby they have lowered their claim to prestige. The graduate is, therefore, reinforced in seeing himself as a teacher of his subject rather than of children.

The influence of age on how the teacher views his role is difficult to assess. In both Germany and Holland the evidence suggests that the effect of age on the attitudes of the two ideal types can be attributed to the historical circumstances of the period in which the teachers grew up and were educated. The educational theories that were current at the time of their training seemed more powerful influences than any hardening of attitudes as teachers grow older.[2] What little British evidence there is would suggest that there are no significant differences between age groups in the way that teachers view their role. However, data from the Plowden Report show that young teachers seemed to be more 'permissive' in their views on

---

[1] J. E. Flood and W. Scott, 'Recruitment to Teaching in England and Wales', 1956, in A. H. Halsey, J. E. Floud and C. A. Anderson, *Education, Economy and Society*, New York, 1961, p. 540.

[2] J. Kob, 1958, *op. cit.*, pp. 571–3; H. W. F. Stellway in *The Yearbook of Education*, 1963, pp. 427–8.

discipline than older teachers.[1] It could be that further research on this topic would show age to be a more important factor than it seems at present, particularly in view of the very different attitudes concerning authority that older and younger generations now seem to hold.

Sex may be another determinant of the way a teacher views his role. There are more men than women graduate teachers and more women than men teachers from colleges of education. The latter, as has been indicated, tend to take more interest in children. In addition, a large proportion of women teachers see marriage as their main career and will have less interest in claiming social status, since they will take that of their husbands', rather than that of their own, occupation. The men, even the non-graduates, will put more stress on their status and hence may feel insecure. The men graduates will also more readily see themselves as academics in exile.

These determinants seem to reinforce each other and to influence teachers so that they will tend to see their role either as academic or child-centred. There is a third ideal type, whose incidence is more dependent upon personality and, therefore, is far less predictable. This is the teacher who views himself as a missionary. He sees his role as rescuing the child from his environment. In the nineteenth century social consciences stirred many teachers to save working-class children from their parents. In the mid-twentieth century a more sophisticated interpretation of the role of the missionary teacher is that he aims to correct cultural deprivation. This concept implicitly assumes the superiority of the teacher's own sub-culture over that of his pupils. Many industrialized societies today are pluralist in nature in that they contain sizeable immigrant groups. In Britain there are the Irish, Pakistanis, Indians, West Indians and various groups of Africans; in Australia there are Greeks, Italians, Turks and Lebanese. Missionary teachers who set out to integrate either ethnic groups into the host culture or sub-cultures based on social classes into their own middle-class sub-culture hold a view of their role that may contradict both social policy and the wishes that are worthy of respect of the members of such sub-cultures.

These teachers are in a rather similar position to those who

[1] P. H. Taylor, *op. cit.*, p. 261, and *Children in Their Primary Schools* (Plowden Report), Vol. II, 1967, p. 561.

advocate a curriculum that aims to change society. In this connection there are some commentators today who see a need for teachers who enter the profession not in search of status but to counter those contemporary trends that they consider harmful to society. Thus one American sociologist, David Riesman, views the teacher as exercising countervailing power against the evils of the day.[1] The teacher is the crusader who will fight for intellectual standards against middle-class mediocrity and the missionary who will check falling moral standards.

When such suggestions are made it is apparent that the role of the teacher under contemporary conditions is no longer an adequate one (J. E. Floud, 1963). In a modern industrial society the teacher, particularly in the secondary modern schools serving large urban areas, may find that he has no common language of morality with his pupils. As Spinley pointed out in her work on personality structure, to which reference has already been made, slum children do not have a highly developed conscience. These children learn by experience, not by percept, and appeals to principles from a teacher or anyone else mean little to them.[2] Yet mainly because of the needs of the economy children stay at school longer and because of the higher material standard of life they are mature physically at an earlier age than thirty years ago. At a time when the cultural gap between the generations is widening and the biological gap is narrowing more tasks are handed to the schools, although the nature of the teacher's authority over the child has greatly changed. The teacher frequently condemns the very conduct that the family will approve. The relationship between home and school becomes strained when the teacher is telling the parents through the child what they should eat for breakfast or how they should dress their family to meet various weather conditions.

Under these circumstances the teacher has little moral authority over the child. Although he may see himself as a missionary the sanctions that the teacher can use are very different from those that were present when moral consensus existed amongst parents. Today the only common factor may be the need for education on utilitarian

[1] D. Riesman, *Constraint and Variety in American Education*, New York, 1958 (espec. Ch. III, 'Secondary Education and "Counter-Cyclical" Policy').

[2] B. M. Spinley, *The Deprived and the Privileged*, London, 1953, p. 83.

grounds. At the secondary level, if the child passes examinations he will gain a better-paid job. In the junior school, to pass the eleven plus will lead to the grammar school and to a chance of rising up the social scale. Under such conditions the ideal types that have been used here for analytical purposes may well prove dysfunctional if they represent common self-images of teachers in the schools. The academic type who loves learning for its own sake and bases his teaching on this idea of his role is unlikely to understand or have great success with pupils whose motives are purely utilitarian. The child-centred teacher may still succeed at primary level, but is unlikely to meet the vocational demands of an adolescent in the secondary school. The missionary teacher will need more than a well-developed social conscience to tackle rebellious youths backed by seemingly amoral parents, or to teach middle-class values or British habits to working-class or immigrant children whose parents give priority to their own sub-cultural ways of life. If teachers see themselves in ways at all near to these three ideal types, they are hindering their own work by casting themselves in the wrong roles. A critical reassessment of what they are trying to do in the light of contemporary social conditions is a regular need for all teachers who want to continue to do effective work.

B. The Adjustment to Teaching

If many teachers play the same or nearly the same role, the life that they lead in the practice of their profession may influence the structure of their personalities. The three ideal types mentioned above have certain common features; for example, all teachers are adults amongst children. Because of these identical experiences teachers may undergo *occupational socialization*. They may be forced to take on the personality of the job. Two other possibilities exist. Firstly, because of its nature the role of the teacher may attract a certain type of personality into the profession thereby ensuring in some respects at least a more or less uniform personality type amongst teachers. Secondly, the teacher under training may learn the responses expected in his particular role as he gradually meets the whole of his role-set. The supposition is that in somewhat the same way as a child becomes Scottish or English through the process of socialization the teacher will take on a similar personality to those already in the teaching world. To test the truth of these three arguments the first step must be an investigation of the psychological traits of teachers. If they are not in some measure the same for all teachers the above arguments cannot be true.

1. The Psychological Traits of Teachers

There have been very few attempts in Britain to discover the traits of teachers (P. E. Vernon, 1953). As long ago as 1931 R. B. Cattell undertook an investigation that demonstrated very fully how difficult this task is.[1] His sample numbered 208 and consisted of educational administrators, inspectors, staff of training colleges, and head and assistant teachers. Cattell asked them to say what they thought were the traits needed in a teacher. From their answers twenty-two major categories were devised. The really important result of the investigation, however, was that the different groups of informants consistently gave very different stresses to their pictures of what were the necessary traits. Administrators at that time emphasized general culture; inspectors named conservatism, orderliness and precision; training college staff demanded intelligence; also different requirements were desired in each sex; men ought to have energy, initiative, discipline and humour, whilst women needed tact, conscientiousness, insight and idealism. In other words the traits demanded consistently varied with the position in the educational system of the informant.

In the USA personality tests administered to teachers in the inter-war years showed them to have much the same interests as other professional people, though there were perhaps some slight differences between men and women teachers. During the same period Valentine found that British teachers were as liberal in attitude as the members of other professions but more liberal than the general public. Within the teaching profession itself there may be differences in certain of the attitudes held. A survey made in the late 1950s of teachers in secondary modern schools in the London area showed that these teachers could be divided into two main groups that were differentiated by their social philosophy.[2] One set of teachers were authoritarian and

[1] R. B. Cattell, 'The Assessment of Teaching Ability', British Journal of Educational Psychology, February 1931, espec. pp. 52-5.
[2] M. K. Bacchus, A Survey of Secondary Modern School Teachers' Con-

the other democratic in their outlook. The democratic group held views that were more favourable than the authoritarian teachers' towards the children's home background. They encouraged social qualities in their pupils, whereas the authoritarian group emphasized moral qualities. Finally, the democratic teachers favoured much less rigid methods of teaching than their authoritarian colleagues. Neither the age nor the social class origin of the teachers appeared to be a determinant of the philosophy held and, therefore, of these differences in attitude.

This work dealt with a very small area of the attitudes held by teachers, but differences were found. Cattell's investigation revealed the difficulties of discovering the psychological traits of teachers and that they appear very differently to various sets of people. The American results showed that teachers held interests that were much the same as other professional people, who have a remarkable diversity of personality type. The conclusion must be that, even though we can envisage teachers as having a definite role, they do not as a group undergo a process of special selection or occupational moulding as a result of playing this role. There does not appear to be a distinct and consistent teaching personality.

2. The Adjustment to Teaching

Those who take up teaching are of very diverse personality, but they must all play a somewhat similar role that, by its very nature, is a difficult one. Clearly in any role-set that is as complex as that of the teacher there is a strong possibility of conflict caused by the fact that the teacher has different expectations concerning his own behaviour from those of the persons with whom he interacts. This has been shown to be the case in a number of studies carried out in England (F. Musgrove and P. H. Taylor, 1969). It was found, for example, that children defined a good teacher as one who was skilful in his teaching methods, whereas teachers saw their own personal qualities as the most important component in their relationship with their pupils. In addition, teachers appeared to hold mistaken views of parents' expectations concerning their role. The teachers in this

---

cepts of their Pupils' Interests and Abilities in Relation to the Social Philosophy and to the Social Background of their Pupils, unpublished M.A. thesis, University of London, 1959.

study stressed intellectual and moral training most and put a lower emphasis on social training and on social advancement through education, but they believed that parents rated instruction and social advancement of greater importance than moral and social training, whereas in fact parents held the same priorities in their expectations of teachers as did the teachers themselves. Such misconceptions ensure that teachers are in conflict with key members of their role-set on issues which are central to their role.

The teacher moves daily from the adult world where his role may be a relatively subsidiary one into a classroom of children where he is dominant, though the equilibrium between himself and his pupils is never stable. In the eyes of the children that he is teaching he moves from friend to judge and back to friend again many times in each day. Each evening the teacher ceases to deal with immature minds and returns to his life as an adult.[1] Some adjustment in personality is needed to cope with what is a demanding task. This adjustment begins in an anticipatory manner during the period of professional socialization that occurs in the college, university, or Department of Education. A recent study examined the ways in which 268 women students in each of the three years of training at an English college of education defined certain important sectors of their future role. These related to the organization of the classroom, the general aims of the teacher, the manner of motivating children and the type of behaviour that teachers would tolerate in their pupils. The same instrument was administered to 183 headteachers and there were found to be no major differences in role conceptions held by those in primary and in secondary schools. The students moved consistently towards a less authoritarian pattern of attitudes during the early part of their training. This process reached a peak in their second year, but during their final year they reverted to a more traditional stance, coming to hold views nearer to those of the headteachers in this study. One suggested explanation that seemed to match the data is that the frames of reference used by college lecturers and by headteachers differ so that professional socialization is a two-phased process. In the first and preparatory stage the college students learn from their lecturers an ideal conception of their role as teacher, but in the

[1] See W. Waller, *The Sociology of Teaching*, New York, 1933, espec. pp. 380–92.

second stage, that of organizational reality, students come to see themselves more as practising teachers, and taking the advice of those in the schools where they do teaching practice they begin to discount theory and emphasize practice.[1]

There is some American evidence that suggests that those entering such service occupations as teaching may have formed during their training an image of the ideal client with whom they will deal. When their expectations are not met in the real work situation problems occur that demand some adjustment. Such a process may perhaps be seen at work in a recent study of 157 postgraduate students who were doing the one-year course for the Certificate of Education in an English university as a preparation for teaching in secondary schools. A far larger number wanted to go into comprehensive schools early in their training than ultimately took up first appointments in this type of school. The discrepancy was apparently not due to a shortage of such posts but rather caused by a change of view during the remainder of their course. The explanation seemed to be that student teachers had an ideal concept of their ability to interest their pupils in their own academic subjects and that this was disappointed when on teaching practice. They were fundamentally men of knowledge and the easiest adjustment to their misconception of classroom work was to take up a post in a selective secondary school.[2] Here again, as in the case of the students in the college of education, there was a gradual adjustment during training to the shock of reality, though they changed more quickly than the students in the college of education because their course was shorter.

After their training students become full members of the teaching profession. We have seen that they have chosen to teach for many and different reasons. Langeveld (1963) has shown that these motives can be twisted through long service in ways that may either help or hinder the teachers concerned. For instance, a teacher who chose this profession because it seemed a safe way of life may easily come to fear life in the world beyond the school; he may tend to limit his

[1] D. S. Finlayson and L. Cohen, 'The Teacher's Role: A Comparative Study of the Conceptions of College of Education Students and Head Teachers', *British Journal of Educational Psychology*, February 1967.

[2] M. T. Whiteside, G. Bernbaum and G. Noble, 'Aspirations, Reality Shock and Entry into Teaching', *Sociological Review*, November 1969.

experience and become tied to teaching. To an outsider such a teacher may appear to be a dedicated person, whereas in fact he is narrow and therefore unable to give his pupils the full benefit of the degree of devotion that he bestows upon them. Again, a teacher who chose his profession because the world of schools was well known to him may become so absorbed in his milieu of school, children and parents that he grows into a 'Peter Pan' teacher who never becomes a fully grown adult. Or, again, he may turn into an educational climber whose ambitions rest upon diplomas for himself and cups or examination successes for his school. In the first case the children are no longer taught by a mature personality and in the second they have ceased to matter to the teacher as children.

Both these motives may, however, adapt helpfully to teaching. The fact that a teacher feels absolutely safe in his work may allow him to put all his energies into fertile uses. This can be true particularly of teachers who are upwardly socially mobile, since they may well be willing to work very hard. In this case the children stand to gain much. Again, the man who chooses to teach since he knows the world of the school well can become a truly devoted teacher to whom his daily work is a labour of love. Once more the motive for teaching has adapted functionally to the test of the classroom.

Throughout this chapter there has been a recurring thread of insecurity in the role of the teacher. Always at the back of his mind is the problem of discipline and under contemporary conditions this is more difficult than formerly when moral authority was greater. The teacher has to keep in mind and adapt to a wide role-set, the membership of which changes frequently; therefore his relationships with, for example, his colleagues alter constantly and are unstable. Many teachers, but especially those who can be included in the academic type, feel insecure in their social status. The teacher still finds himself to be something of a social stranger. He feels that he must be a paragon of virtue as a teacher, but knows himself to be as near falling from grace as the next man. The adjustment to the sum of these threats to his security may be that he emphasizes conformity. His class must behave alike; to differ is dangerous and even unpredictable. Thus, many new techniques of teaching that rely on individuals working on tasks of their own choice or at their own speed rather than at a rate dictated for the whole class by the teacher are seen as unacceptable because apparently uncontrollable. He must be unadventurous to escape the notice of those around him; in this way even sins of omission may go unheeded and his isolation becomes less pronounced. Social forces make this one possible adjustment, but the effect of conformity on the children in the teacher's class must be examined. The teacher may crush their creativity and produce children who are trained to think in a conformist manner. In this way the teacher's own personal adjustment to his role is harmful to the needs of the children and of contemporary society.

There are other ways in which the teacher's adjustment to his role may hamper his efficiency. Since he is continually on a pedestal before his class he may grow into a pedant and lose contact with the children. This can also happen if the teacher feels joy in using his power over his class. The distance between himself and the children widens. Again, the organization of any institution demands some routine. The timetable of the school and the annual pattern of his teaching may encourage a rigidity in a teacher that will not help him to meet new conditions or difficult children who do not fit his preconceived ideas of how they should behave.

Finally, the majority of teachers begin their career with high ideals, but they will all fail with some children. If a teacher does not have a personality marked by a sense of optimism he may react to the failure to live up to his ideals by a retreat into cynicism. This is an adjustment to the problems of teaching that is particularly harmful to the children in his class. The teacher who has no hope will never engage the full interest of the children. In each of the cases described the teacher has adjusted to the circumstances of his profession in a way that hinders efficient teaching. Teachers have some chance of avoiding this, if they know that these hazards exist, and if they regularly examine themselves to see how they are adjusting to the circumstances of their professional life.

C. Conclusion

To the general public teachers probably seem conformists and isolated from the real world, but there is reason to believe that the role of the teacher is changing and that teachers are coming to be seen as ordinary people who teach rather than as cultured paragons. Teachers see themselves in various ways. Two common self-images are the academic and the child-centred types, neither of which seems to meet the needs of the schools in contemporary Britain. It is only in the last few years that we have begun to examine the role of the teacher in this country. It may be that in Britain we are less prone to self-conscious analysis than the Americans, or it may be that we have less money to spend on such work, but there is an importance in more exact knowledge of the role of the teacher. The image of the teacher influences vocational choice and hence the attraction of a profession that is undermanned and seems likely to remain so in the near future.

The traditional stereotype of the teacher with definite traits in his personality, mostly unpleasant, seems to be untrue. Yet forces exist that play upon anyone who teaches and to which an adjustment must be made. The teacher who begins his career with the soundest possible of motives may in time change so that he is no longer helping the children as much as he might. This conclusion emphasizes the need for continual self-assessment by practising teachers to see whether their idea of what they are doing meets their pupils' needs. If it does not, the teacher is not having the maximum possible effect on the children.

BIBLIOGRAPHY

J. E. Floud, 'Teaching in the Affluent Society', *The Yearbook of Education*, London, 1963.

E. Hoyle, *The Role of the Teacher*, London, 1969.

J. Kob, 'Definition of the Teacher's Role' (1958), in A. H. Halsey, J. E. Floud and C. A. Anderson (eds), *Education, Economy and Society*, New York, 1961.

J. Kob, 'The Teacher in Industrial Society', *The Yearbook of Education*, London, 1963.

M. J. Langeveld, 'The Psychology of Teachers and the Teaching Profession', *The Yearbook of Education*, London, 1963.

F. Musgrove and P. H. Taylor, *Society and the Teacher's Role*, London, 1969.

P. E. Vernon, 'The Psychological Traits of Teachers', *The Yearbook of Education*, London, 1953.

W. Waller, *The Sociology of Teaching*, New York, 1932 (reprinted 1961), espec. Part V.

PART III

The Social Functions of Education

13

Introduction

In an earlier chapter we considered the family and its place in the social structure. It was found that the family, as an institution, served certain functions. It is possible to analyse most social institutions in this way and to discover in what ways they help to maintain the society in which they exist. These are their social functions. Therefore we may ask the question, what are the social functions of the educational system? Just as we look at a car engine and say what each part of this machine is doing, so we may examine the educational system as a whole or one part of it, for example, one individual school, and decide what functions it is performing. Furthermore, in the same way that machines do not always run smoothly, so it may be that social institutions do not fulfil their functions in an efficient manner.

Such an analysis can never be entirely free of value judgements, but at least assumptions can, as often as possible, be made clear. The social scientist should be willing to bow to the philosopher and learn from him the skills of classifying the aims of education. But once this is done he can undertake as unbiassed an analysis as he can of how the educational system is functioning. From this he can help in the understanding and efficient working of the country's educational provision.

This analysis will not only be of the internal working of the various parts of the educational system from primary school to university, but also of the relations between these parts and between the educational system and other social institutions, such as the family or the economy. It may be found that the way in which education is organized is not meeting the aims assigned to it. The sociological term used to describe this state is *dysfunction* and comes by analogy from the field of medicine. Just as illness brings dysfunction to the body, so there may be dysfunction in the social system. Furthermore, this element of dysfunction may be either *latent* or *manifest*.

When we look for the functions of any social institution, we tend to focus on the way in which that institution helps the rest of the social system at one moment. The picture is static, but we know that society is in flux. Institutions once established begin to have lives and to create values of their own. In consequence we must remember that we are examining a system prone to change. Equilibrium is rare; tensions are common. Often there is a balance between the consequences of contemporary social organization. In some ways it is functional and in others dysfunctional. Where, however, there is no balance, a political decision may be necessary to rearrange the institution so as to meet the nation's present aims.

It is convenient to consider the social functions of education under five headings:

(i) The transmission of the culture of the society; here the need is basically the conservative one of passing on the main patterns of society through the schools.

(ii) The provision of innovators; someone must initiate the social change that is necessary for a society to survive under modern conditions. Such change may be, for example, technical, political or artistic.

(iii) The political function; this may be looked at in two ways. There is firstly the need to provide political leaders at all levels of a democratic society and, secondly, there is the demand that education should help to preserve the present system of government by ensuring loyalty to it.

(iv) The function of social selection; the educational system is central to the process by which the more able are sorted out of the population as a whole.

(v) The economic function; here the need is that all levels of the labour force should be provided with the quantity and quality of educated manpower required under the current technical conditions.

These five functions should be considered as the tools of analysis that will be used in the final part of this book in an endeavour to see what the educational system is really doing. It is suggested that to apply these same tools to some of our contemporary educational disputes might clarify the issues considerably. More especially it would show where there were no facts upon which to base a decision and therefore direct attention to those places where research was needed.

14

Stability and Change

There is a very delicate balance in any community between stability and change. Though new techniques are constantly altering the material conditions in which we live, many of the values by which we govern our lives are based on Christianity, a religion which is nearly two thousand years old. Both techniques and values are part of the culture which a society transmits to its next generation. In a primitive society changes in the culture were rare. Today, for reasons which are often economic or political, few societies can maintain such stability. If, however, change were to grow very rapid, any continuity of culture might prove difficult to achieve. The tension between stability and change is well illustrated by what happens when a country decides to industrialize and to switch from being a traditional society to a society where much that is conventional must go. It can be seen that here the problems of culture transmission become acute. How much of the old social structure should be preserved and handed on to the next generation? How much will the new generation accept and pass on to its children?

In primitive societies the coming generation learn the ways of their culture within the extended family system. We saw this in our study of the family. Today in Britain much of this function of the family has been passed over to a special institution, namely the school. A very clear example of this process can be taken from English educational history; during the nineteenth century the public schools grew as upper and upper middle-class families came to rely on these, mainly boarding, schools to form the character of their children.[1]

---

[1] F. Musgrove, 'Middle Class Families and Schools', *Sociological Review*, December 1959 (also in P. W. Musgrave (ed)., *Sociology, History and Education*, London, 1970).

The important position that all schools play in Britain today in passing on culture can be appreciated.

Another aspect of the equilibrium between stability and change is the consideration of who pushes a society on to the road of change. These men are the innovators. In the British industrial revolution the innovator was often self-taught, but under modern conditions much specialized knowledge is needed to achieve change in almost any field. It can be seen that for this reason alone the provision of innovators has to be considered as one of the functions of education.

Any consideration of stability tends to raise the problem of change and vice versa. Certainly the educational system of a modern community has a function in respect of both. It is because they are so closely connected, though opposites, that the function of providing stability through transmission of culture and the function of assisting change through a supply of innovators have been placed together in this chapter.

A. Culture Transmission

1. *Conserving the Culture*

When looking at primitive cultures which are very different from our own, as, for example, those described by Margaret Mead, it is relatively simple to appreciate their particular customs and see how their children learn these patterns of behaviour. It is more difficult to examine our own culture and discover which parts are passed on by the family and which by the school. The extent and nature of culture transmission through the school can perhaps best be shown by a series of examples. Some of these will be extreme cases, since these throw a very clear light on just what is happening.

Let us take the case of a five-year-old British child who comes from an Agnostic home. When he goes to his primary school, this child will spend much of the latter part of each autumn term preparing the classroom for Christmas. It is almost impossible that the child will not learn something of the Christmas story from a Christian viewpoint and this learning will be reinforced yearly till the child leaves school. It is difficult to imagine this process not taking place. By law State-aided schools must give religious instruction, and the religion taught is almost always Christianity. A child may be withdrawn from religious instruction if his parents demand it. But even in such a case this aspect of our culture would almost inevitably be transmitted to the child. The classroom walls will be covered with pictures or decorations, many of which his classmates have made. His friends will eagerly talk of what they have done and this may include the making of a nativity scene in the corner of the classroom. The new songs learnt will be carols. The theme of Christmas will recur throughout all his work and play. How can he escape learning about it?

A second example of the same extreme type is the case of the British school in a foreign land, such as the Argentine, or even in a Commonwealth country, such as Malaya. In this school a British child will not only learn the English language which, as will be seen later, is an important vehicle for transmitting the culture and which he will be accustomed to using in his own family circle, but he will learn much that will make him a Briton and which his family's restricted pattern of experience cannot provide. Perhaps the most obvious example is seen in the games that he will play; cricket overseas is a well-worn joke. Less obvious is the particular way in which the British of the social class to which the child belongs mix with others of their own age and sex. The triumph of the British school abroad is that the British at home shall say of its old scholars, 'You would never have thought that he was brought up abroad.'

As a child grows older he is constantly learning new patterns of behaviour and at the same time expanding his vocabulary. These two processes bear a unique relation to each other in any single culture. Under modern conditions much of both types of learning occurs at school or under its influence. In this way what is considered polite, whether in actions or in words, is often 'picked up' at school and may well be considered wrong in the family. Much of the work that is done in the classroom under the heading of 'English' is of the nature of moral education and therefore attempts to transmit cultural values.

Our language is full of metaphors and, particularly in poetry, of images that are peculiar to us as a nation. Children undertake many comprehension exercises during which these cultural images are attached to words and analogies are explained. One has only to try to read contemporary American or Australian poetry to children to realize that what is ostensibly the same language carries very different meanings, references and values, all of which are part of an alien culture. Or again, one should note the difficulty of using American children's books, even when illustrated, in English schools. In Scotland and in Wales some schools play an important part in preserving the national cultures by teaching the national tongue and emphasizing the national literature so that, for example, the poetry of Burns is given more attention in Scottish than in English schools. The young child is of an age at which he is unable to appreciate that culture transmission is taking place during an English lesson, whilst the parents are either unaware or in some respect wish the process to occur.

From the examples given it is clear that on the whole culture transmission is conservative. The teachers in the schools tend to pass on what they have been given. Conformity to what went before is stressed. The schools help the family, which plays a more predominant part in infancy, to pass on the national culture, which may be taken to include the national character. This last point is best exemplified from American educational history. The task of the typical American city school, especially on the eastern seaboard, has always tended to be the creation of good American citizens from the children of the most recent immigrants (M. Mead, 1951). They have to learn not only a language, but a national character. The symbol of this task is still the Stars and Stripes on the teacher's desk. In passing it is worth commenting that this task has become more common since 1945. For example, immigrants into Australia, the so-called 'New Australians', have had to be made into Australians, and Jews from all over the world into Israelis; also in Britain the assimilation of white and coloured immigrants has brought problems of an educational nature.

2. *Immigrants*

Immigrants have always formed a substantial minority of our labour force, but during the nineteenth century they were largely Irish, so that, although there were religious problems, assimilation was not complicated by differences in colour or in language. In 1964 it was estimated that there were about 820,000 coloured persons in Britain, or just over 1·5 per cent of the total population. The greatest part of this number were recent immigrants. There were 430,000 West Indians, of whom 60 per cent were Jamaicans, 165,000 Indians and 100,000 Pakistanis. This rapid influx of migrants, all coloured, was concentrated in such large cities as London, Birmingham, Liverpool and Leeds, and brought as its consequence a number of social problems, particularly in the fields of housing and education. In some schools more than a third or even a half of classes consisted of immigrant children. Those from the East were Hindus or Muslims by religion and had very different culture patterns both from their host culture, the British, and from such other immigrant groups as the West Indians, Africans or Cypriots. Furthermore, many of the Christians amongst the West Indians found the practice of their religion in Britain very different from that of their home country. The motives for migrating tended to differ by ethnic group. Thus, many West Indians aimed to assimilate into the host culture and to be seen as British citizens, whilst many Indians aimed to earn more than they could in their home country, but wished to remain a socially distinct grouping (G. Bowker, 1968).

In this situation the schools have a difficult task in passing on the host culture, if such is their aim. The immigrant child finds that the habits and behaviour learnt from his parents, and hence valued highly by him, are despised sometimes by his teacher and almost always by the community at large. Much of the behaviour that he has learnt at home is totally inapplicable in his new land, and this applies both to migrant children and to the majority of children born of immigrant parents after their arrival in Britain. For example, there are the problems due to language, obvious in the case of Indians, but, though less obvious, no less real for West Indians, whose English is in many ways syntactically different from that spoken in Britain. Minor matters like school dinners cause difficulties, since the children are unused to the food and styles of eating. Many immigrants have names that seem odd to the native British and the large numbers of Singhs and Khans can even cause administrative frustration, though this is more often due to doubt over children's ages because registration of births is either unknown or inefficient in their country of origin. However, perhaps the major problem is the prejudice against the incomers amongst British parents who feel the hostility to coloured persons, apparently usual in Britain, and also hold the possibly well-founded view that a high proportion of ill-educated children, particularly from a culturally very different group, will lower the quality of education given to their own sons and daughters.

In 1965 the DES issued *The Education of Immigrants*, in which it specified the 'integration' of immigrants as a social aim in the fulfilment of which the schools had a large part to play, though it did not closely define this term. Initially the schools had, on the whole, attempted to fulfil such a policy by trying to help immigrants to become British, but, though this course coincided with the motives of many West Indian parents, it clearly conflicted with the desires of most Indians and Pakistanis. However, there have always been a number of schools whose aim has been, on the one hand, to teach migrants enough to enable them to live successfully in Britain, whilst at the same time respecting their ways of life and religion, and, on the other hand, to try to lower the level of prejudice amongst British children against coloured persons. In one school in Huddersfield the religious festivals of the various ethnic groups in the school are respected and used as starting points for the groups to teach each other, with the aim of breaking down stereotyped attitudes based on ignorance and a lack of thought.[1] In as much as teachers succeed in these two aims, their function is to change in some respects both the cultures concerned, since the immigrants become a little more British and the British a little less prejudiced.

However, it must be remembered that prejudice also exists amongst coloured immigrants both towards the British and towards each other. Thus, in work done in 1963 Kawwa found that, though there was more negative prejudice against coloured persons amongst children in London than in Lowestoft, where immigrants were very few in number, yet the pattern of prejudice in Islington, London, reflected the pattern of ethnic groupings in the catchment area of the comprehensive school in which his study was undertaken, and in which 15 per cent of the pupils were migrants. Here the Cypriots, who were seen as culturally more different from the English than the West Indians, were the target for the prejudices of both the other immigrants and the English. In later work carried out in 1965, Kawwa compared two large groups of English and immigrant

---

[1] T. Burgin and P. Edson, *Spring Grove*, Oxford, 1967.

children in a primary and a secondary school, and found ethnic prejudice to exist in children as young as seven. English children held the stereotyped views of immigrants displayed in such comments as 'They're dirty', or 'They take our houses and jobs', which clearly seemed to have been learnt from their parents. Immigrant children in their turn saw native children as unfriendly and inegalitarian. In the secondary school children chose their friends within their own ethnic groups. Yet the situation may be more complex than this. From work done in Sparkbrook, Birmingham, it seems that what happens is that children, even in early adolescence, make friendships and mix with each other across ethnic divisions whilst in school, but that they do not carry these friendships out of the school into their leisure activities. An easy mixing takes place at school, but segregation at home. In this context, as in many others, familial sanctions seem to overcome behaviour learnt in the schools, which are in the eyes of parents of all groups, white or black, seen to be undermining both the accepted pattern of culture and parental authority by sanctioning such friendships.[1]

In all these instances, the schools are acting either on the one hand to pass on the existing culture in greater or lesser measure to new members who may or may not have been born in the community, or, on the other hand, they are in some small way changing the present pattern of culture. Such innovation may or may not be the policy given to the educational system.

3. Changing the Culture

The educational system may, however, be given a much more positive role in transmitting culture. A political decision may be taken that the existing way of life ought not to continue, and the Government may want to use a social institution which is as central to this purpose as the educational system in an attempt to change

[1] For Sparkbrook see J. Williams, 'The Younger Generation', Ch. X in J. Rex and R. Moore, *Race, Community and Conflict*, Oxford, 1967. For a general survey see R. J. Goldman and F. M. Taylor, 'Coloured Immigrant Children: A Survey of Research, Studies and Literature on their Educational Problems and Potential – in Britain', *Educational Research*, June 1966. See also T. Kawwa, 'A Survey of Ethnic Attitudes of some British Secondary School Pupils', *British Journal of Social and Clinical Psychology*, September 1968.

the culture. The Russian schools were in this position in the 1920s, though by today an existing culture is being transmitted. One of the clearest examples of an attempt to alter the culture of a country was that made in Germany by the Nazis after they came to power in 1933. In this case the full extent of the term 'education' can be seen. The Nazis used every type of school for every age range and all the facilities for further education, including universities and technical colleges. They used the existing institutions for adult education and created new ones. Finally, they used the apprenticeship and training system in industry, always considered a part of the educational system in Germany. Though this attempt failed, it is a reminder of how many and varied are the institutions which we lump together under the heading 'the educational system'.

In Britain we may think that what the Russians succeeded in doing and what the Germans attempted to do was morally wrong, but we should remember that a similar role is sometimes suggested for our schools today. The argument runs somewhat as follows: the modern adolescent is not of the type that, according to some, is good for Britain today, or according to others, of whom they approve. He must be changed, and the schools must play a big part in this policy. To put it bluntly, the child must be saved from society. It is a worthwhile exercise for any teacher to examine his role and see whether he is neutral or positive in the way in which he passes on his country's culture. And can he justify either his neutral or his positive position?

The child stands between two powerful influences, the school and the family. Every teacher needs to remind himself constantly that the family is often the stronger of the two influences, especially when the child is young. Yet paradoxically teachers of children in primary schools probably have more direct influence on their pupils than teachers at any later stage, more particularly because of the greater influence of the peer group amongst children of the secondary age. But at all stages the influence of the school and later the university or college is great, especially in the introduction of ideas to older pupils. An inspiring teacher can create what the Crowther Report has called 'intellectual discipleship'. The great French sociologist, Durkheim (1956, p. 89), spoke of the teacher as 'the interpreter of the great moral ideas of his time and his country'. It is clear that these ideas may be Marxist or Christian, but the teacher in his role as teacher will pass them on to the next generation.

4. Sub-cultures

(i) *Regional Differences*. So far we have spoken as if it was one culture that was being passed on by the schools. We must now face the question of whether the educational system does or can transmit only one culture. Let us take a concrete example. In several parts of rural Britain there are secondary schools in villages that are close to RAF airfields. These schools must cater for two types of pupils, the children of the local people and the children of the RAF personnel. Children of the former type are country born and bred, whilst the majority of the latter type come from the great industrial conurbations. In fact, both of these divisions represents a sub-culture, the rural and the urban. They are both within the overall British culture, but each has distinctive differences of its own. Can the school give the same way of life to both types of child? In one case of which details are known this proved to be impossible. Despite their period under the influence of a country school the city children still showed in their work, more especially their English compositions, the marks of their strong attachment to their own sub-culture. Deep differences in the ways of thought of the two types of children were seen. The city children had a greater factual knowledge of the technical world of today and on the surface were more sophisticated; the village children showed a deeper understanding of the ways of the country and because of this had a subtler feeling for life and death, growth and decay. Whilst the city child appeared the more mature, in reality the country child was so in his appreciation of the feelings and emotions around which life revolves. The school could not here change what had been begun, nor could it combat the influence of living in an airfield to which the city child returned after school each day.[1]

Sub-cultures exist within our society. T. S. Eliot (1948) has argued that the tensions produced by their existence, provided that they do not cause great conflict, bring gain and that, therefore, the resulting whole is greater than its parts. R. Hoggart (1957) has

[1] B. Jackson, 'Report from a Country School', *Universities and Left Review*, Autumn 1958.

traced the way in which the traditional rural English culture was taken by migrants during the nineteenth century to the great northern industrial cities and how by today the traces of this traditional way of life have in some respects disappeared, though in others they remain. A school set in the midst of any sub-culture will find it difficult to pass on the culture in any form other than that in which it is interpreted by that sub-culture. This is particularly true when the differentiation is mainly along material lines, as is perhaps so in the case quoted of the rural and urban sub-cultures. It would be hard to teach a rural way of life against a background of tall chimneys.

(ii) *Educational Sub-cultures.* There is another aspect of the passing on of one culture which must be considered. This is the problem known today as 'the two cultures controversy'. In its modern form, which is relevant to all levels of education, including higher education, it was sparked off in 1959 by C. P. Snow (1964). In brief the argument runs that specialization in education is nowadays so intense that even in the final years at school, but certainly by the time higher education has been reached, it has become impossible for those following arts courses to understand and communicate at any depth with those following science courses and vice versa. The effect created by specialization goes further than difficulty in understanding the material with which the other side is dealing, but extends to the fact that the two sides are learning totally different modes of thought.[1]

The validity of this argument in such an extreme form can be questioned, but there is an element of truth in it. For perhaps the greater part of the last hundred years the claims of science to a place in the school curriculum have been overlooked despite the fact that the contemporary culture was growing more scientific throughout the period. The influence of this neglect is still with us. It is therefore true to say that in organizing a curriculum which fits children and older students for the modern world the whole of the present culture must be considered. To use the word coined by the Crowther Report, 'numeracy' as well as literacy is important if the schools are to come near passing on the culture in this respect.

[1] C. P. Snow treats the same problem in his novel *The New Men*, London, 1950 (Penguin), though here he introduces an intermediate sub-culture, that of the engineers.

(iii) *Social Class Differences.* There is another difficulty, similar in some ways to that of the rural and urban sub-cultures. This problem lies in the fact that social classes may be considered as sub-cultures. This affects the schools in various ways, but one important aspect is found in the relation between teacher and taught. Very often the teacher is middle class and hence has middle-class values. Even if he has come from a working-class background, the teacher will in all probability aspire to the middle class and hence hold the values of that class more strongly. Since the majority of pupils in schools come from the working class and this is especially the case for most secondary modern schools, the teaching situation is normally such that a member of one sub-culture tries to communicate with members of another sub-culture. Very often, as we saw when considering social class learning, the teacher is trying to teach his pupils a way of life and set of values that is alien to them.

It is useful here to consider a special case, that of 'the scholarship boy'. This is the child from the working-class home who achieves social mobility through the educational system. This has been the way of social advancement of many teachers and therefore has an especial interest in this context. Does the scholarship boy stay loyal to his class of origin or transfer his allegiance to his achieved social class? Jackson and Marsden (1962) made a pioneer study of this problem in a large industrial community in the North of England. They concluded that on the whole such children transferred their loyalty, sometimes in an exaggerated fashion, to their new and higher class. This did not happen without soul searching and often was accompanied by emotional difficulties. But it is clear that the grammar school education which is so necessary for achieving upward social mobility not only gives the child the factual knowledge that he must have, but has as well a stereotyping effect on many children. It tends to turn out young adults who have middle-class values, whatever the social class from which they originally came.[1]

As we already know, the majority of the children in the grammar schools come from the middle class, as do their teachers for the most part. Even to a child of eleven it is apparent that to succeed in this environment he must adopt certain new values and modes of be-

[1] For a novelist's picture of the life of a scholarship boy to manhood see Raymond Williams, *Border Country*, London, 1960 (Penguin).

haviour. Support for him in this course often comes from home, especially from his mother. This takes the form of encouragement to succeed without a full realization of what this will entail for the child in a change of values, leading perhaps to difficulty of communication between parents and child. In extreme cases the cost of success is not just inability to communicate, but that the child does not wish any longer to see his parents. It is a relatively easy task for the grammar school to assimilate a minority of working-class children and initiate them into a new sub-culture. In comparison the attempt to introduce an overwhelming majority of working-class children to the values and ways of life peculiar to the English middle class seems an almost impossible task, if in fact this is what the teacher wants to achieve.

(iv) *Differences by Types of School.* In Chapter 5 we saw that there were a number of different types of schools at both primary and secondary levels whose styles of operation and whose curricula were so different that each could be seen as transmitting different patterns of culture. It therefore seems likely that the organization of British education, especially at the secondary level, may further complicate the way in which the culture is transmitted. In general, children at first attend a primary school that is common to the majority including, for at least a year or two, many of those who are going to enter the private school system. From about eleven secondary education is given in several types of school. A brief re-examination of the main types of school will show that dysfunction is caused by this method of organization, at least in respect of the particular function of the educational system here under consideration. Each type of school chooses from what is available in the culture as a whole and passes on only what it wishes.

The public school exists to train an elite. This has always been so and is so today. In medieval times Winchester and Eton were founded to train a priestly elite, during the great expansion of these schools in the nineteenth century the elite was a political one, whilst today it has become largely a managerial elite with perhaps a bias more towards commerce than industry. The clients of these schools pay so that their children shall be taught the qualities of personality thought necessary for leadership. Certainly many of the products of these schools seem to assume that they will be leaders.

The maintained grammar school has imitated the public school in many respects. It has taken over what are often considered the virtues of the public school; a sense of duty is stressed and training for taking responsibility is given. But the majority of the pupils of these schools have not been able to assume that their path onwards after school was assured. Therefore, if it was one's duty to use one's abilities well, but one had to make one's way, success in school and more particularly in examinations became important. The ethos of the new grammar school came to be marked by duty and competition.

The secondary modern school was a product of the 1944 Act and the attempt to give a secondary education to all. It is here that the clash of two sub-cultures can be seen most clearly. The teachers, products of the grammar schools, who believe in the values that they learnt there, have tried to teach a way of life based on these values to mainly working-class pupils. Over the last century the hard experience of unemployment and industrial strife has taught the working class to trust in a way of life based on solidarity and cooperation, not duty and competition. The coming of full employment may alter the ethos of the working-class life, but as yet it is difficult to assess how much the secondary modern school has achieved. Many teachers might question whether in some cases it is not the middle-class values that should give way to those of the working class.

The three types of school considered in so brief and generalized a way are passing on very different versions of the British culture. The secondary technical school may provide a fourth version, but even less evidence exists about it than for the other schools mentioned. One of the most important consequences of this pattern of educational organization relates to the curricula of the various types of school. We have seen that these schools form a hierarchy paralleling the status of the majority of their pupils. Each type of school not only reinforces or passes on patterns of behaviour that vary with the nature of the social class of its pupils and their parents, but also divides up the contemporary stock of knowledge so that certain parts of that stock have become associated with specific strata in society. The classics and such vocational education as relates to the major professions have been taught to pupils largely drawn from or destined for the higher reaches of the social class system and largely because of this Latin and Greek have been granted high status, whilst handicraft and that vocational education relating to manufacturing industry have, in a similar, but inverse fashion, come to be given low status. A somewhat similar division is traditionally extended to the affective, as well as the cognitive, subjects, so that certain artistic, musical and dramatic forms are seen as of higher status than others, and as part of the education of those of high social status. Knowledge, like people, can be, and in Britain has been, stratified.[1]

It has been suggested that these dysfunctions in the transmission of culture could be corrected if the secondary system were organized on the basis of the comprehensive school, the argument being that a single type of secondary school would transmit one basic common culture. However, in Chapter 5 we saw from Ford's recent work that in respect of such a major part of the British culture as the normal views held about social class, different versions of the culture were still being passed on in the comprehensive school which she studied, and from Miller's slightly older work, that a stratified version of the stock of knowledge still formed the basis of the curriculum in the comprehensive school in Birmingham in which his research was undertaken. The conclusion must once again be that the subcultures transmitted by the tripartite system are in very large measure learnt in the various streams of the comprehensive school. Thus, this new type of school, as now organized, functions to perpetuate many of the cultural divisions associated with the system of organization which it is replacing. Nor is it easy to see how the comprehensive school could ever overcome the problem of social class learning, since the fundamental differences in thought processes caused in this way occur long before the child reaches the secondary stage. Further, as long as parents can contract out of the State system and buy their children a different culture in the private system, the transmission of one single culture cannot be achieved. Nor, perhaps, should this be our aim for several reasons, one of the most cogent of which is the need to provide religious education of different types and to respect the ways of life of the various groups of immigrants that we now find settled amongst us.

[1] M. F. D. Young, 'An Approach to the Study of Curricula as Socially Organised Knowledge' in R. Brown (ed.), *Sociology of Education*, London, 1971.

(v) *Sub-cultures within the School*. There is one final difficulty which must be examined. Within schools themselves it is possible to identify sub-cultures. Often there exists a group whose main aim in school is to play games well, whilst at the other extreme there is a group whose whole aim is academic work. Again, in some schools, particularly in the poorer urban areas, there is a small group whose interests seem centred in activities best described as delinquent. The work by Coleman (1961) mentioned in Chapter 6 is relevant here. Coleman identified in the American high school three main sub-cultures, which he named the fun, academic and the delinquent sub-cultures. The children who formed the fun sub-culture put a low value on academic success and intellectual matters, but gave much importance to social success; to the boys athletic prowess and to the girls good looks were what really mattered. It was on the whole not the aim of the teachers to perpetuate this set of values, which seem to have been imported from life outside the school. Yet this system of values now exists within these schools and is therefore willy-nilly passed on to many children. An academic sub-culture also exists in the American high school. Here we find a very different set of values marked by a stress on things of the mind, though it was the case that neither sub-culture was mutually exclusive.

The fun culture in the shape of organized games has for some time been consciously used in British schools with definite objects in view. It had been assumed that games trained character. In the present state of psychological knowledge there is more justification for two other of the aims sometimes given, namely that by organized games loyalty to the school can be increased and that healthy exercise lets off much emotional steam, thereby easing the problems of keeping discipline. However, this aspect of the fun culture, games, has often come to have such importance in many British schools as to encroach seriously on the academic sub-culture. Games mattered and work did not. Intellectual pursuits such as poetry and art have not a very high standing in our culture. How much of this is due to the cult of games in our secondary schools? Certainly it is true that teachers must be careful what values they attach to various school activities, since they hope to transfer these values to their pupils.

Sanctions that are external to the schools may well be strengthening the academic sub-culture. Industry and trade are coming to put more stress on proof of academic success; children have to pass examinations to find a good job. Examinations are now more common in the secondary modern schools. It may well be that the academic sub-culture is being sought, as has happened often in the past, not for itself, but for vocational reasons.

Coleman found that the delinquent sub-culture was marked by avoidance of and rebellion against the school. This was not mere adolescent negativism, but a conscious total rejection of the school. It was found in Britain that, when the school leaving age was raised from fourteen to fifteen, the peak age for juvenile delinquency also rose, so that it still occurred in the final year at school.[1] There seems to be a conscious revolt against a system where the adolescent is treated as a child. This rejection is symbolized by the boy who had just left school and was asked by his former headmaster what he thought of the new buildings. 'It could be marble, sir,' he replied, 'but it would still be a bloody school.'[2] If the delinquent sub-culture is strong in a school, the transmission of the present culture becomes very difficult. The children who become members of the delinquent group will learn to reject much or even all that the school stands for, and thereby most of what the majority of adults would think worth while. An extreme example of this process occurs in the Approved Schools, where the only pupils are those classed by the courts as deviants from the generally accepted culture of this country. The aim of these schools is to establish the values of the majority in the minority. But these institutions fail in as much as a large proportion of their pupils who are first offenders leave these schools only to be re-committed. The teachers in such schools try to pass on a set of values from which the majority of their pupils dissent. As has been indicated earlier in many cases their values and resulting behaviour are not deviant in their own home environment. In these schools the delinquent sub-culture is so strong that in many cases it, rather than the school culture, wins the adherence of those whose crime might have been their only one, but who become regular criminals.[3]

[1] D. J. West, *The Young Offender*, London, 1967 (Pelican), p. 15.

[2] *Half Our Future* (Newsom), 1963, p. 2.

[3] A perceptive novel relevant to this paragraph is Alan Sillitoe, *The Loneliness of the Long Distance Runner*, London, 1959 (Penguin).

It must be added that Coleman found few traces in the American high school of the vocational sub-culture which is to be found in many institutions of higher education, such as the university with its medical or law schools, the college of education with its stress on teaching, and the technical college. It may well be that this sub-culture, with its stress on values relevant to success in one's chosen career, is to be found in Britain in the secondary technical school. These values may provide a substitute for those of the fun or delinquent sub-cultures.

The function of transmitting culture is a complex one. Much of this process, and particularly that part relating to the passing on of the stock of knowledge, is now carried out in the educational system, but the creation of institutions has in some cases built in dysfunctions which are often not recognized. Sub-cultures can provide a healthy tension, but this is not always the case. We have to consider whether our educational aims are such that when we recognize dysfunction we should reform the institutional framework which our analysis reveals to have caused it.

B. Innovation

The function of providing innovators clashes with that of transmitting culture. Innovation brings either new ways or new ideas and therefore challenges what was formerly considered to be usual. The educational system here plays two parts. It provides the innovators and also ensures that the necessary changes take place with the minimum of friction. Opposition to change is common where traditional ways have ruled for a long time; this is the case in many societies now meeting industrialization for the first time. But change is not welcomed in some complex industrial societies either because it will hurt vested interests, or, as in Britain, because the traditional is held in high regard.

1. The Schools and Change

This twofold role of the educational system is particularly important in modern Western economies. Even before 1939 research of a scientific nature was being applied to industry; this had raised the rate of introduction of new industrial products. But the pursuit since

1945 by successive Governments of a policy aimed at full employment has lowered the level of unemployed labour and capital in the economy to such an extent that the rate of industrial innovation has been further increased. The American economist, J. K. Galbraith, has suggested that in a modern high consumption economy change is essential to provide employment for all; new cars with slight differences from the previous model must be sold in order to keep the industry in full employment. In brief, this is Galbraith's *Dependence Effect*.[1] The place of advertising in this process is clear. What part can the schools play if change is to occur as easily as possible?

There has been a move towards more general education at many levels of the educational system, and this matches the need of workers for as broad a base of knowledge as is possible to meet future alterations in methods of production which will demand from them many changes of job during their working lives. As more children are staying at school beyond the minimum leaving age, they pursue their general education for longer. This in itself is an advantage, but it also means that adolescents may possibly choose their first occupation more wisely since they are somewhat more mature. The new universities have tried to introduce broader degree courses in many fields of study, and in the sixth forms of secondary schools many headmasters are trying to reduce the tendency to early specialization that marks British education.

Much more direct help in adjusting to change is given by that part of the educational system that provides technical education. Since the 1956 White Paper on Technical Education the Government has spent far more in this field.[2] The links between education and industry must be good so that teachers in technical colleges can know the changing needs of the economy. Though unofficial links between industry and education exist on some examining bodies, on the whole there are not strong channels of communication. In Germany the situation is very different. Communication is assured because representatives of management, the unions, the Government and education sit together on official committees that are responsible for laying down and revising the syllabuses for the examinations taken

[1] J. K. Galbraith, *The Affluent Society*, London, 1958 (Pelican).
[2] See M. Argles, *South Kensington to Robbins*, London, 1964, espec. Ch. 8.

by all German craftsmen before qualification as a skilled worker.[1] In Britain the Industrial Training Act of 1964 laid down that boards responsible for vocational education at every level of the labour force shall be set up in each industry. The Government has appointed a number of boards covering most sections of British industry and has, therefore, started to establish the machinery needed to keep technical education in line with the needs of the economy. This system is geared to teaching younger workers, but recently more attention has been given to the creation of facilities to help older workers to meet change by training them for new jobs.

We do not know much about the education of recent innovators. During the industrial revolution many were self-taught, but this is no longer common in industry, if only because of the extensive knowledge needed to understand present-day techniques. Recent research in the field of psychology has, however, revealed a disturbing possibility. Our teaching methods, certainly up to the age of sixteen, tend to demand the one right answer and throughout are characterized by examinations which encourage standard answers. It may be that we turn children who are potentially creative into adults whose only wish is to succeed through conformity. Psychologists now believe that some people have an innate mode of thinking such that they tend to give the expected answer or follow the usual line of thought, whilst others have a mode that enables them to diverge easily from the conventional. It is suspected that the emphasis in our schools may teach the 'diverger' to think in a more conformist manner and thereby crush potential creativity.[2]

We may not know the educational background of our innovators, but recent work in the USA has revealed two facts that we may suspect to be true in Britain. Despite the growth of research in large teams about half of industrial innovations still seem to be made by individuals.[3] This emphasizes that, if the schools do stunt the creative potential of individuals, they are acting in a dysfunctional way in that they are stopping the flow of innovators. Secondly,

[1] See Lady G. Williams, *Apprenticeship in Europe*, Ch. II on Western Germany, London, 1963.

[2] For an account of work in this field see J. W. Getzels and P. W. Jackson, *Creativity and Intelligence*, New York, 1962.

[3] J. Jewkes and others, *The Sources of Invention*, London, 1958.

there seems to be no difference in the quality of the output of American scientists from schools or colleges in which the expenditure per pupil is high and those where it is low.[1] Anyone with experience in British education might go so far as to say that the correlation in Britain was inverse!

The educational system has itself changed so as to ease adaptation to continuous technical innovation. The institutional framework that links the economy with education is growing stronger. The movement towards staying longer at school and towards less specialized courses at all levels of education is helping to meet change on the side of production. But what little we know of the education of our present innovators leads us to believe that here the educational system is acting in a dysfunctional way in that it may well be checking the supply of innovators. This would seem a serious fault in a country traditionally as conservative as Britain.

2. *Autonomous Change*

The educational system is a social institution which can develop autonomously. The dysfunctional attitudes towards science cited above developed within the educational system itself. Often schools, which were started at least in some measure to assist social change, have become sources of ideas that have hindered change. A recent example, which will be discussed fully in Chapter 17, is the way in which the supply of scientists from the schools has risen greatly since 1945, but many of the children have learnt unconsciously to see their future careers as spent in research rather than in industry where the need for scientifically trained young workers is perhaps greater. The task of checking the autonomous growth of attitudes dysfunctional to the smooth acceptance of change is difficult, but a first step is analysis to find where such attitudes exist.

It must be realized that, whereas industry makes some attempt to plan the direction in which it is going to change, the educational system itself causes much unplanned cultural change. This can be seen in three ways. There is one obvious example. Universities are a source of new knowledge and ideas, which are usually the result

[1] For schools see an unpublished survey in Connecticut in J. S. Coleman, *op. cit.*, p. 235, and for colleges see R. H. Knapp and H. B. Goodrich, *Origins of American Scientists*, Chicago, 1952, pp. 45-6.

of research pursued for its own sake rather than because of any possible commercial application. It is not only in the field of pure science that discoveries are made that bring cultural change. It might be argued that one of the most beneficial of inventions in this century has come from a social scientist, namely Keynes' discovery of the mechanism of the trade cycle. Important new ideas are also generated in the arts faculties. A very good example is the influence of the school of literary criticism that grew up in Cambridge under Dr F. R. Leavis in the 1930s. We have seen that this has influenced not only the way we look at literature and teach it in schools, but has changed the sense of values inherent in this teaching, and hence influenced the way we look at newspapers and advertisements.

Another source of unplanned change is the sheer spread of education. More children are staying longer at school and this must affect their values and tastes. This could have an impact on the publishing industry; the growth of the paperback has proceeded simultaneously with the spread of education both in Britain and the United States. Perhaps more important is the effect of longer education upon attitudes held. In both the United States and Germany it has been found that the longer the education that people have had the more tolerant their attitudes seem to be.[1] The cause of this is uncertain, but it may be due to deeper knowledge or to a greater breadth of social contacts. When we encourage or legislate for longer education, we are never sure what the eventual effects will be.

The final example of unplanned cultural change also stems from the greater length of educational experience. When the majority of the population attended the elementary school up to fourteen, they underwent an educational experience that was fairly common to all. It was pointed out in the last section that secondary education in Britain today provides a variety of experience and thereby instils different sets of values. If a larger proportion of the population go beyond the secondary stage, many more people will not only experience the various types of secondary schools, but also the differing sub-cultures of the university, the college of education or the technical college. This could be of more importance relatively to women than men, since women are seriously under-represented in many of our institutions of higher learning. Longer education is itself a

[1] S. M. Lipset, *Political Man*, London, 1960, pp. 109–11.

powerful instrument for further differentiating culture. It could therefore make the problem of culture transmission a more complex one.

3. Conclusion

Once again a consideration of social change and innovation has led us back to the problem of providing stability. As was observed at the beginning of this chapter the two are closely linked. The very decision to hand part of the task of socializing the young to an institution other than the family builds in the chance of change. As more educational institutions are set up, so sub-cultures can be born within them. This can result in healthy tension, but it can also lead to dysfunctions which may be latent until a careful analysis is made. The results of such an examination may drive us to justify a particular sub-culture; this will force us out of the realm of sociological analysis into the field of politics or philosophy, since we must then consider our aims in education. In one particular sphere, namely the position of coloured migrants, recent developments in Britain force us to think about the social aims that must be settled prior to determining what we do in the schools, since we cannot know how to teach white or coloured children, together or apart, until we know whether our policy is to integrate migrants to our own way of life, or to aim for a pluralist society in which all cultures are given equal respect. Our knowledge of the effects and sources of change is very limited, particularly in the field of education. The very least that we can do is to be aware all the time that in the modern world this is an important problem and has a relevance to what and how we teach.

BIBLIOGRAPHY

(i) *Culture Transmission*
G. Bowker, *Education of Coloured Immigrants*, London, 1968.
J. S. Coleman, *The Adolescent Society*, New York, 1961.
Émile Durkheim, *Education and Sociology*, Glencoe, Illinois, 1956.
T. S. Eliot, *Notes Towards the Definition of Culture*, London, 1948.
R. Hoggart, *The Uses of Literacy*, London, 1957 (Pelican).

B. Jackson and D. Marsden, *Education and the Working Class*, London, 1962 (Pelican).

M. Mead, *The School in American Culture*, Cambridge, Mass., 1951 (for an extract, see in A. H. Halsey, J. E. Floud and C. A. Anderson, *Education, Economy and Society*, New York, 1961).

C. P. Snow, *The Two Cultures and a Second Look*, Cambridge, 1964.

(ii) *Innovation*

B. R. Clark, *Educating the Expert Society*, San Francisco, 1962 (Ch. I).

Sir F. Clark, *Education and Social Change*, London, 1940.

15

The Political Function

In its political function the educational system has two tasks. If the political unit as it is now constituted is to survive, there is a need that all its members, especially the new generation coming to the age when it can exercise political power, shall be loyal to the assumptions underlying the present system of government. This consensus is often taken for granted, but one of its main sources, whether consciously pursued or not, lies within the educational system. Secondly, there is the necessity that the country shall be led. Whatever is the type of government that exists in the country, its leaders must come from within it if it is to remain independent. The schools can play a major part in both the selection and the training of leaders (R. Rose, 1964).

A. Consensus

Whatever the regime that rules a country, its leaders will hope to gain the acceptance of that country. This should help to ensure the continuance of the regime and this will be so whether the country is democratic or not. Since Britain is a democratic society, it is natural to give more attention here to this type of political system. The assumptions that underlie a democratic system demand a high level of political sophistication. Most important are the tolerance of minorities by the majority who for the time have power, and the acceptance by the minorities that the majority has legitimate power. It has been said that one of Britain's greatest political inventions is the office of Leader of the Opposition, a politician paid by the State to ensure that an opposition exists able to take office if voted into power. Certainly the Leader of the Opposition symbolizes many of the basic assumptions of a democracy.

Research work during the 1960s in the USA has shown that

various agencies play a part in the political socialization of the child, but both the family and the school seem of major importance. Work in this field has only recently begun in Britain. In a study in Exeter of 627 boys and girls aged eleven to seventeen at grammar and modern schools and of 327 of their parents, some attempts were made to compare the effects of the family and of the school upon children's political views and knowledge. The experiences undergone in their families appeared to have little influence except on those children who perceived their parents' preference of political party, in which case there was some slight, but by no means pronounced, tendency for them to follow their parental example. Three reasons were suggested as likely to be at the root of this lack of effect by the family. Firstly, politics had a low salience in the interaction between parents and their children, since only 16 per cent of the parents claimed to be 'very interested' in the subject and 29 per cent were 'not very interested'. Secondly, much American work (F. I. Greenstein, 1965) has shown that children seem to develop during childhood and early adolescence attitudes that accept a rather benevolent view of political figures and institutions; thus, only 27 per cent of the children surveyed in Exeter said that the country would be better off without political parties. Lastly, there was some evidence to show that schools, rather than families, affected the political socialization of children of this age group.

This influence of the school related, however, only to particular facets of the process. Most children had somewhat similar views when asked to evaluate a number of political questions. For example, though their awareness of social class was somewhat limited, they were able to predict accurately how the occupants of such positions in the labour force as company director or bricklayer would probably vote. In addition, as may be expected in view of their benevolent political attitudes, none of them were very critical of the present British political system. Similar findings were reported in research into the political development between the ages of twelve and fourteen of 480 children in Aberdeen. Boys and girls had very favourable views of the Prime Minister, a public figure who was found to have great salience for children of this age range, and of the Lord Provost (Lord Mayor), in that at both twelve and fourteen never more than 12 per cent in the first and 22·8 per cent in the latter case thought that these political figures did 'not work as hard as most people'. However, they were, perhaps, more critical of the Queen, since at twelve 42·3 and at fourteen 28·6 per cent placed her in this category. Though intelligence could not be connected with holding different or more critical attitudes, the more intelligent of these children had more political knowledge than those with an IQ of 95 or less, and this paralleled the situation in Exeter where children at the grammar schools were more knowledgeable than those at the secondary modern schools. Those in the latter type of school rated lower on what is termed *political efficacy*, namely the belief that citizens have the power to influence decisions made within the political system. In Aberdeen, just over a half of the children at both twelve and fourteen felt that their families were politically powerful, and during this age range, within which in Scotland the move is made from primary to secondary school, the middle-class boys, namely those of whom more were in grammar schools, moved towards a great belief in political efficacy, whilst the working-class girls became less sure of their efficacy.

The main conclusion of the work in Aberdeen seems to be that the primary role of sex was latent in political learning, since by fourteen the children had been socialized more fully into the political roles of the sexes, namely that women have less to do with and a lower interest in politics, than into their social class political role. In view of the work done in Exeter, the move to secondary school might have had something to do with this development, since the main conclusion there was that, though political socialization was the result of a complex interaction between the child and his family, school and possibly certain other agencies, yet in respect of certain cognitive and affective discussions, the school appeared to have more influence on this process than did the family.[1]

The question may be asked whether the various types of British school, and particularly the public school, politically socialize their pupils in different ways. Little is known about this question. However, in 1966 a comparison was made between some of the political

[1] R. E. Dowse and J. Hughes, 'The Family, The School and the Political Socialization Process', *Sociology*, January 1971; P. W. Musgrave, 'Aspects of the Political Socialization of some Aberdeen Adolescents and their Educational Implications', *Research in Education*, November 1971.

values held by 231 boys aged fifteen and above at Winchester and 238 boys in the sixth form of a nearby grammar school. On most of the measures used the boys from the public school were surprisingly like those at the grammar school. Both groups saw political decisions as important, personal matters to which their experiences at school were relevant and all felt a definite sense of political efficacy. The outstanding differences were that the boys at Winchester placed a 'much lower moral evaluation . . . on the office of politician' and to a lesser extent were more reluctant 'to acknowledge a strong duty to participate in politics'.[1] In the light of the historical position of Winchester and other public schools in supplying political leaders these are surprising findings. The similarities between the schools may be due to a threshold effect; beyond a certain minimum level such values as political efficacy may be little affected by schooling, particularly amongst children whose families are supportive of education. Possibly this pioneering research did not tap the major dimensions of difference.

The decision that the schools should have a definite part in promoting political consensus can be a conscious decision. The part the school plays in Russia is a good example. In our view much of the history taught in Russian schools is given a bias with the intention of making the children loyal to the Communist regime so that they will see the world in the way that the rulers of Russia wish them to do. However, it is probable that most countries do much the same thing unconsciously in their own schools. History textbooks provide many examples. For instance, in describing the War of the Spanish Succession, British books tend to mention only British victories and omit French ones. French books tend to minimize or omit the part played by Marlborough. Both sides claim to have won the war. In the case of the Hundred Years War British texts make much of Crécy, Poitiers and Agincourt, so that British pupils are left wondering how we came to lose so many of our French possessions by 1453. Spanish textbooks have omitted any mention of the Armada.[2]

[1] D. McQuail, L. O'Sullivan and W. G. Quine, 'Elite Education and Political Values', *Political Studies*, June 1968, espec. p. 265.

[2] E. H. Dance, 'History Textbooks and International Revision', *History Today*, April 1956. For further examples see J. W. Hunt, *English History Through Foreign Eyes*, London, 1954.

It may be thought that it is easiest to build up loyalty to the country in such school subjects as history, geography and the teaching of the mother tongue, and that this process will be more powerful when the child is at the secondary stage. But this is not so. The textbooks of many countries could be quoted. A careful study of anthologies of verse for young children with their stress on national folk heroes would be relevant at this point. But here examples from German textbooks will be given.[1] An elementary reading book dated 1906 will show how the ideal of militarism, then considered a political necessity by the rulers of Germany, was inculcated into the young child:

'We want to play soldiers,' said Albert. 'Yes, soldiers,' cried the others. He divided them into two armies, four boys in each. Charles led his army to a large sand heap. Albert had to storm this with his soldiers. Shouting, 'Hurrah! Hurrah!' they ran up the sand heap, came to grips with the enemy and took them prisoner. Thus Albert won the war with his soldiers.

Or, again, under the Nazis elementary arithmetic was used to teach the young child the political aims of the new regime. The child became familiar with large numbers by reading how 13·25 millions were called up by Germany in the first world war and 11·25 millions by Germany's allies. These men carried on the 'heroic' fight, against the 47·5 millions of the league of Germany's enemies. Language can be used in an emotional way even in elementary arithmetic textbooks.

These examples are very obvious and were part of a conscious policy; the same process occurs in Britain unconsciously. If one makes a historical examination of the relevant journals and official reports, there are only rare references to be found to the conscious use of education to create political consensus. They can be found in the official reports issued in 1917–18 at a time when there was considerable political unrest of an extreme left-wing nature. They can occasionally be found in the speeches of moderate trade union leaders reminiscing about the slump of the early '30s; loyalty to the democratic way of life was preserved for these men in some cases through attendance at classes of the Workers' Educational Associa-

[1] These and many other examples will be found in R. H. Thomas and R. H. Samuel, *Education and Society in Modern Germany*, London, 1947, *passim*.

tion. However, consensus is maintained in many ways (R. W. Connell, 1971). Partly it is a matter of culture transmission; the great stories of the nation that are told from the earliest years in school are important here – the Armada and Trafalgar. Partly it is determined by the questions teachers ask and omit to ask; are there no disadvantages to our *laissez-faire* system? Is 'the West' always right and Russia always wrong?

The connections between education and democracy are well documented in certain particular instances. Thus it has been shown that in the case of various countries those with a longer education tend to vote more regularly than those with less education (S. M. Lipset, 1960). This raises the difficult question of whether a basic minimum of education is essential for a stable democracy. In the case of Britain it is true to say that one of the main influences that brought about the establishment of a State-aided system of elementary education in 1870 was the extension three years earlier of the vote to the male urban working class. It may well be that the experiment in India of running a democracy in a country still marked by mass illiteracy may, if successful, disprove this connection. However, Lipset has shown that degrees of democracy correlate positively with several indices of education. He compared firstly stable democracies with unstable democracies and dictatorships in Europe, and, secondly, democracies and unstable dictatorships with stable dictatorships in Latin America; the division into these categories had necessarily to be somewhat arbitrary. Lipset found that in both comparisons the more democratic group had a higher index on four educational criteria. These were the percentages of literacy, and the percentages in primary, post-primary and higher education. Though the statistics were by their very nature not strictly comparable, the differences between the two groups, both on average and when considering the ranges, were in each case so great as to leave the general conclusion in little doubt; the more educated countries were the more democratic. Certain exceptions at once come to mind, more particularly France and Germany. These exceptions raise the problem of national aims in education. As has been shown above, for much of the last century the German educational system has been used to further undemocratic ends.

One of the most influential of modern philosophers of education has built his entire philosophy around the need for a full education in a true democracy. John Dewey, particularly in his *Democracy and Education* (1916), argued that, if a democracy was to survive, the educational system must teach certain knowledge about the society and its traditions, and inculcate certain qualities so that citizens will both wish and be able to participate in the ruling of their country. It is hoped that such an education would lead to a greater tolerance of views of others and provide a basis for more rational political choice. There is a suspicion amongst political scientists that less sophisticated people have a simpler view of politics and are, therefore, more likely to fall under the power of extremist political leaders. It has already been pointed out that there is a connection between length of education and the degree of tolerance of opposing views. But more particularly, the fear is that it is the working class, because of their shorter education, who will surrender to extreme political views. Hoggart pointed out that the education of the working class probably gives 'little idea of a continuing tradition'. This class will not have the same wide general perspective as the more educated middle class, nor will they have the same sense of a past, a present and a future, which is an important element in political continuity. Evidence on the latter point comes from Spinley's work; it will be recalled that she found that her sample of working-class children tended to live for the present and were unable to forgo present pleasures for future benefits. Psychologists have found that this kind of limited or fixed frame of reference is one condition for easy suggestibility, which is in itself a major explanation of political extremism. Spinley also found that because of their upbringing these children were more prone to use violence and to rebel against authority.

However, very recent work has thrown some doubt on this thesis since rather different results in this field have been reported when different indices are used. More particularly, Lipsitz has shown that members of the working class who have more education tend to have less authoritarian attitudes than those with little education. Furthermore, Zeitlin, working in Cuba since the revolution, indicates that the interest shown in politics seems to be an important independent influence on authoritarian feelings. Where political interest was found to be high, a lower level of authoritarian feelings has been reported; thus pre-revolutionary Communists and deeply committed revolutionaries, who in both cases came from the working class and by definition showed high political interest, were rated low on authoritarianism.[1]

To sum up the argument, many working-class children come from a poor home background, have an education of a poor standard and leave school as soon as they can. This start in life is followed for many by a job in which they mix with adults from a very similar background. Limited educational experience is followed by low mental stimulation. This restricted frame of reference could well be a breeding ground for extremism. The Communist Party has always seen the leadership of the slumbering masses as one of its historic roles. Work done in Jamaica and amongst Negroes in the USA is relevant here. The effect of the school on political socialization seems to be strongest amongst those with least knowledge; the family in the lower social classes is as weak an agent of socialization into political, as it is into many other roles.[2] Education may not be a sufficient condition for democracy, but it certainly is a necessary condition for its survival.

B. Leaders

When we talk about 'leaders' in a democracy, to whom are we referring? We certainly include political leaders such as members of the Cabinet. We should include Members of Parliament and the more active members of the mainly hereditary House of Lords. The higher grades of the Civil Service must be added, since they are a part of the governing machinery of the country and have considerable powers of their own. Mention must be made of the counterparts of these national leaders at local government level, namely councillors and aldermen, and the full-time officers, such as the Director of Education, who carry out the policy determined by our democratically elected representatives on the local council. It will be noticed

[1] M. Lipsitz, 'Working Class Authoritarianism; A Re-examination', *American Sociological Review*, February 1965; M. Zeitlin, *Revolutionary Politics and the Cuban Working Class*, Princeton, 1967, pp. 262–5.

[2] K. P. Langton, *Political Socialization*, New York, 1969 (Ch. 4, 'Formal Environment: the School').

that economic leaders are omitted; they will be considered when we examine the economic functions of education.

1. *National Leaders*

Where are our political leaders educated? There is a description of their education which is almost a caricature. It runs as follows: a private preparatory school leads to a public school followed by Oxford or Cambridge University. The distinctive point of this education is that it is an education apart from those who are to be led. Further, it is not only the pattern supposed for Conservative Party leaders, but also for a considerable number of Labour leaders, more particularly for the intellectuals of the party. The trade unionist section of the Labour Party must be excepted, since by the present convention British trade union leaders must rise from the ranks of the unions that they lead. How true is this stereotype of leaders educated in the main apart?

Work by W. L. Guttsman (1963) has shown the changing social background of our political leaders over the last century. The Cabinet has become less predominantly aristocratic in its recruitment and is now recruited more from the upper-middle and middle classes. Yet there still persists a strong aristocratic connection. There also remain traces of the great 'political families', the younger members of whom have an earlier start in politics, often because of greater financial independence. By our present constitution a certain number of Cabinet members must sit in the House of Lords, though there is the possibility that the Labour Party could fill these positions by appointing life peers, rather than hereditary aristocrats. There was a lag of a generation between the changes in the constitution that broadened the social composition of the House of Commons, and the subsequent changes in the social composition of the Cabinet. The lag was not just a question of political connections, but the new political generation had to serve its apprenticeship before reaching high office and positions of leadership. The old political elite had been marked by an aristocratic connection with the more exclusive public schools. The new elite seems to have been drawn principally from the professional classes and more especially from lawyers. Business men are under-represented, perhaps because of the greater difficulty in their case of combining the earning of a living with

Parliamentary duties. The intellectual level of the new elite is high. Some have been to the old public schools, but a fair proportion come from the new public schools that grew up in the nineteenth century in answer to the demand of the new middle class. Oxford and Cambridge are well represented amongst these new men, whose careers at university indicate more interest in things academic than the old aristocratic elite had shown at these same universities in the nineteenth century.

(i) *The Cabinet*. When Baldwin formed his first Government in 1923 he said that one of his first thoughts was that 'it should be a Government of which Harrow should not be ashamed'. Similar sentiments were attributed to Macmillan in the 1950s except that in his case it was Eton and not Harrow that was important. In 1951 82 per cent of ministers in the new Conservative Government had attended public schools; ten years later the proportion was 76 per cent. The public schools still seem to be the educational source of an important section of our political leadership; they are still considered to give the worthwhile lessons in loyalty, obedience and leadership that are thought necessary for public life. Later in this section consideration will be given to the validity of the claims that these characteristics can be taught.

(ii) *Members of Parliament*. Cabinets are drawn from Parliament and largely from the House of Commons. What types of school have Members of Parliament attended in recent years? In the case of the Conservative Party the position was almost the same in 1955 as between the wars. In 1955 75 per cent had gone to public schools and 16·5 per cent to other secondary schools, whereas the inter-war averages were 78·5 per cent from public schools and 19 per cent from other secondary schools. For the Labour Party the proportion who had been to public schools rose from 9 per cent in between the wars to 19 per cent in 1955, and from 15·5 per cent to 29 per cent for those attending other secondary schools; these increases were at the expense of those who had attended elementary school only. In 1955 the percentage of Members of Parliament of all parties who had been to public school was exactly 50 per cent.[1]

[1] J. C. Dancy, *The English Public School*, London, 1963, p. 112. A public school here is defined as one of the approximately 200 Headmasters' Conference schools.

(iii) *The Civil Service*. Before considering the consequences of this recruitment the third component of political leadership must be examined. There are two main avenues of entry to the senior, or administrative, grades of the Civil Service; entry may be by open competition through a qualifying examination, followed by either further written papers or by a series of tests and interviews lasting two days, or by promotion from the executive or clerical grades. Entry by examination would be thought to supply a genuine career open to the talented. However, during the inter-war years more than 80 per cent of the entrants to the senior grades by this method of entry and about 50 per cent of the entrants by other means came from the independent public schools. During the years 1944–52, 56 per cent of entrants by open competition attended independent public schools, 17 per cent direct-grant schools, many of which are in fact Headmasters' Conference schools, and 28 per cent maintained grammar schools. For more recent recruits, namely for those entering by examination between 1960 and 1964, the situation seems little changed. Three-fifths of candidates, but over four-fifths of those who were successful, came from Oxford or Cambridge universities. Though an almost equal proportion, namely 38·1 and 42·7 per cent respectively, of candidates for entry came from local authority and independent schools, yet of those who were successful 30·8 per cent came from local authority schools, 50·8 per cent from independent and 18·2 (17·6 of candidates) per cent were from direct-grant schools.[1] The picture here is similar to that of Parliament. There is a fall in the public school representation and a rise in that of maintained grammar schools, but a substantial proportion, about half in both cases, came from the public schools, using a wide definition of the term.

It must be realized that there is one possible justification for this situation to continue, or at least, not to undergo rapid change. Those who are our leaders can possibly mix more easily with those who have the same upbringing as themselves. In this way proper communication will ensure efficient government. However, two powerful

[1] R. K. Kelsall, *Higher Civil Servants in Britain*, London, 1955, gives full details of the education of this group (percentages rounded off); C. H. Dodd, 'Recruitment to the Administrative Class, 1960–64', *Public Administration*, Spring 1967.

arguments exist on the other side. The first is purely on the functional level. There is no guarantee that men or women educated apart in special schools for a small proportion of the country and drawn predominantly from one class will have any understanding of those whom they will govern and from whom they have been segregated almost completely since birth. Secondly, despite the contemporary political aim of equality of opportunity in all spheres, it appears that those who attend the public schools still have a greater chance of success in national politics.

2. Local Leaders

The rise of the Labour Party in local politics has made a considerable change in the educational sources of local leaders. From the few relevant surveys[1] in this field the expected stereotype seems to be true. Most local Conservative leaders, whether on the council or the committee of the local party, are drawn from local managers, small business men or shopkeepers, many of whom have been to grammar school and a few of whom have gone to public schools. This seems to be the case in both urban and rural areas. Most local Labour Party leaders come from lower managers, and from clerical and skilled manual workers, few of whom have been to grammar schools, but a greater proportion of whom in the near future will go to grammar schools or the upper streams in comprehensive schools because of the greater stress on formal educational qualifications at this level. One of the social problems of the near future will be to provide a replacement for the old type of local Labour leader, particularly of the type connected with the trade union. In the past these men have been mainly recruited from the able men whose social background in childhood prevented their having the education for which their ability fitted them. Today, persons with these characteristics stay at school much longer and often then rise up the social scale. In the USA trade unions feed such men back from the universities into the higher levels of union and local politics, but in Britain on the whole convention as yet will not allow this.

The equivalent at local level to the national Civil Servant is the

[1] See A. H. Birch, *Small Town Politics*, London, 1959; T. W. Brennan, E. W. Cooney and H. Pollins, *Social Change in West Wales*, London, 1954; M. Stacey, *Tradition and Change*, London, 1960.

local government officer. The senior grades, for instance the Director of Education or Town Clerk, must by the nature of their occupation have had a long formal education. In one large Midland city Musgrove (1963) found that 76·9 per cent of the senior local government officers had been to grammar or public schools. At the middle levels of the local government service it would seem that many make a career who have left grammar school at sixteen. The grammar and public schools were also found to provide the education of many local leaders, both men and women, in voluntary organizations such as the scouts and guides, and the Red Cross.[1]

3. *Education for Leadership*

It has been made very clear that at national level a majority of our political elite is educated at public schools and at local level at maintained grammar schools. The influence of the public schools on the aims and organizations of the grammar schools is well known; some aspects of this were discussed in Chapter 9. One of the most important claims of the public schools has been that they can train boys to become leaders. They aim to give our future leaders the sense of duty and responsibility to their country which will ensure that their former pupils will use their talents as leaders, and these schools further believe that they can inculcate the social skills needed by leaders. In other countries, such as the USSR and to a large extent the USA, political leaders are not educated apart. Can the British system be justified?

The early attempts of psychologists to study the nature of leadership concentrated upon the character traits displayed by those considered to be leaders. The results were inconclusive. In a critique of twenty studies made up to 1936 seventy-nine different traits were reported.[2] Only one trait was common to as many as ten of the studies and that was intelligence. Similarly, in Britain intelligence was found to be the most efficient predictor for choosing officers in

---

[1] See Rosalind C. Chambers, 'A Study of Three Voluntary Organisations', in D. V. Glass (ed.), *Social Mobility in Britain*, London, 1954, for a contrary conclusion in the case of voluntary organizations consisting mainly of women.

[2] C. Bird, reported in T. H. Newcomb, R. H. Turner and P. M. Converse, *Social Psychology: The Study of Human Interaction* (2nd ed.), London, 1966, p. 474.

the armed services during the 1939–45 war (E. James, 1951). Many of the twenty studies reported traits that were obviously contradictory.

As a result of the failure of this type of investigation, psychologists have turned their attention away from the concept that the leader is a person who fulfils a special role in a group of people with a shared set of values (T. H. Newcomb, R. H. Turner and P. M. Converse, 1966, and G. Homans, 1951). The only factor common to all leadership situations is that the other roles in the group are dependent upon the leader's role to fulfil the aim of that particular group. But in different situations a different set of qualities is required to fill the role of leader. For example, the role of the army captain in action demands different traits from that needed by the scientist leading a research team. To a school teacher it is clear that the headmaster of a public school must have different qualities from the headmaster of a secondary modern school. The conclusions to be drawn here are that the character traits demanded in leaders vary from situation to situation, but that the position of the leader is marked by the structural dependence of the roles in the group on his role. Possibly the only personality trait that may be demanded in a leader is that of intelligence.

There are groups that need leaders at all levels of society. We should not be surprised to read that adolescent boys in Liverpool organized a football league with matches every Saturday morning, each team in charge of a boy captain; they did this without any help or encouragement from adults.[1] Again, an investigation compared leadership amongst two school classes of thirteen-year-old boys in Glasgow. The first group was from one of the best fee-paying schools, whilst the other was in one of the toughest non-selective secondary schools in the city. It was found that the general trait of leadership was distributed in each group according to the curve of normal error.[2] At all socio-economic levels men and women fill the role of leader.

The claim of the public schools to train leaders has usually been

[1] J. B. Mays, *Growing up in a City*, Liverpool, 1951, Appendix A, pp. 169–73.
[2] J. Kelly, 'A Study of Leadership in Two Contrasting Groups', *Sociological Review*, November 1963.

based upon the fact that they could bring out the qualities essential for leadership in boys. We can now see that this is impossible, since different qualities are required in different situations. It is even difficult to argue the case put by the public schools in their own terms since no one has been able to agree what are the traits that are vital in leaders. What then can the educational system do to educate the potential leaders that exist at all socio-economic levels? It would seem that any policy of educating for leadership must be based on the foregoing analysis.

In the first place at every level of leadership intelligence seems necessary. Any educational system that selects by intelligence, whether between schools or within them, will influence the supply of leaders. Entry to the grammar school is largely determined by measured intelligence, and therefore these schools are bound to be the main source of leaders for many of the higher positions of leadership in Government, industry and other spheres. As long as we have a selective system of secondary schools, it must be arranged to find the maximum number of intelligent children who may become leaders. But leaders are also required in the lower ranks of society. In secondary modern schools a number of children, usually of working-class origins, who left school at the minimum school leaving age, did have the experience for what it was worth of filling positions of leadership, whether as prefects or as officers of school clubs. However, it would seem that in the comprehensive school such opportunities may now be rare, since in a recent study of one comprehensive school just under 80 per cent of the prefects came from middle-class homes.[1] Therefore attention to the education of leaders is needed in all, not merely selective schools.

A second lesson to be drawn from the analysis of leadership is that no one will take the role of leader unless he feels impelled to do so. The motive is essential. The public schools did give many young men a deep sense of service, particularly of a political nature, and this, rather than any special training in the necessary character traits, led such men to grasp the role of leader that was offered to them in many different situations.[2] Under the social conditions

[1] D. N. Holly, 'Profiting from the Comprehensive School', *British Journal of Sociology*, June 1965.
[2] R. H. Wilkinson, 'The Gentleman Ideal and the Maintenance of a

found in Britain up to 1939 few others had the education, the income, the time and the will to take these roles, and traditionally leadership went to the class who patronized the public schools. Under modern conditions it is therefore necessary that at all levels of intelligence there should be people who want to be leaders in the many spheres of action open to them. It is here that the comprehensive and the secondary modern schools have a place in educating for leadership. Many of their pupils must leave school with the desire to lead and the interest that will supply a motive to leadership in some activity that is open to them.

Finally, the prefect system was supposedly an agent in training leaders. Originally, as we have seen, it rested on domination by force, but in its present less authoritarian form it can have a place in educating leaders. Children who are prefects have the chance to lead others in all the activities in a school. If the many activities in any school could be systematically divided and children given the chance to lead in each sphere, far more children than under the present unitary prefect system would have the chance of acting as leaders.[1] This experience would be valuable only if the lessons learnt in the particular situation at school could be transferred to other situations on leaving school. Transfer depends upon conscious thought. Therefore the vital lesson in all school leadership situations must be pointed out to the children, namely that the dependence of the led is common to the role of all leaders.

C. Conclusion

Obviously the educational system has two important parts to play from a political point of view. As was shown in the first part of this chapter it must ensure that the political leaders at each level are followed even by those in loyal opposition. Democracy is a system of government that demands a fair standard of education to ensure its continuance. Secondly, the educational system must be organized so that those with the intelligence necessary to lead at whatever level

Political Elite', *Sociology of Education*, Fall 1963 (also in P. W. Musgrave (ed.), *Sociology, History and Education*, London, 1970).

[1] For further consideration of this topic see K. G. Collier, *The Social Purposes of Education*, London, 1959, Chs XI and XII.

or in whatever sphere of society, can have the chance to do so. At present this is basically part of the selective function of education to which we now turn.

BIBLIOGRAPHY

R. W. Connell, *The Child's Construction of Politics*, Melbourne, 1971.

F. I. Greenstein, *Children and Politics*, Newhaven, 1965.

W. L. Guttsman, *British Political Elites*, London, 1963.

G. Homans, *The Human Group*, London, 1951 (espec. Ch. 8).

E. James, *Educating for Leadership*, London, 1951.

S. M. Lipset, *Political Man*, London, 1960.

F. Musgrove, *The Migratory Elite*, London, 1963 (Ch. 5).

T. H. Newcomb, R. H. Turner and P. M. Converse, *Social Psychology: The Study of Human Interaction* (2nd ed.), London, 1966 (espec. Ch. 15).

R. Rose, *Politics in England*, London, 1964 (Ch. III, 'Political Socialization').

16

The Selection Function

A political aim common to many countries is that of ensuring equality of opportunity. This aim is often held especially strongly in the case of education. Certainly no political party in modern Britain could afford to forgo the provision of equality of educational opportunity as one of its main policies, though the interpretation of 'equality' does change through time.[1] Politically the educational system is seen as a possible way of selecting some children and giving them a better start to their adult life than others. However, we are trying to view the working of the educational system in a non-political manner. Here we must attempt to answer two questions, namely what is the selection function and how is it being fulfilled in Britain today?

At any time the population of a country contains children who have different abilities and personalities. It is essential that by the time they are adults these children shall be able to use their talents to the utmost. This may be justified in several ways. One may argue on moral grounds that each child ought to be given the chance to develop fully, or on psychological grounds that only by a full use of his talents will the child grow to be a mentally healthy adult. Again, there is the economic case that in the modern world no country can afford to neglect the greatest of its resources, the native talents of its population.

In this context we can consider the educational system to be acting in a way akin to a sorting mechanism. Children with many individual differences are helped to the starting places for their adult lives which are most suited to their own particular qualities. If the educational system is undertaking the selection function well, then the country will make full use of the personal and intellectual

[1] J. Evetts, 'Equality of Educational Opportunity: the Recent History of a Concept', *British Journal of Sociology*, December 1970.

qualities of its people. It is the sum of these qualities that is sometimes called the pool of talent or the pool of ability. For reasons which will become clear the *pool of capability* is perhaps a more apt term.

A. The Pool of Capability

In recent years some thought has been given to the more exact analysis of the pool of capability (P. E. Vernon, 1963). Interest has been stimulated in two ways. There has been a political interest based on the desire that able children of all social classes should be given the fullest education of which they are capable. There has also been competition on an international scale to achieve higher economic productivity. This has directed attention to the comparative output of technicians and technologists from the institutes of higher education in various countries including the USA, Russia and Britain. This interest in the pool of capability has led to attempts to measure the size and distribution of the reserves of ability. Statistical exercises endeavouring to answer this problem for Britain have been made, for example, by the Crowther (Vol. II, 1960) and Robbins (Appendix I, 1963) Committees. Similar work has been done in Sweden and Holland (P. de Wolff and K. Harnqvist in A. H. Halsey (ed.), 1961).

The initial attempts to measure reserves of ability were based on the use of tests, usually of IQ, which were considered to have a value for predicting future academic success. A typical method was to calculate the proportion of the population of a given IQ that was thought to be the minimum requisite for a given level of education, for example, to achieve success in a grammar school course as measured by passing five 'O' levels, or for university entry. This proportion was then compared with the proportion that was in fact undergoing that level of education at that particular time. Any shortfall would indicate the order of the reserves of ability. Such a calculation has been called an assessment of reserves in the narrow sense. Usually the sole criterion is IQ, whereas it is well known that many other considerations are important for the progress of children at school or of undergraduates at university. Apart from the influence of the home and the rest of the environment there is the whole complex of personality factors. Many teachers know that relatively dull children succeed at school because of perseverance or the support of their parents, whilst more intelligent children can do less well than expected due to some defect in personality or a lack of parental interest. It is for such reasons that Vernon wishes to talk of 'the pool of capability' rather than 'the pool of talent'.[1] The statistical measurement of reserves of capability must obviously be a much more complex task.

Although no adequate allowance has yet been made for personality factors, measurements of reserves in the broad sense have been made. The population has been divided into strata, usually by social class, and the distribution in these strata of measured intelligence or some such measure of school success as passing a given examination has been calculated. If it is assumed that the highest stratum covers the optimal conditions for all the possible variables, then the shortfall in the lower strata can be calculated. Some calculations have attempted to allow for the effect of removing the economic hindrances to success at school. It is hoped that such methods can be extended to the measurement of the reserves of special abilities such as those needed by mathematicians and scientists. This is partly dependent on further improvements in the psychological tests used to measure such special aptitudes. When thinking about these methods it is worth while reminding ourselves constantly that it is usually ability and not capability that is being used as the criterion. In this connection we should remember that 'merit' has been defined as 'IQ plus Effort'.[2]

Some indications can be given of the quantity of capability that now appears to be wasted in Britain. The very framework of the analysis used will show some of the causes of this waste, since it will make clear the way in which this country fails to allow many individuals to develop and use their capabilities to the full. It is possible in this context to make comparisons between countries, the sexes, geographical regions within the same country, social classes and between types of school.

[1] P. E. Vernon, letter in *British Journal of Educational Studies*, November 1958.

[2] M. D. Young, *The Rise of the Meritocracy*, London, 1958, p. 94 (Pelican). For an attempt to measure the way selection taps the pool of capability differentially, see D. F. Swift, 'Meritocratic and Social Class Selection at Age Eleven', *Educational Research*, November 1965.

1. *International Comparisons*

There is immense difficulty in international comparisons of educational statistics, mainly because of differences in standards. Yet the fact that in 1957-8 in the USA 16·65 per cent of the relevant age group gained first degrees compared with 2.92 per cent in Britain cannot be attributed entirely to the somewhat lower standards of some American universities. Again it is known that in the early 1960s 13 per cent of the relevant age group in Sweden passed the university entrance qualification compared with the 6·9 per cent of boys and girls who gained two 'A' levels in England and Wales in 1961.[1] This difference can hardly be attributed to a higher level of innate intelligence among the Swedes than among the British. Some measure of the possibility of university expansion is indicated by this comparison, but calculations by Professor Harnqvist (A. H. Halsey (ed.), 1961) suggest that even in Sweden there are reserves of capability, since he believes from his figures that at least 28 per cent of boys and girls could attain university entrance standard.

2. *Inter-Sex Comparisons*

It is generally held that there are no significant differences in the innate intellectual potential of men and women. Differences in kind may exist, but not of level. Yet in 1961, whereas 8·7 per cent of boys in the relevant age group left school with two 'A' levels, only 5·1 per cent of girls achieved this standard.[2] The same type of inter-sex difference can be found at 'O' level, though of a smaller order of magnitude. Yet it is also known that once women are at university they do on average as well as men.

Any attempts to calculate reserves of capability are complicated when comparing the sexes by the fact that girls often study a different curriculum from boys even in co-educational schools. This can be seen clearly in the table below which shows the proportions of different types of sixth forms in maintained schools in England in 1959. This tendency is as pronounced in the universities where the proportions of young men come near matching the occupational structure, whereas a much higher proportion of women are in arts rather

[1] A. H. Halsey (ed.), *Ability and Educational Opportunity*, 1961, pp. 192–3, and *Higher Education* (Robbins), Appendix I, p. 7.

[2] *Higher Education* (Robbins), Appendix 1, p. 7.

than science or technology faculties. Though there is no doubt that
this matches the structure in women's occupations, the swing to the
arts appears to have gone further than economic needs would

	Science	Arts	General
	%	%	%
Boys' Schools	59	39	2
Co-educational Schools – Boys	72	21	7
Girls	23	64	13
Girls' Schools	23	56	21

Source: *15 to 18*, Vol. I, 1959, p. 253.

demand. There is, therefore, a tendency built into the school system
to divert young women into one particular educational avenue which
may be dysfunctional, if one is considering the optimum use of
available capability. Marriage and consequent withdrawal from the
labour force also complicate the issue and make calculations, for
instance, of the reserves of women teachers a very difficult task.
However, these complications should in no way be allowed to obscure
the fact that in Britain, and indeed in many other countries, women
do not receive an equal chance compared with men to be educated
beyond the minimum school leaving age. It is, therefore, amongst
women that one of the largely untapped pools of capability lies.

3. *Geographical Comparisons*

In view of the very different social characteristics of the areas for
which the local education authorities in Britain are responsible, it is
not surprising that the proportion continuing school beyond the
minimum school leaving age of fifteen varies throughout the country.
Explanations for this might be sought in the fact that there is
difficulty in matching the rate of change of the population in any
area to such a 'lumpy' piece of capital investment as a new school.
Each local authority has reached its present pattern of provision by a
different historical route. The problems of educational provision
are not the same in rural and urban areas. Social class differences in
measured intelligence exist and often characterize a local authority's
catchment area; thus, different patterns of the distribution of measured intelligence will be found in Southport and in Salford. Yet
after allowing for all such considerations the recorded variations

between areas in Britain in 1960 seems unduly high. Amongst counties Cardiganshire had the highest proportion of seventeen-year-olds at school with 27·9 per cent, Lincolnshire (Holland) the lowest with 5·5 per cent; the highest county borough was Merthyr Tydfil with 15·2 per cent and the lowest Bury with 2·5 per cent.[1] Such large regional variations, which on the whole mirrored the provision of grammar school places, can in no way match differences in the distribution of capability or even of measured intelligence, nor for that matter do they bear any relation to the availability of fee-paying schools.

If we contrast the performance of pupils in local education authorities that provide many places in selective secondary schools with those where there are few places, we can see some of the effects of these regional inequalities of opportunity. In Douglas' (1968) study of children in secondary schools he compared areas providing places in selective schools for between 13 and 23 per cent of pupils with areas where between 26 and 36 per cent of children were found such places. In the areas of low provision the percentages completing fifth form were 38 for boys and 32 for girls compared with 43 and 44 respectively in the areas of high provision, whilst the percentages gaining General Certificates were 25 for boys and 21 for girls in those areas with low provision against 27 per cent for both boys and girls in those areas with the higher rate of provision of selective places. Thus, the girls seemed to be at a greater disadvantage than the boys as a result of lower provision, though both sexes were influenced to some extent, particularly before entry to the sixth form.[2]

These differences are often founded on local attitudes towards education. An analysis of similar regional inequalities in France has shown that the southern third has on average higher attendance rates in secondary education than the rest of France (J. Ferez in A. H. Halsey (ed.), 1961). This was attributed partly to the strong cultural tradition left by the Roman civilization in this area and partly to the fact that the small-scale vineyard owners of this area see in education an escape from their own economic uncertainty, whilst the industrial areas of northern France have provided a more certain demand for labour amongst those who could leave school at the

[1] *Higher Education* (Robbins), Appendix I, p. 65.
[2] J. W. B. Douglas, *All Our Future*, London, 1968, pp. 80 and 213.

minimum age. A further comparison was made between the dispersed rural areas and the concentrated urban and suburban areas. In the latter the provision of secondary schooling does not demand boarding facilities or long journeys, both of which are needed in rural areas and demand exceptionally favourable attitudes towards education.

In the USA place of residence has been found to influence the desire for university education.[1] In Wisconsin the intelligent sons of prosperous farmers were less liable to want to go to university than were equally intelligent urban boys, since higher education was regarded by the farmers' sons as irrelevant to their chosen career of farming. Their sisters, however, could not easily find an occupation at home and chose a career, such as teaching or social work, for which higher education was necessary.

Little is known of this nature with regard to Britain. Yet similar forces must be at work. It is in an analysis of this kind that we must seek the answer to the question why it is that both the five counties with the highest proportion of children staying at school until seventeen and the five counties with the highest proportion entering higher education are Welsh. When the proportions vary between local education authorities as much as those given above, it can be clearly seen that here is another source of inequality and of unused capability.

4. Social Class Comparisons

The argument about the reserves of ability is often stated in terms of social class. Sometimes crude comparisons are made between the proportions from various social classes at different stages of the educational system, for example, the percentage of children of manual workers at university. Apart from the by now familiar warning against confusing ability with capability, there are two other considerations to be taken into account. Comparisons between the measured intelligence of the various social classes may for many purposes need to be corrected to allow for the skewed distribution of IQ by social class. But perhaps of more importance is the influence of social class learning as described in Chapter 4, which works so that

[1] W. H. Sewell and others, 'Social Status and Educational and Occupational Aspiration', *American Sociological Review*, February 1957.

many able children from working-class homes cannot gain the experience necessary for the full development of their intelligence.

It is possible to quote statistics that show clearly the differences between measured intelligence and academic attainments in each social class. For example, during the course of its inquiry the Crowther Committee examined a representative sample of 5,940 National Service recruits to the Army. It found that in the top 11 per cent of measured intelligence the proportion who gained the entry qualifications necessary for higher education, namely two or more 'A' levels or an Ordinary National Certificate, was 68 per cent in the case of children of fathers in professional or managerial jobs compared with 52 per cent for those whose fathers were in clerical employment, 45 per cent for the children of skilled manual workers and 31 per cent in the case of children of semi-skilled and unskilled workers. It is not so much amongst the very able that these differences are so apparent. Thus in the second level of ability 69·1 per cent of the children of fathers in professional and managerial occupations are in independent, grammar or technical secondary schools, whilst only 26·3 per cent of the children of fathers in unskilled manual work are; at the first level of ability the respective percentages are 96·2 and 77·2.[1]

Using this type of statistic it is possible to calculate the reserves of ability 'in the broad sense', but such a figure would be very artificial, since the academic achievements of children in the upper social classes have improved greatly in recent years, but there has been only a small reduction in the differential rate of achievement between the social classes. All classes have been affected more or less equally by the recent expansion in education. Therefore any calculation of the reserves of ability made in the future may well yield a higher estimate than at present, assuming that this differential rate of achievement diminishes. It is clear, however, that there is a dysfunction in the British educational system so that it is not playing its proper part in sorting out the capability available in all the social classes of the population. After the next brief section it is to this problem that the rest of this chapter will be given.

[1] *15 to 18* (Crowther), Vol. II, pp. 120 and 122.

5. *Type of School*

The four comparisons made so far have all relied on factors external to the educational system. It is possible to tackle the problem in a different way. This examines the educational achievements of children who have the same apparent capacity as measured by intelligence tests or by some form of teacher's report, but who have taken different routes through the secondary school system or have left before taking certain examinations. The difficulty inherent in this type of estimate can be seen from the fact that in the report on *Early Leaving* (1954) heads of a sample of grammar schools in England and Wales thought that 33 per cent of their entry were capable of a course leading to two or more 'A' levels, but by 1962 well over 40 per cent of their pupils had begun such a course. In fact in 1960-1 26 per cent of all grammar school leavers had obtained two or more 'A' levels. Rapid change can confound most calculations in this field.

At the moment little is known of the effect of different types of secondary education on children of equal measured intelligence at the time of entry. In a recent sample of 5,362 children it was shown that there is a considerable overlap in the IQ scores of children in different types of secondary school. The ranges within which 90 per cent of the children's IQ scores fell were: grammar schools 106–127, technical schools 100–122·5, independent schools 85–124, secondary modern schools 76–107·5.[1] It is known that in some independent schools children attain much higher academic results than might be expected from their IQ scores. There is also the possibility that children may lose points of IQ through the experience of being placed in the lower streams of a primary school (J. W. B. Douglas, 1964). The possibility will be discussed later in this chapter that the very act of putting a child in a certain type of school may provide him with the experience that can help to develop or hinder the growth of his intelligence.

6. *Conclusion*

The problem of the pool of capability viewed from an educational standpoint is whether the schools and other educational institutions

---

[1] J. W. B. Douglas, *The Home and the School*, London, 1964, p. 21 (T Scores converted to IQ points as on p. 7). S. Wiseman, *Education and Environment*, Manchester, 1964, pp. 21–4 and p. 132, found a similar overlap in his work in the Manchester area.

are so organized that they help to bring about the full development of the capability potentially available to the country. Perhaps the best way to epitomize what has been said is to take an imaginary, but not atypical case. What is lost to the country when the daughter of an unskilled labourer just fails the selection test for the grammar school at the age of eleven and becomes a member of the top stream of a single-sex secondary modern school in an urban area with a ready demand for unskilled young women in the local labour force? Mention of selection at eleven leads straight to the other main problem of this chapter, namely, how does the educational system carry out the function of selection?

B. Selection

The function of selection in Britain cannot be considered apart from the structure of the educational system. There are two important factors to be borne in mind. Firstly, there is the division into the private and State sectors. There is also the present division in the State sector between, on the one hand, a comprehensive primary system that caters for all children of whatever measured ability up to the age of eleven, apart from certain special cases such as the educationally subnormal, and on the other hand, the secondary schools that are rapidly differentiating into various versions of the comprehensive school, but on the whole the influence of the grammar, technical and modern school is still strong. The roots of this system are based in British educational history, but it would certainly seem to have been the intention of the new Ministry of Education in the early part of the post-war era that the 1944 Act should be interpreted in this way by the local authorities responsible for its local implementation. It is within this structure and under the influence of its connections with other social institutions, more particularly with the economy and the social class system, that the function of selection is carried out.

1. *The Private System*
Before examining the State system brief mention must be made of the private sector, which for many is characterized by the public schools, though schools other than these are included within the

private system. The important part that the public schools still play in providing political leaders has already been described, and in the next chapter it will be found that these schools play a somewhat similar role in the provision of leaders for the economy. Therefore, although in 1969 only 5·0 per cent of all children at school were in independent schools, these schools – or rather that number known as the public schools – have a social significance far outweighing their numerical importance in the total educational system.

One of the main institutional reasons for this significance is the special relationship of the public schools with the universities. In fact this was almost inevitable. Because of the way the British educational system has grown, the proportion of sixth-form places provided by these schools has always been high, though it has diminished considerably during the last decade. In 1962 32·3 per cent of all boys in sixth forms were in those independent schools recognized by the Ministry of Education as efficient and, if direct-grant schools are included with the independent schools, the proportion rises to 49 per cent. In 1969 the comparable percentages were 16·8 and 26·1. For girls the proportions in 1962 were lower, namely 19·2 per cent for independent and 34 per cent for direct-grant and independent schools. By 1969 the percentages for girls were 11·2 for independent and 20·9 for direct-grant and independent schools.[1] In the years between 1918 and 1939 boys and girls from independent schools had just over twice the chance of going to a university that children from maintained grammar schools had and, more surprisingly, the chances seem to have moved against the children from the State system during this period. In 1960-1 there was still a greater chance that a boy or girl leaving an independent school would go to university than one from a maintained grammar school, since 19 per cent of leavers from independent schools and only 13 per cent from maintained grammar schools went to universities; if the direct-grant schools, many of which rank as public schools, were included, the proportion would rise from 19 to about 22 per cent. However, by 1968/9 the percentages had risen to 21 for independent, 25 for independent and direct-grant, and 18 for maintained schools.[2]

[1] Ministry of Education, *Annual Statistics*, Vol. I, 1962; Department of Education and Science, *Annual Statistics*, Vol. I, 1969.

[2] *15 to 18* (Crowther), Vol. 1, p. 200; J. E. Floud in D. V. Glass (ed.),

Clearly the expansion of sixth forms in maintained schools is changing their relationship with the universities and putting them more nearly in the same position as the independent schools.

Although many children attend the State primary schools up to the age of eight or nine before going on to private preparatory schools, it is possible for a child to complete his education without ever entering a State school. In an important study, mainly statistical in nature and made in 1964, Kalton found that 97 per cent of pupils in those independent boarding schools and 84 per cent of pupils in those direct-grant day schools that were members of the Headmasters' Conference came from families where the father was middle class. Providing his parents can afford to send a boy through the private system the question of selection scarcely seems relevant. There is an examination, the Common Entrance Examination, at around thirteen years of age on passing from the preparatory to the public school. This would seem to operate more as a test of attainments than as a selective mechanism, though all children do not enter their first choice of school. The majority do, and those who are not accepted at once appear to find places elsewhere in the private system.[1] 36 per cent of Kalton's sample in independent boarding schools had an IQ of 130 or more. However, at the other extreme 20 per cent had an IQ of less than 115, of whom 2 per cent scored under 100. In the favourable conditions of these schools children of lesser ability may achieve high educational results. Thus, in one group of boys who went to independent schools after failing the eleven plus, 70 per cent passed five or more subjects at Ordinary level of the GCE and more than a quarter passed two or more subjects at Advanced level.[2]

Without entering the field of political polemics, only two valid points may be made. As long as the private system exists, and there are valid arguments of a philosophical nature that it should continue

---

Social Mobility in Britain, London, 1954, pp. 114 and 136; and *Higher Education* (Robbins), Appendix I, p. 229; Department of Education and Science, *Annual Statistics*, Vol. I, 1969.

[1] G. Kalton, *The Public Schools*, London, 1966, p. 25; J. C. Dancy, *The English Public School*, London, 1963, p. 39.

[2] G. Kalton, *op. cit.*, p. 30; P. L. Masters and S. W. Hockey, 'Natural Reserves of Ability – Some Evidence from Independent Schools', *Times Educational Supplement*, 17 May 1963, p. 1061.

to exist, parents who can afford it have a chance of opting out of the State system to buy for their children the prestige which is still perhaps conferred by these schools on their former pupils, whether they have capability or not. Again, the children who attend these schools for one reason or another still seem to have a disproportionate chance of entering higher education and, as long as children of the same measured ability do not have the same chance of developing it, the educational system is not carrying out the function of selection with the maximum efficiency. Resources of teaching power are being used in one part of the system which from the viewpoint of the system as a whole might be deployed to greater purpose elsewhere. Capability is lost to the country and inequality of opportunity exists.

2. The State System

When examining selection it is to the State system that most consideration must be given. This is the way by which the majority of our children gain their education. Despite the changes that are being made in procedures for allocating children to secondary schools, many still sit an examination at about eleven years old as a result of which they are placed either in one or another type of secondary school or in a higher or lower stream in a comprehensive school. The school or the stream in which they are placed will in most cases determine the type of occupation that they can take up as an adult. Certain educational qualifications lead to certain jobs, and the majority of the jobs carrying high social status demand qualifications that are usually gained in the grammar school, higher streams of a comprehensive school, technical college or university. It has already been seen that the British educational system is not organized so that it makes the most of the capability available in this country. We must now try to discover where it is within the system that dysfunction occurs. One fruitful way of doing this is to take each of the stages in the educational system in turn, paying particular attention to the points of transfer between the different institutions involved.

(i) *Primary Schools.* When children first go to school at five years of age they enter the infant school. Here the classes are not divided by ability level. There may be parallel classes in the larger schools in order to divide the children into groups of a teachable size. The children remain in such unstreamed classes until they go to the junior school at seven. In many of these schools the children are divided into streams by ability some time between the ages of seven and nine. This is the first selection process in our educational system. The arguments used to justify organization of the junior school in this way are that the brighter children will be given the chance to develop more fully and more quickly, whilst the less able children will have all the advantages of proceeding at the rate most suited to their ability. Admittedly there are innate differences in the potential capability of children that can sometimes be discovered by this age, and certainly by eight many of the effects of social class learning have influenced the development of children's intelligence. But if it can be shown that the IQ scores of the children in the upper streams improve whilst those in the lower streams deteriorate between the ages of eight and eleven, that period when the children are in the junior school streams, some of the basis for streaming would be removed. In fact, it could then be said that streaming acts as a self-fulfilling prophecy, bringing about what it predicts.

It is just this that seems to be shown by the recent work of J. W. B. Douglas (1964). He found that there was a big overlap between the IQ scores of the children in his sample who were in the upper and in the lower streams of junior schools. Yet at all levels of measured intelligence children in the upper streams gained points of IQ between the ages of eight and eleven, whilst children in the lower streams lost IQ points. To give examples, children in upper streams with IQs between 87·5 and 92·5 gained 8·6 points, whilst children of the same measured ability in lower streams lost 1·5 IQ points. For the IQ range 98·5 to 101·5 the upper stream gained 6·7 points against a loss of 2·4 points by the children in the lower streams. In the range from 107·5 to 110·5 the upper stream gained 3·4 points compared with a loss of 2·9 points by the children in the lower stream. It must be noted in addition that it is the less able children in the upper streams who at every level improve more than the abler children in the same streams, whilst in the lower streams the range of ability remains more or less the same throughout the time spent in the junior school.

There is great difficulty in interpreting statistics of this type. There are problems both of a theoretical nature inherent in the comparability through time of the measures used[1] and also of a more practical nature because, for instance, many of the unstreamed schools are in rural areas or are schools with poor records of past academic success. The Plowden Committee set up a large-scale project using two samples of fifty carefully matched schools to investigate the effects of streaming in the junior school. This study was cross-sectional rather than longitudinal in design, and hence comparison between the various age groups is dangerous. However, although there were some differences between streamed and unstreamed schools amongst the eight- and nine-year-old children in scores on a test of verbal ability, there were no such differences amongst the ten-year-olds, nor did the latter age group show any marked differences on a verbal/non-verbal test of ability. The children in streamed schools did score more highly on attainment tests relating to the subject of mechanical arithmetic, usually taught in a more traditional manner, whilst those in unstreamed schools did as well as their peers in the streamed classes on tests of reading attainment, often associated with more progressive methods of teaching. Furthermore, as has been found before by other workers in investigations of activity methods of teaching, there was some evidence to show that the children in the less structured unstreamed schools were catching up with the children in the streamed schools where more traditional methods were probably more often used. Even within each category of schools it seems that the attitudes of the teachers towards the method of teaching employed has some effect on attainments and on a measure of anxiety shown by the children.[2] It can therefore be seen that contradictory evidence about the effects of streaming exists and that more research is needed before a reasonably definite judgement can be passed, but certainly we should bear in mind that merely to change the structure of a school may not have the desired effect if the teachers concerned do not favour the structure within which they are working.

(ii) *Entry to Secondary School*. The methods used to allocate children to the different types of secondary school vary very much

[1] For some problems of interpreting Douglas' results see G. Horobin, D. Oldman and W. Bytheway, 'The Social Differentiation of Ability', *Sociology*, May 1967.

[2] *Children and their Primary Schools* (Plowden), Vol. 2, pp. 573–6 and 581.

from one local education authority to another. Most, however, still incorporate some form of a test of measured intelligence. It was found in Middlesbrough and southwest Hertfordshire (J. E. Floud and others, 1956) that more or less all the children of the same measured intelligence reached grammar school regardless of their social class, though when southwest Hertfordshire dropped the use of an IQ test, a bias in favour of the middle class appeared (J. E. Floud and A. H. Halsey, 1957). Allowing for regional differences in the rate of provision, social class chances of entry to the grammar school thoughout Britain today are probably not grossly unfair using measured intelligence as the criterion. Even to state this points to the fact that with secondary education organized on the tripartite system the country's use of capability varies according to the way that the number of grammar school places is adjusted to meet changes in local demographic conditions.

In addition, because of the influence of social class learning and the differences in parental attitudes towards education, chances of entering the grammar school still vary greatly for children of equal measured intelligence, but of different social class. Thus Douglas (1964) found that, whereas 40·1 per cent of upper middle-class children with an IQ of 106 or less were in grammar schools, only 7·9 per cent of lower working-class children of the same measured intelligence gained entry to these schools. What is more, once children reached the grammar school, their average IQ score seemed to change as compared with that of those children in the secondary modern school in much the same way as happened in the streams of the junior school. The average scores of those who went to a grammar school rose, and the average scores of those at the secondary modern school fell. The decline was most pronounced for children from the manual working class with the highest test scores; those in the range 112–115 IQ points lost about 6 IQ points by the age of fifteen (J. W. B. Douglas, 1968).

Some children are, therefore, placed in secondary modern schools whose achievement could be higher in the ethos of a different type of school. It may well be that it is not only the development of intelligence that is crucial in this selection process, but that different levels of aspiration are internalized in the different types of schools. Studies of the vocational aspirations of children in modern schools show them to be realistic and to accord well with the measured intelligence of the children concerned. In a survey in Ealing in 1951 it seemed that children tended to aim at the highest level normal for the social group to which they belonged.[1] Another investigation made in 1956 (T. Veness, 1962) found that boys and girls in secondary modern schools were less preoccupied with their future work than were children in other types of school. Such motivation or lack of it could partly govern the academic attainments of a child and thereby determine whether or not the child had the experience necessary to develop his intelligence fully. If the children of slightly above average or average intelligence are educated apart from other children of their intelligence, but together with children of below average intelligence, they may well come to hold the lower aspirations of those who form the majority of their school fellows. These 'more realistic' hopes may be inappropriate to the more able pupils in a secondary modern school or to children of a slightly higher level of ability in those areas where provision of grammar school places is low.

For some children who are placed in a secondary modern school at eleven there is a second chance for selection, either for transfer to grammar school or for entry to a secondary technical school, in both cases before the age of thirteen. These possibilities do allow for a recovery of some of the capability lost at eleven, and it should be said that the use of the best available selection methods at present may involve errors in the allocation of approximately 10 per cent of the candidates, or in the late '50s of about 60,000 children.[2] Moves to the grammar school are not common; Douglas (1968) found that only 2 per cent of his sample moved from secondary modern to grammar schools, most of whom were middle-class children, whilst another 2 per cent, mainly girls, moved to independent schools. Often the presence in the curriculum of such subjects as French or algebra make transfer impossible. Moves are possible to grammar school sixth forms for pupils who do well in 'O' level in secondary modern schools. The other possibility is a place at the secondary technical

[1] M. D. Wilson, 'The Vocational Preferences of Secondary Modern Schoolchildren', British Journal of Educational Psychology, June and November 1953.

[2] A. Yates and D. A. Pidgeon, Admission to Grammar School, London, 1957, p. 192.

school. Courses in these schools often begin at thirteen; in Douglas' sample 3 per cent moved from secondary modern schools to schools of this type. Many parents or children consider this to be a second chance for selection for an education which can lead to a job of relatively high status and perhaps a chance of upward social mobility. Since the recruitment to these schools has in the main become part of the selection mechanism rather than dependent upon the desire for a particular type of education,[1] it could be that the practical occupations served by these schools will be deprived of people of high measured intelligence, and this could affect the cultural and political unity of the country. It is perhaps unfortunate that the secondary technical school, which could be so well fitted to give an education suited to a technological age, should have come to be considered the school that gives the second chance to many after the intellectual cream has been skimmed off at eleven.

(iii) *Leaving at Fifteen*. At the present time the minimum legal leaving age is fifteen, though in 1972 this is to be raised to sixteen. The main weight of leaving at fifteen is from the secondary modern school, but there are some children who leave the grammar school at this age. Early leaving is once again a selective process. Fifteen per cent of children with an IQ of 113 or more in Douglas' (1964) sample had left full-time education by the time they were sixteen and, as might have been expected, almost four-fifths of these leavers were working-class children. At a higher level of measured intelligence more than 6 per cent of children with an IQ of 120 had left; it is from people of this level of intelligence that potential university students must be recruited.

Though few parents today think, as George Orwell put it in the 1930s, that 'the notion of staying at school till you are nearly grown-up seems merely contemptible and unmanly',[2] many children still leave as soon as they legally can because their parents press them to go to work. A common reason is the need to start earning, thereby relieving the economic pressure on the family. Other children leave because they see their friends going from school, and they go too, almost in sympathy and regardless of contrary advice from the school.

[1] P. J. Kemeny, 'Dualism in Secondary Technical Education', *British Journal of Sociology*, March 1970.

[2] G. Orwell, *The Road to Wigan Pier*, London, 1937 (Penguin ed.), p. 104.

These social forces are very strong, particularly in areas that lack social variety. Thus in 1951 in Dagenham, an area characterized by great housing estates and a preponderance of working-class families, the rate for children leaving school under fifteen, as was then possible, was the third highest out of 157 British towns, and the proportion of its population between fifteen and twenty-four in full-time education was the lowest, being 3·8 per cent. The reasons for leaving were partly economic, but in an interview the local head-master laid great stress on the pressures to conformity.[1] To stay at school when the majority of one's contemporaries have left or to have intellectual or cultural interests means that the adolescent boy or girl has to be different from his peers, and this demands unusual qualities. In this case social attitudes increase the wastage of capability.

(iv) *Entry to the Sixth Form.* Even amongst those who stay on beyond the legal minimum leaving age there are able children who leave grammar school at around sixteen, namely at the point of entry to the sixth form, the start of the course that is almost essential for any higher education beyond eighteen. There will always be some children who either on their own initiative or on the advice of their parents wish to leave school at this age to enter employment. A good example is the case of a boy taking up a technical, as opposed to a craft, apprenticeship. His 'O' level passes together with a practical training should make him into a good technician. As long as facilities are available for the further education of such able children this cannot be called a loss of capability or unfair selection. Whether there are adequate facilities for the further education of this type of leaver will be considered later.

It has been said (W. D. Furneaux, 1961) that even in the public schools there is some selection at entry to the sixth form. In these schools this is done 'by discouraging the further attendance of those who do not measure up to a rather "upper class" archetype of "a good type of boy" '. However, in the maintained grammar school such leaving was found in the 1950s to be connected with the econo-mic circumstances as well as the attitudes and lack of knowledge of parents (*Early Leaving*, 1954). It has occurred amongst working-class children in spite of the fact that the children have realized to the full the connection between success in the grammar school and their

[1] P. Willmott, *The Evolution of a Community*, London, 1963, pp. 115–17.

chances of upward social mobility (H. T. Himmelweit, 1954). There is a new, and as yet unmeasured, form of premature leaving at this point. Both boys and girls are leaving grammar schools and transferring to local technical colleges to do the equivalent of a sixth-form course. They do so because they consider themselves to be treated as old children in the sixth forms of grammar schools, whereas at the local technical college they are treated as the young adults they consider themselves to be. This transfer, brought about by the different atmospheres of the two institutions, does not constitute a loss of capability, but it may indicate an unnecessary duplication of courses and thereby use resources in an inefficient manner in that, for example, there may be two half-filled science courses with the same curriculum in the same area.

The proportion of children staying at school after sixteen having the same level of measured intelligence but coming from different social classes varies in the expected direction. In the sample investigated by the Robbins Committee it was found that amongst children with an IQ of 107·5 or more, 92 per cent of the children of the upper non-manual class, but only 60 per cent of children from the lower non-manual class was still at school by this age; for children with an IQ of 94 or less the percentages were 27 and 3 respectively. This difference in proportion leads to a social class differential in success at 'O' level. In fact this is greater than might be expected allowing for the social class distribution of IQ. The important level of success here is five 'O' levels, as this is the usual requirement for entry to the sixth form. In 1961 the proportions of children at maintained grammar schools who gained five or more 'O' levels were as follows: for the children of the professional and managerial class 72 per cent, clerical 60 per cent, skilled manual 55 per cent and semi-skilled or unskilled 37 per cent. Further, the proportion of candidates with five or more 'O' levels from professional and managerial homes, who were in the bottom third of the intake to grammar school at eleven, was higher than the proportion from working-class homes who were in the top third of the eleven-plus intake. In addition, the proportions with this level of success from all social classes have risen through the 1950s in such a way that it would seem as if there has been little narrowing in the social class differential.[1]

[1] *Higher Education* (Robbins), Appendix I, pp. 51–3.

It can, therefore, be seen that there are great differences in the social class chances of entry to the sixth form and that it is here as well as at eleven that unfairness and loss of capability occur due to the way the selection process works. The effect is that the proportion of working-class children who stay through the sixth form to the age of eighteen, at which 'A' level is normally taken, is lower than the proportion of middle-class children who actually achieve two or more passes at 'A' level. Yet it must be stressed that once in the sixth form there is no significant difference in the achievement at 'A' level of children from working-class homes, whether they come from the upper, middle or lower third of the ability range admitted to grammar school at eleven.[1] The selective effect of the handicaps that operate up to sixteen, including the difficulties caused by homework conditions and by attitudes within the family that are unhelpful to education, seem to cease to operate once the sixth form is reached (W. D. Furneaux, 1961). Apparently, if the child is unusual enough to overcome these hurdles before sixteen, he will have no difficulty in continuing to do so up to eighteen.

(v) *Entry to Higher Education.* The higher one passes up the educational system, the more complex becomes exact analysis of the selection process, since there are more alternatives open to the student. He may, for example, wish to go to university, a college of education, a polytechnic, or one of the various types of technical college. In addition, there are many eighteen-year-olds who want, and by any criterion ought, to leave the full-time educational system to enter their chosen vocation, whether this is in industry, commerce or the armed forces. There is a legal compulsion upon local authorities to supply education to all those who are within the ages when a child must be at school, but after sixteen the position becomes less clear and certainly in Britain the State has never undertaken to provide higher education to all who want it. As the provision of secondary education has grown in this century, so the proportion of first-generation grammar school parents has risen; they in their turn have swelled the demand for more education for their children. So in the 1950s the supply of places in universities never met the demand from qualified applicants. In fact in the late 1950s the chances of reaching university possibly moved

[1] *Higher Education* (Robbins), Appendix I, pp. 45-6.

against children with the necessary qualifications, so great was the demand.[1]

This increase in the competition for higher education led to multiple applications to universities and colleges of education or to combinations of the two. It also led to a rise in the supply of higher education by such institutions as technical colleges, for some of whom this title almost became inappropriate so great was the weight of their work of a non-technical nature. Clearly rigidities in the supply of places of various types in higher education have resulted in students modifying their vocations or their demands for a particular type of higher education. It seems that unsuccessful applicants to university have entered teacher training and further education. In the latter case they have been easily absorbed, but in teacher training, despite a great rise in provision, the standard of entry has had to rise to ration out the scarce places.[2]

Some indication of how the selection process has worked by this level is given by the following figures which relate to a sample of twenty-one-year-olds born in 1940-1. Of those with an IQ of 130 or more at eleven whose parents were in non-manual occupations, 41 per cent were in full-time higher education compared with 30 per cent of the children of parents in manual occupations. The gap in attendance became greater with lower measured intelligence; for the IQ range 115-129 the percentages were 34 and 15, and for the range 100-114 they were 17 and 6 respectively.[3] Yet, as in the case of the sixth form, once at the university students seem to achieve equally well regardless of social class.[4]

(vi) 'The Second Way'. This is the name given in Germany to the route by which intelligent adults or adolescents can achieve higher education despite their lack of the equivalent of a grammar school education. Is this concept relevant to Britain? Mention has been

---

[1] A. Little and J. Westergaard, 'The Trend of Class Differentials in Educational Opportunity in England and Wales', *British Journal of Sociology*, December 1964, pp. 310-11.

[2] *Higher Education* (Robbins), Appendix I, pp. 125-6.

[3] Ibid., p. 42.

[4] See J. G. H. Newfield, 'The Academic Performance of British University Students', p. 120, and R. R. Dale, 'Reflections on the Influence of Social Class on Student Performance at the University', both in *The Sociological Review: Monograph No. 7*, Keele, 1963.

made twice above of the need for adequate facilities for the further education of those who leave school early to go into industry or commerce. It has been traditional in Britain for children who either failed to achieve their full capability through the usual educational channels, or for those who were not even granted this opportunity, to use the facilities provided by further education as their second way. There are very adequate facilities of this nature in Britain, and they have proved very flexible in the face of the varied needs put on them by the country's rising demand for education of all types. Their flexibility has partly offset the rigidity of other institutions. It does seem that the participation of persons from the working class in both full- and part-time work at all levels of the system of technical education has been growing slowly since 1945.[1] But it must be stressed that this second way is a long, arduous and even inefficient route.

The evidence collected by the Crowther Committee showed that of all the students who start the course for a National Certificate without prior exemption, which is usually gained by passing 'O' or 'A' level examinations beforehand, only 26 per cent eventually gain an Ordinary National Certificate and only 10 per cent a Higher National Certificate. The former examination is at technician, and the latter at technologist level. For those who are exempt from the first year of the course the proportions of successes rise to 51 per cent and 26 per cent at the respective levels. At the lower level of the craftsman, the City and Guilds five-year courses are relevant. Here, in a sample of five courses in the field of engineering, 28 per cent passed the examination that marks the end of the third year and a mere 6 per cent that at the end of the fifth year. However, many of the students in both sets of examinations took longer than the minimum periods to succeed. Many of those whose attendance was unsuccessful, if judged by the criterion of passing the examination, must have learnt much of a useful and educative nature. Yet these failure rates are very high. The main reasons for failure were found to be weakness in mathematics and having to rely on evening classes only, a very

---

[1] I. Hordley and D. J. Lee, 'The "Alternative Route" – Social Change and Opportunity in Technical Education', *Sociology*, January 1970, espec. pp. 35–42; S. Cotgrove, *Technical Education and Social Change*, London, 1958.

real strain on an adolescent. In fact, the two reasons are to an extent interconnected. Students who leave school at fifteen cannot achieve a high standard of mathematics, a subject which demands more time, regular practice and individual tuition than can be given to it in the compressed type of course necessarily prevalent in part-time education. The selective effect of these courses can be seen from figures relating to students on National Certificate courses in 1956 and 1958. Not only did many fail, but the farther along this route students went, the more difficult it became for students from the lower social classes to succeed. Thus between the first and fifth year of the course for the Higher National Certificate the proportion of students with fathers in administrative and professional occupations doubled, rising from 10·6 per cent to 20·3 per cent, whilst that for students whose fathers were in skilled work dropped from 31·5 per cent to 25·4 per cent, and for those with fathers in semi-skilled work from 18 per cent to 13 per cent.[1]

(vii) *Summary*. It would seem to be inevitable that at some point in any educational system where places are in short supply in institutions of higher education, selection must take place in order that the training may begin of those who are to fill the positions of responsibility in a society that needs a high level of education in its potential leaders. However, it is apparent that in Britain the organization of the educational system is such that selection begins in the primary school and goes on up to the point of entry to the sixth form. The initial selection in the primary school into streams may well hinder the full development of capability. The next selection at eleven, whether made by placing children in different types of secondary school or in different streams within one comprehensive secondary school, divides children into successes and failures, many of whom, regardless of their measured intelligence, come to think of themselves and their future in the light of this allocation. This results in a greater loss of capability than might be expected because there is an overlap in IQ scores between children in the different types of secondary school or in the different streams of the comprehensive school. In the tripartite system this overlap is due to the very different rates of provision of grammar school places throughout the country, which can also be regarded as due to institutional rigidity. The existence of a

[1] *15 to 18* (Crowther), Vol. I, Chs. 30 and 31.

second way does not seem to recover much of the capability already lost. This selection process, albeit unintentionally, works against certain social classes so that there is a social class bias in the proportion of those undergoing education beyond sixteen. This is a dysfunction which is largely inherent in the present organization of the educational system, and it must cause a considerable loss of capability.

3. *Conclusion*

Before concluding this chapter there is one possibility that must be considered, though for Britain it is as yet a hypothetical one. It is possible that the increase in educational opportunity may be so great that aspirations for upward social mobility are generated in excess of the number of high positions that are available to the population of the country. In this case it is no longer a case of selecting the most able out of all those qualified to go on to higher education. All will go anyway. Nor is it so necessary to develop the potential capability of the country; this is being done. The function of selection is replaced by that of 'cooling out'[1] those with excessive aspirations for mobility. There is one area in the world where this has become the problem, namely the state of California in the USA. Here more than half the population continues in education beyond the age of eighteen. A large proportion of these students go to junior colleges. An important part is played in these colleges by the counselling department. As soon as is possible, those students are discovered who have reached their highest academic attainment level and who are not capable of going on to take a university course. These students are counselled towards courses that end at junior college. This is done in such a way that the minimum possible psychological disturbance is caused.

This is a problem that is only marginal to Britain, since the main form in which it is met is amongst some of those wrongly selected for grammar school. Such children have been placed in an ethos that leads them to hold aspirations that are higher than their capabilities will bear. Of this problem little is known, though a somewhat

---

[1] R. Clark, 'The "Cooling-out" Function in Higher Education', *American Journal of Sociology*, May 1960 (also in A. H. Halsey, J. E. Floud and C. A. Anderson (eds.), *Education, Economy and Society*, New York, 1961).

similar and possibly more important dysfunction of the grammar school has been discerned (F. Musgrove, 1963). The educational system selects with some efficiency the type of child who can succeed in the grammar school. This school has become the recognized avenue of upward social mobility, particularly in that it leads to the higher levels of the labour force. Yet there is some evidence that the type of child that can succeed in the grammar school may not necessarily be the type with the psychological qualities that are needed for undertaking a career in the jobs to which the grammar school now leads. It is almost as if the educational system is now organized to select the children who will succeed in tasks that the grammar school has evolved autonomously, but which have no necessary connection with the future of its pupils. A similar comment might be made on many courses given in the Arts Faculties of universities.

This problem is typical on the many possible conflicts between education in its individual and social contexts. We have been examining the function of selection and to do this is to view education in its social context. It is clear that the position in Britain is complicated by the private system. However, a consideration of the way the educational system undertakes selection shows firstly that, looked at in various ways, there is a pool of capability which is not at the moment fully used. Secondly, given the present structure of education, which is still much influenced by the tripartite system, we may ask, are the most capable children selected? It seems that the often rigid form of organization makes it difficult to meet demographic change and hence brings about a loss of capability. Within the system children of lower social class still appear to be at a disadvantage, though this is not so gross as formerly. But one can ask a deeper question. Once the children are segregated, even assuming absolutely 'fair' initial selection, is such segregation in itself dysfunctional? The answer, based on studies of the results of streaming, seems to be that this could be so. The cumulative nature of both processes may be summed up in one set of statistics: when the sample of children born in 1940-1 investigated by the Robbins Committee had reached the age of twenty-one, those who were children of fathers in non-manual occupations had greater chances of academic achievement than those who were children of fathers in manual occupations at each IQ level and at each stage of the educational system. The one exception was for the most able at the end of their course in the fifth form. The ratios were as follows:

Social class chances of academic achievement by I.Q. at eleven

IQ	Degree Level Courses	At least Two 'A' levels	At least Five 'O' levels
130 and over	2·06	1·43	0·97
115–129	2·12	1·64	1·24
100–114	3·00	1·50	1·68

Source: Higher Education (Robbins), Appendix I, p. 43.

Segregation at primary and secondary levels hinders development of capability and leads to low aspirations. The selection process fulfils the prophecy upon which the system is founded, but equally surely it lessens the capability available to this country.

BIBLIOGRAPHY

(i) *The Pool of Capability*

A. H. Halsey (ed.), *Ability and Educational Opportunity*, OEEC, 1961 (espec. Chs. 2, 5 and 6).

P. E. Vernon, 'The Pool of Ability', *Sociological Studies in British University Education, Sociological Review: Monograph No. 7*, Keele, 1963.

15 to 18 (Crowther), Vol. II, London (HMSO), 1960.

Higher Education (Robbins), Appendix I, London (HMSO), 1963 (espec. Part Three).

(ii) *Selection*

J. W. B. Douglas, *The Home and the School*, London, 1964.

J. W. B. Douglas, *All Our Future*, London, 1968.

J. E. Floud, A. H. Halsey and F. M. Martin, *Social Class and Educational Opportunity*, London, 1956.

J. E. Floud and A. H. Halsey, 'Intelligence Tests, Social Class and Selection for Secondary Schools', *British Journal of Sociology*, March 1957 (in A. H. Halsey, J. E. Floud and C. A. Anderson (eds.), *Education, Economy and Society*, New York, 1961).

W. D. Furneaux, *The Chosen Few*, London, 1961.

H. T. Himmelweit, 'Social Status and Secondary Education since the 1944 Act', in D. V. Glass (ed.), *Social Mobility in Britain*, London, 1954.

F. Musgrove, *The Migratory Elite*, London, 1963.

T. Veness, *School Leavers*, London, 1962.

Early Leaving, London (HMSO), 1954.

15 to 18 (Crowther), Vol. I, London (HMSO), 1959 (espec. Part Six).

17

The Economic Function

By this stage the importance of the connection between education and the economy has been made clear. We must now examine in some detail the ways in which the educational system helps to maintain the economy. In order to do this we must first examine some aspects of the contemporary British economic system (P. W. Musgrave, 1969).

A. The Economy

The British economy is seen by most people as capitalist in nature and in one crucial respect, the private ownership of most economic property, this is a correct view. Yet a large sector of the economy is nationalized and much central planning now takes place, so that the contemporary version of capitalism is very different from the *laissez-faire* system of the nineteenth century. Here four factors, central to the economy today, will be described, namely the distribution of the labour force, the size and ownership of units of production, the achievement of full employment and, finally, the direction of change in the economy.

1. *The Labour Force*
In 1776 Adam Smith wrote what is often regarded as the first modern book on economic theory, *The Wealth of Nations*. He began this work with a chapter on what he called the *division of labour* and he chose the manufacture of pins as one example of this process. One man carrying out the whole process 'could scarcely, perhaps, with his utmost industry, make one pin in a day, and certainly could not make twenty'. But he noted that the job was now divided up into a number of branches, each of which was done by a specialist. In

one factory that Adam Smith had visited ten persons in this way 'could make among them upwards of forty-eight thousand pins in a day', or 4,800 each as against 20 made by the one relatively unspecialized man. Thus the division of the job amongst many labourers who each specialized in a small part of it brought a great rise in productivity.

This is the principle upon which most industry is now organized. Craftsmen do not operate in this way, but a modern economy is characterized by mass production rather than by craft industry. There are, therefore, today a very large number of semi-skilled occupations in our labour force. It is possible to enumerate these occupations under main headings that are usually chosen on an industrial rather than an occupational basis. This gives an indication of how the labour force is employed in any country and provides a rough picture of the occupational structure.

In the UK in 1966 out of a population of 54·5 millions there were 26·2 millions in the labour force, of whom just under 9 millions were women. The broad outline of the occupational structure as it relates to civil employment was as below (figures in '000s):

Primary		Secondary		Tertiary	
Agriculture ⎫ Fishing ⎬	488	Manufacturing industry	9,179	Transport communication	1,651
Mining	635	Construction	1,769	Distributive trades	3,067
		Gas, electricity water	434	Professional, commercial, services	5,514
				National and local government	1,399
1,123		11,382		11,631	
(4·7%)		(47·1%)		(48·2%)	

Source: *Annual Abstract of Statistics*, 1967, pp. 113–16.

On the basis of these figures a broad comparison can be made with an underdeveloped country and this will indicate a way of analysing the occupational structure. The labour force of an underdeveloped country will contain a far larger proportion than in the UK in the economic sector that develops first, namely the agricultural group of occupations. This category has been called the *primary* sector. As a country begins the process of economic development, it will shift part of its labour force out of the primary sector into the manufacturing or the *secondary* sector. At this stage only a small proportion of its workers will be employed in the service industries, such as banking, insurance or distribution. As a country moves towards economic maturity the proportion employed in this final or tertiary sector grows. It can be seen that in the UK the tertiary employment by any count is large. Some idea of the changes that have occurred in Britain over the last century can be judged by comparing the rough figures for 1881 with those given above. The proportions then were approximately 13, 50 and 37 per cent in the primary, secondary and tertiary sectors respectively. Comparison with the percentages in the table clearly show the trend towards a smaller primary and a larger tertiary sector in the British labour force.

2. *The Size and Ownership of Units of Production*
The impression given by classical economic analysis is that the size of economic unit, whether for production or distribution of

Size and number of manufacturing establishments in Great Britain, 1961

Number of Employees	Number of Establishments	%	% of Total Employees
11–99	40,049	72·6	20·5
100–499	12,213	22·1	32·2
500–999	1,693	3·1	13·7
1,000 and over	1,206	2·2	33·6
	55,161	100·0	100·0

Source: *Annual Abstract of Statistics*, 1967, p. 122.

goods, is small. An individual who wanted to set up a new business enterprise could make a start easily since the amount of capital required would be relatively small. An examination of the size of industrial units in the above table will show the contemporary trend. The usual criterion for measuring size of units is the number of employees, though this is not equally applicable to all types of economic activity.

Clearly most people work in establishments with more than 100 employees, but the majority of manufacturing units employ fewer than 100 workers. Yet even in 1961 a large but unknown number of factories employed fewer than eleven employees. The total of these small units was believed to be around 140,000. These are the small units of the modern economic system. They still exist, but there is a definite tendency for the amount of capital needed to enter most industries today to be so high that the private individual cannot start a manufacturing business on his own out of his personal resources. This must modify the traditional analysis of capitalism and poses the question of who today owns and controls these large enterprises.

In a major study of ownership of British companies, Sargent Florence investigated a representative sample of 1,700 joint stock companies of varying size. He found that in 1951 the average share-holding was about £500. In the fifty-three largest companies there were approximately 10,000 shareholders, but in many cases there was a concentration of ownership which enabled small groups to control the policies of some companies. This situation, however, seems to be growing less common, since Sargent Florence found that the average proportion of the total shares carrying votes held by the largest 20 per cent of the shareholders declined from 30 per cent in 1936 to 19 per cent in 1951. Furthermore, since there is an increasing flow of savings into pensions schemes a larger proportion of shares is now held by such large institutional investors as insurance companies. Thus, Sargent Florence concludes that 'two-thirds of the large companies in 1951 were probably not owner controlled'.[1] One may then ask, who are the directors of the large companies who control the economic behaviour of a large part of the labour force? One survey made in 1951 of 1,173 directors of large public companies showed that between 50 and 60 per cent started their careers with the advantage of a business connection in the family. Nineteen per cent were directors of firms of which their fathers were directors before them, though only 8 per cent were leaders of firms that had been in the same family for more than three generations.[2] Even allowing for this 50 or 60 per cent, many of whom may not have had a large

[1] P. Sargent Florence, *Ownership, Control and Success of Large Companies*, London, 1961.

[2] G. H. Copeman, *Leaders of British Industry*, London, 1954, pp. 95–6 and 98.

financial stake in the companies that they were controlling, there still remains a large number of directors who can be regarded as professional managers. Particularly at a slightly lower level there are many managers who have made their careers in such companies, who have much power and a relatively high income, but own no shares in the companies for which they work.

3. The Achievement of Full Employment

Since the beginning of industrial capitalism in Britain in the mid-eighteenth century there has been an alternation of active and depressed business conditions that economists have named the *trade cycle*. The whole cycle of boom and slump varied in length but averaged seven to eight years. The proportion of the working population still unemployed at the top and bottom of the cycle also varied. Conditions were very bad in the inter-war years when the rate of unemployment averaged 12 per cent of the insured labour force, rising to 23 per cent in 1932 and never falling much below 10 per cent even in the best year of the late 1920s. The incidence varied and the old staple industries, particularly shipbuilding, suffered most. Since these industries tended to be concentrated in particular regions, some areas such as Clydeside, the Northwest and Northeast, were more hard hit than areas such as the Southeast, where the newer type of industry was already growing important.

During the inter-war years economists gave much thought to the causes of the trade cycle. They noted that its course was disturbed by wars, and that it never occurred in wholly planned economies. In 1936 J. M. (later Lord) Keynes, the Cambridge economist, published his book, *The General Theory of Employment, Interest and Money*, which provided the key to the understanding of the trade cycle. Out of Keynes' work came the idea of a full employment policy. If there are unemployed resources in an economy at any time, this is due to a lack of demand backed by the money to buy goods. The Government can create the deficient demand in two ways. It may make conditions favourable so that business men will undertake more activity, thereby employing unused resources including labour. Secondly, the Government itself can expand its own activities by, for example, undertaking public investment. Both policies will create wages which will be spent so that the demand for other goods and services is increased. This in turn will help to bring still unused resources back into work so that unemployment is reduced.

In 1944 the three political parties forming the war-time Coalition Government issued a White Paper on Full Employment Policy in which they all pledged themselves to use Keynesian-type policies to maintain full employment in Britain after the war. Since 1945 there has never been, until recently, more than just over 3 per cent or less than just under 1 per cent unemployment, though regional variations still exist; the North, Scotland and Northern Ireland have continuously had higher rates than London, the Southeast and the Midlands. However, the unemployment figures have risen dramatically to over 4 per cent in 1972.

Full employment was defined in 1944 by Lord Beveridge in his book, *Full Employment in a Free Society*, as '3 per cent unemployment'. There will always be some workers in the process of moving from one job to another in a modern economy. When cyclical unemployment was reduced to a mere trace of its pre-war severity, the object of policy was to lessen the impact on the individual worker of such 'technological' unemployment as is inevitable when changes in industrial techniques cause redundancy. With the aid of unemployment benefit and retraining facilities the period out of work accompanied by a lower income can be shortened, so that the individual worker suffers the minimum of the indignity of unemployment. Keynes pointed to a fundamental fault in the working of the capitalist system that prevented it from running smoothly. The logic of his theories indicated some Government intervention to ensure full employment. In Britain the benefits of a so-called 'free economy' were considered great enough to keep intervention to a minimum, and the rate of unemployment that could be tolerated politically seemed to have settled at Beveridge's figure of 3 per cent, though the tolerable rate in the USA is double and in Australia less than half the British rate.

4. The Direction of Economic Change
(i) *Specialization*. The Classification of Occupations that was used for the 1961 Census of Britain showed approximately 35,500 different occupations. The sub-division of labour is now very great. One Midlands manufacturer of men's clothing has broken down the

making of a waistcoat into sixty-five separate units of work. The farther this process goes, the more specialized, but the less skilled, does the work become. The production line becomes the standard method of large-scale manufacture; a line of highly specialized workers is stationed before a slowly moving conveyer-belt along which the product passes, gradually assuming recognizable shape as each worker adds the piece for which he or she is responsible. Little knowledge of the materials used is necessary. Speed, precision and dexterity are the qualities demanded.

From this it may be imagined that the ratio between the skilled part of the labour force and the unskilled is falling. However, there are two forces at work in the opposite direction. Firstly, there is the great growth in the tertiary sector of the labour force. Many of those employed in these occupations are in work of an administrative or clerical nature. This is true within manufacturing industry itself. Large production lines working on a mass-production basis require careful control and present complex problems of management. Nothing must be allowed to stop production, since idle machinery makes no profit.

There is a second force working to preserve the ratio of skill. Production lines are complicated trains of machinery. Some very skilled men are necessary to maintain the machines essential to modern industry. Thus the percentage of maintenance men is rising. Many of these men are craftsmen who not only need the skills to repair complex machines, but also must be able to diagnose just what has caused the breakdown. In a typical steel company the number of craftsmen as a percentage of the total labour force rose from 7 to 11 per cent between 1925 and 1953.[1] An exact balance of the forces operating on the need for skilled workers is difficult to assess, and it must be left until we have considered the move towards automation.

(ii) *The Changing Nature of Industry*. In addition to the economic tendencies so far mentioned there are three changes which affect the very nature of British industry. Firstly, the industries based on science are growing more predominant. This encourages a second but logically separate trend, the move towards a greater use of research and science throughout industry. Lastly, connected with this

[1] *Men, Steel and Technical Change*, Department of Scientific & Industrial Research (DSIR), London, 1957, p. 8.

but again partly autonomous, is the application of new techniques to industry, exemplified particularly by automation (J. H. Dunning and C. J. Thomas, 1966).

(a) *Science-based Industries*. The old staple industries upon which Britain's prosperity in the nineteenth century was founded were not renowned for the application of science to their processes. It may have been that at that time their nature and the state of scientific knowledge was such that it was not possible to apply science to the textile, coal and heavy engineering industries, though this is doubtful. But by the mid-twentieth century other industries are basic to our survival as an industrial power with a high standard of life. The chemical industry has become important both in itself and as a supplier of raw materials to other industries; many of the industries using and producing the new synthetics, such as plastics, clothing fibres and detergents, are based on raw materials provided by the chemical industry. The survival of old as well as the welfare of new industries has come to depend on an industry of a highly scientific nature. In 1963 this industry employed 6 per cent of those working in manufacturing industry.

The character of the engineering industry has also changed greatly. Within this heterogeneous statistical category there has been a switch to lighter products and, more particularly, the electrical engineering industry has become important. In 1953 the engineering, shipbuilding and electrical goods industries together employed 30·0 per cent of the workers in manufacturing industry; by 1963 the proportion had grown to 33·6 per cent. But during the same ten years the proportion of workers employed in electrical engineering rose from 23·9 per cent to 28·6 per cent of the whole engineering group. Since 1900 two new industries have arisen, namely the aircraft and vehicle industries (vehicles 8·6 per cent and aircraft 3·1 per cent of all workers in manufacturing industry in 1963), both of which rely heavily on science and high standards of precision.[1]

(b) *Research and Science*. In 1867 Marx pointed out in *Das Kapital* that capitalism, unlike earlier systems of production, does not regard existing technical methods as definitive. Competition forces the search for new products and methods. This process has been accelerated by the coming of full employment. Change is more

[1] Figures for 1953 and 1963 from *Manpower Studies No. 1, 1964*.

worthwhile in surer markets where sales seem more likely. At the high British standard of life many consumers have to be persuaded by advertising that they need a new product or that it is essentially different from what it replaces and so must be bought. Rapid obsolescence and replacement by the new but slightly different article become integral processes in a fully employed advanced economy. Change is now built into our economic system.

Behind this search for new and 'better' products is the science-based activity of research. The decision to commit manpower and resources to research is an economic one largely dependent upon the search for profits, though whether industry's attitude towards science is favourable or not will also be seen later to be important. Recently there has been a rise in expenditure on research and development; from 1955-6 to 1961-2 the proportion of the gross national product spent in this way rose from 1·7 per cent to 2·7 per cent. Though only about a third (33·6 per cent) of the funds were supplied by private industry as opposed to the Government, almost three-fifths (58·0 per cent) of the actual work was carried out by private industry. The amount spent varied considerably from industry to industry, but those referred to above as the science-based industries were the ones with the highest expenditure per employee.[1]

(c) *Methods*. The stress on science in industry has extended beyond an increasing application of the results of pure scientific research to industry. There has been a growing application of scientific methods of management. This had begun early in the century in the USA when F. W. Taylor had introduced what came to be known as the Scientific Management Movement. The aim was a realistic assessment of economic efficiency at every level of industry. Initially the application of Taylor's ideas were often inhumane. Since 1945 much of British industry has begun to use more scientific but humane techniques of management. The rational layout of the management structure, particularly in large companies, is now given more attention. It is more common to find emphasis put on accurate methods of cost accountancy and on the application of systems of wage rates to individual jobs, so that the worker is given maximum incentive. These new techniques of management require complex calculations, as do the increasingly difficult problems posed by stock

[1] *Treasury Bulletin for Industry*, February 1963.

control in large organizations, and the use of computers may, and often has, become necessary.

(d) *Automation*. Almost a symbol of these changes is automation, the product of a new and scientific industry that implies up-to-date management techniques. The term *automation* is usually applied to an industrial plant that has a very high ratio of capital equipment to labour employed and is in addition characterized by transfer mechanisms. Firstly, the plant is a chain of machines that were formerly separate, but are now linked by transfer mechanisms that pass the semi-finished product from one process to the next without the use of any manpower. Secondly, throughout the train of machines there is a succession of feed-back mechanisms that automatically send information to other stages of the process, if the product is not meeting the specification. Automation, it can be appreciated, may lessen the manpower needed, certainly reduces the decision taking and skill of the traditional type required by the operative, and probably improves the quality of the product.

B. The Educational System and the Economy

We must now examine in some detail the way in which the educational system helps to maintain the economy. Very briefly the economic function of the educational system is to provide the labour force with manpower that matches the needs of the economy and to give future consumers the knowledge that they will require. We shall proceed by examining first the qualitative and then the quantitative aspects of this problem. Quantity and quality are not independent of each other, since the quality, or level of skill, of the bulk of the labour force will be one of the determinants of the quantity of supervisory staff, for instance, of the number of foremen, that are necessary. Thus in the British, German and American iron and steel industries the same processes, involving very similar machinery and operating with fairly comparable productivity, are run by labour forces with very different proportions of training and skill. To generalize, in the USA the emphasis is put upon qualifications amongst supervisory staff, in Germany amongst managers, whilst in Britain the labour force itself is highly skilled.[1] However, for

[1] P. W. Musgrave, 'The Educational Profile of Two British Iron and Steel

T S E—L

simplicity of analysis we shall consider the qualitative and quantitative aspects separately here.

1. Qualitative Considerations

In an advanced industrial society such as Britain we tend to take for granted the fact that we have an efficient labour force. We forget that in the eighteenth and nineteenth centuries men and women had to be recruited to industry and we overlook that in many countries this process had to be achieved by force. Once in industrial employment workers must be committed to this way of life and perhaps to one occupation or even one employer for a period of time. The 'here today, gone tomorrow' attitude found among workers in some underdeveloped countries is a considerable handicap to efficiency in industry. Workers at all levels of the labour force must have the skills, attitudes and knowledge appropriate to contemporary techniques, and they must be willing to use these attributes to the utmost if the economy is to prosper. This willingness can come only from a strong desire to work hard and to produce. Such a desire is fostered by the conscious or unconscious attachment to a set of commonly held assumptions. The labour force of an industrial country must be both skilled and 'committed' (C. J. Kerr and others, 1962).

(i) *Knowledge and Skills.* In the first place, then, the educational system must play its part in laying the foundations upon which industrial skills can be built. The sheer factual knowledge needed to do most of the highly specialized jobs that many workers do today is very small. If the worker can read instructions, carry out easy calculations so that he will produce only the required number of articles and fill in a simple report form or work ticket, this will be sufficient. The '3 Rs' at a relatively low level are enough. To master such jobs may take only a day or two, and after this brief training period is over little thought is required to do one's daily work. In pre-industrial days the life of a peasant or craftsman, though far from idyllic, was in some measures an education in itself. Life today is not built round work as was then the case. Nor do jobs today allow the exercise of the faculties of judgement and initiative that most humans need for psychological health. Work no longer provides either satisfaction or the feeling of being someone that matters. The worker must look elsewhere, perhaps to his family or friends, for the fulfilment of these needs.

In the field of technical education the industrial skills themselves will sometimes be taught. An example is typewriting. Can we go so far as to say that the connections between the economy and the educational system must be so arranged that what is taught at school matches what industry requires? Many would argue that education should be directed to an end such as 'the good life' and not harnessed to the needs of industry. However, once the ultimate end is given, it is true to say that the educational system can be organized so that it gives more or less attention to the requirements of the economy.

There is no conflict between the present needs of the economy and the broader aims of education over much of the curriculum. Both demand the thorough teaching of the elementary techniques of the '3 Rs' together with some knowledge of the social subjects such as history and geography. When work may be trivial and leisure long, the place of the aesthetic subjects is important in answering the need for men to live a richer life (G. H. Bantock, 1963). Without any attempt at cynicism it may be observed that, if such an education forms the basis for future happiness, then contented men will make better workmen.

There are some recent developments in education that are helpful to the economy. Such are the tendency to stay longer at school, the development of technical education and the rising proportion of adolescents granted day release. New institutions have grown up outside the educational system. In many large firms youths are taught by instructors who are experienced craftsmen and who have often also had training in the imparting of technical skills. A new type of school has been born with its own hierarchy of headteacher (the education officer) and assistant teachers (craft instructors). There are similar developments at managerial level, usually at the level of the industry rather than of the company (industrial public schools?). Since the passing of the Industrial Training Act, 1964, such practices have slowly spread to a large sector of British industry. This Act has helped to systematize the place of industrial education within the national structure of education.

Changes within school subjects themselves can be of importance. An obvious example is the revolution in the teaching of mathematics in both primary and secondary schools. Any improvement in mathematical competency has a direct relevance for future members of a modern labour force. Here we shall consider in rather more detail two instances of the way the present teaching of school subjects can have indirect economic consequences. The first will be functional for the economy and the second is dysfunctional.

We can isolate a part of the curriculum which we can call education for consumption. This attempts to teach children to discriminate between the many choices open to them. Discrimination in consumption ensures that the economy uses resources efficiently. The schools have come to play an important part in fulfilling the need for education for consumption. A seminal work was published as long ago as 1933, *Culture and Environment* by F. R. Leavis and D. Thompson. The authors aimed to apply the methods developed in the practical criticism of English literature to a criticism of the whole environment surrounding the individual.[1] The influence of this book has been great, and today secondary schools run courses that aim to teach children to examine advertisements for the use of emotive language and question-begging statements. Leavis and Thompson wrote mainly for sixth forms, but teachers are giving lessons with the same aim to fifteen-year-olds in secondary modern schools. Syllabuses for the CSE in Commerce are often relevant, containing, for example, a section on 'Buying Wisely' – which includes 'The Comparison of Price, Quality and Value', 'The Use of Advertisement' – and on 'Protection of the Consumer'. This is an example of teaching that is often pursued with a frankly moral aim, but which has economic consequences. In as much as children become more discriminating consumers, the schools are contributing to the efficient running of a *laissez-faire* economy.

A survey by the Oxford University Department of Education (1963) indicates that the attitudes conveyed unconsciously through the present teaching of science may have effects for the economy of the opposite nature. Firstly, the academic attainments and vocational aspirations of 1,459 sixth-form boys were investigated. Secondly,

[1] For some more recent comments on education in this context see R. Williams, *Communications*, London, 1962 (Penguin), pp. 100-11.

1,434 sixth-form boys in seventy-six grammar and public schools completed questionnaires; the aim was to find out what opinions the boys held about scientific and technological occupations. From these two sets of data it was hoped to find out what effect school science teaching has on a boy's choice of his future occupation. It was found that a far greater proportion of boys whom their headmasters considered capable of gaining first-class honours degrees chose careers in pure science as opposed to careers in technology. Comparison was then made with certain European countries. In Sweden the most able boys appeared to take courses in applied rather than in pure science; in Holland proportions were more equal; in Western Germany, though more able boys went to pure science courses, the proportion was in no way as great as in Britain. It seems that science teachers who are products of pure science departments in universities perpetuate in their own pupils the attitudes they had learnt as undergraduates. This can be seen from the second part of the investigation in which the boys were asked to rank in order of prestige nineteen professions, including technological occupations such as civil engineer and metallurgist. Doctors and nuclear physicists were given the highest prestige. No engineers or technologists appeared in the six most chosen occupations. When asked about the kind of scientific career that they wished to pursue the largest proportion gave research as their first choice (35 per cent). To the British sixth-former the image of the white-coated physicist doing research in his laboratory is a force that powerfully affects his occupational choice and the attitudes that govern his approach to his job. Comparisons were made with France and Germany where the results were by no means as pronounced as in Britain. The German 'sixth-former' gave much prestige to a technological career. The British schools would seem to be imparting an attitude that is dysfunctional to the economy, since too few able boys are choosing technological employment.

The economic function of the educational system is not restricted to teaching skills and to matters of the curriculum, though these are perhaps easiest to understand and, providing the means of communication between education and the economy are good, problems in this field should be easily solved. Of far more importance are the attitudes that the schools often transmit unconsciously, and to which attention must now be given.

(ii) *Attitudes*. The need for men and women at all levels of the labour force who have some knowledge and training in science must by now be very clear. The nature of the most rapidly expanding industries and their dependence on research, particularly under conditions of full employment, has been described. The labour force must therefore not only have scientific knowledge but must exhibit attitudes that are favourable towards science, change and education (P. W. Musgrave, 1967).

(a) *Science*. The conversion of British schools and universities to the teaching of science in the nineteenth century was a slow and difficult process (E. Ashby, 1958) and largely as a result a negative approach to science has much hindered many British industries.[1] The modern economy, as has been seen, is based on science, and development depends upon research in the field of pure science to lay bare the theoretical principles relevant to its working. This research is usually undertaken in a university, namely in an institution that is within the educational, and not the economic, system. Upon the principles that are discovered can be built a technology round which will grow the whole structure of technical education backed by curricula, textbooks and examinations. Therefore the work of pure scientists is the source upon which applied science is built, but a fair proportion of intellectually bright young men and women ready and able to use the results of contemporary research must go into industry. The important point is that of balance. If we examine the way that the UK and the USA employed their stock of qualified scientists in 1956, we find the percentages were as follows: in industry USA 60, UK 38: in Government USA 20, UK 12; in education USA 20, UK 50. Allowing for the difficulties of international statistical comparisons we may say that Britain employed twice as many of her pure scientists in schools, colleges and universities as the USA, whilst the USA employed half as many more of her scientists in industry as the UK did.[2] The determinants of these comparative differences must to some extent be rooted in the attitudes to pure and applied science passed on in the schools, to which reference has just been made.

[1] C. F. Carter and B. R. Williams, *Science in Industry*, London, 1959.
[2] G. L. Payne, *Britain's Scientific and Technological Manpower*, London, 1960.

The world of science in Britain is very inbred and attitudes are easily passed from one generation to the next. However, few of the scientists are in the community outside education to spread a knowledge and understanding of modern science throughout industry and commerce, and those within education may well, albeit unconsciously, be transmitting unhelpful attitudes. Those who were not science specialists at school must not lack the knowledge that they need as producers and consumers. In addition all must have attitudes favourable to the application of science to industry and commerce.

(b) *Change*. Innovation in any field, whether artistic or scientific, depends on existing knowledge. The wider this is spread, the more easily can additions to knowledge be made and the easier will be applications of new knowledge. The scientific knowledge necessary for the invention of the Bessemer Converter, which ushered in the age of cheap steel in 1856, was known at the start of the nineteenth century, but it was not known widely or in the right places, so that application was not easy. When the invention was eventually made, there was enough understanding for the new process to be taken up by the industry quite quickly, though lack of scientific knowledge was one reason that prevented the new product from being accepted in some quarters as rapidly as should have been the case. For both consumption and production a high level of literacy and numeracy is even more essential in the mid-twentieth century, when change is apparently more rapid than was the case a century ago.

Since the educational requirements of most occupations are constantly altering, there is difficulty in specifying the academic content of a curriculum to meet change. The most serviceable education would appear to be a general one out of which specialization can grow. The deeper the specialization the further the general education must be carried. The specialist requirements of a metallurgist need a longer general education, especially in general science, than is necessary for a first-hand melter on a steel furnace. A broad general education will assist adaptability since a worker will be more able to understand future changes in his field and to relate them to his own particular job. If the job is changed, the worker can return to the basis provided by his general education to start out afresh. If the steel industry switches to a new process, the metallurgist with a broad education can more easily cope with this change, as can the operative on the furnace at his own level of education.

Very little is known about how schools affect attitudes towards change. Adaptability is a factor of personality whose source has not been deeply explored. The willingness to accept change is a necessity for young workers who are just entering industry and for older workers who may have to move to new jobs because of technical innovation. In Western European countries since 1945 younger workers have tended to receive higher pay than older men. The benefits of technical change seem to go to the younger men with the formal qualifications.[1] We must therefore consider how to teach the present generation in school to meet change, but in addition we must give older workers every chance of retraining themselves to meet new techniques. The revolution demanded in the views of operatives and managers is great if a worker or a manager aged forty-plus is to go back to school to relearn his job or to learn a totally new one. The educational techniques involved in teaching such pupils would seem to be very different from those at present used in technical education.[2]

(c) *Education*. Unless education is given a high priority, the proportion of the national income spent on education will not be large enough to create an educational system adequate for the type of demands that the economy puts upon it. Thus, during the nineteenth century when education had a low place on the national agenda, the schools did not educate enough men at any level, but particularly at managerial level, who understood the scientific advances of the time. Furthermore, during this same period the schools and universities gave their pupils an attitude towards industry such that able young men of the upper middle class were very unwilling to enter industry.

The educational system and the economy are two social institutions that are closely linked in any society, though many do not realize the nature of their mutual relationship. Industry in Britain has tended to put its faith in the practical man and in effect to say to the schools, 'You teach the three Rs and we'll do the rest.' In the schools there has been little knowledge of or sympathy with the industrial and commercial life of the nation. Any social institution can oppose the general direction of the development of the society that contains it.

[1] OEEC, *Steel Workers and Technical Progress*, Paris, 1959, p. 27.

[2] See C. E. Belbin, *Training the Adult Worker* (DSIR), London, 1964.

But today there seems on the whole to be a consensus in industrialized society that the economy should be used to make persons wealthier. In this situation the place of the educational system is clear. The schools must teach and shape personality in a way that recognizes economic developments. If children, particularly, though not entirely, of a low socio-economic status, are to cope with greater leisure, an increasing triviality of work, and rapid technical change, then there is scope for research and thought of a more sociological nature in the schools concerning the topics discussed in this section.

(iii) *Commitment of the Labour Force*. Any consideration of the values that the members of the labour force of a country must hold if they are to be wholly committed to industry must take into account the type of the economic system and the stage of its development. In a traditional society such as medieval Europe or Japan before the 1860s a conservative approach to the economy was necessary; an apprentice or a peasant in the fifteenth century learnt how to conserve tradition, not how to forge it anew. In all probability a capitalist country in the early stages of industrialization needs a different set of values from one that is more fully developed. Britain today has an economy of a mixed nature characterized by rather more *laissez-faire* than Government intervention, but also marked by large productive units. There seem to be three important sets of values that, when held by the labour force, smooth the working of a semi-capitalist economy (E. Ginzberg, 1956). These are the value attributed to a successful life, more particularly as measured by whether or not high wages or salary are earned, the value given to equality of opportunity so that the able can 'get on' and, finally, the value put on change. We have just given some consideration to the question of how change is viewed and shall now turn to an examination of the part that the educational system plays in transmitting the first and second of these values.

(a) *Success in Life*. Theoretically the mainspring of a *laissez-faire* economy is the attempt by all to buy as cheaply as possible and to sell as dearly as possible. It is assumed that a man will try to earn as high a wage or salary as he can, though allowance must be made for any advantageous conditions of work such as great security in the job or good chances of promotion. In theory the various wage rates direct labour to the highest return and ensure efficiency, since the employer will only pay what a man is worth to him. In fact the wage system does not work as smoothly as this, but what matters here is whether the labour force strives primarily after monetary rewards or gives the wage a low priority as part of its total reward.

In the USA children are imbued with the money-making spirit from an early age. The family plays a large part in the child's early years in encouraging him to work for money on every possible occasion. In the school each generation is inspired with the model of the self-made man. It is not without significance that many Americans work their way through university, whilst British undergraduates receive grants at one of the highest rates in the world. In the 1950s about 60 per cent of graduates in the USA came from what the British would call the working classes, a much higher proportion than in Britain. Much of this educated manpower goes into industry where rewards are high. The economy of the USA may base its efficiency on great natural advantages, but its industry makes the most of this competitive position by ensuring that its management is capable and committed to its economic assumptions.

European management has different attitudes towards money-making. Financial achievement is seen as only a part of the satisfactions yielded by the job; the true essence is considered to be doing the job itself.[1] The place of the school in the initial formation of such values can be vital. To most teachers in grammar schools an emphasis on money-seeking is unpleasant and conflicts with many of the ideals that they wish to impart, particularly that of service. There is a tradition in the public schools, which can be traced back to Arnold of Rugby, that the occupation into which a young man ought to go should be marked by the giving of service to the community. Such a choice of occupation was truly a vocation and often did not lead to the highest monetary reward consonant with the capability of the man entering the vocation. The connection established by these schools with the learned professions rather than with industry pays tribute to this tradition. The grammar school inherited this ideal in some measure, though, as we saw from King's work quoted in Chapter 5, a spirit of competition and thrust may replace the ideal of service as the modern grammar school comes to be seen more as a way into the higher levels of industry. Until very recently the

[1] D. Granick, *The European Executive*, London, 1962.

grammar school educated the majority of secondary modern teachers and hence transmitted some of the same tradition of service into this new form of school and also into the comprehensive school. A recent development in these schools has been the growth of schemes such as the Duke of Edinburgh's Award; here again unpaid service to the community is rated highly.

Many of the values taught either consciously or unconsciously in the secondary modern schools do not match the needs of a semi-capitalist system. Carter found that among secondary modern school leavers in Sheffield the values taught at school had always seemed irrelevant to life as it was actually lived. Beauty and the things of the spirit were insisted on at school, whilst the children often met ugliness and materialism at home and later at work. Teachers advised their pupils to show enthusiasm and loyalty in their future work, but the children found that their workmates scorned these qualities. So the children tended to ignore the advice of the schools, both before leaving school and after starting work.[1] This is a good example of the strains that are possible between education and social institutions. Here the schools are not helping the economy, but they can claim that they aim to redress what they see as bad in a materialist world.

In the upper levels of the labour force the ideal of service has directed many capable men from industry into the Colonial and Civil Services, and into the professions and politics. A case can be made that until recently industry has been somewhat starved of capable men. Service and security of employment were put before money and risk. As well as an ideal of service the public schools inculcated a strong corporate spirit that continues into adult life and is symbolized by 'the old school tie'. The connections encouraged by this spirit are used for finding jobs and placing business deals. There also exists a strong corporate feeling in the British working class. This is not a consequence of education but was born in the industrial struggles of the last hundred years and is symbolized by loyalty to the trade unions.

In the last chapter we saw that the British working class is early conditioned to failure in school examinations and more particularly in the eleven plus. Selection to the secondary modern school, or

[1] M. P. Carter, *Home, School and Work*, Oxford, 1962 (see espec. Chs. 5, 6 and 13).

perhaps even placement in the lower streams of a large comprehensive school, acts as a form of vocational guidance. The aspirations of the children not selected for grammar school are formed in a climate of opinion that limits their horizon. However, conditions vary very much by locality; the types of employment available to school leavers are very different. How do strictly local economic circumstances alter ambitions? It seems likely that in an area where one industry is predominant, as is often the case in the older industrial areas of the north of this country, the choice of ways of earning a living that is open may not meet the varied choices of school leavers. In Carter's survey in Sheffield, a city where employment is predominantly in engineering or the iron and steel industry, 20 per cent of the boys first chose jobs in the city's main industries, but 40 per cent actually obtained their first jobs in these industries. After a year 27 per cent were still in this category. In the case of the girls, the proportions choosing, entering and remaining in either office or shop work were more or less constant, but many who wanted to do other work ended up in factories or warehouses. Only 7 per cent chose this work, but 21 per cent found themselves doing it after a year. Where a wider range of occupations is available, a match between choices and vacant jobs is more likely. In one such case, namely Ealing, the Youth Employment Service could place 61·4 per cent of boys and 78·5 per cent of girls in their chosen occupations.[1] Vacancies within broad industrial categories more or less matched choices, though within each category there were difficulties. For example, within the occupations categorized as building too many boys wanted to be carpenters.

All these children, therefore, had been placed in a school where their ambitions were aimed towards a range of occupations that could have been below that of which many were capable. Some were unable to do what they wished, a situation hard to avoid under modern conditions. But what is of particular relevance here is that, when asked what were their reasons for their choice of vocation, only 7·6 per cent of the boys and 6·4 per cent of the girls mentioned good pay. Evidence collected in the late 1940s showed that amongst a

[1] M. D. Wilson, 'The Vocational Preferences of Secondary Modern Schoolchildren', *British Journal of Educational Psychology*, June and November 1953.

sample of 300 men aged eighteen and nineteen attitudes towards job incentives varied with measured intelligence. Those with below average IQs looked to the immediate satisfaction of the job itself; though they rated pay highly, the most important incentive to them was the satisfaction found in the job itself, and they were willing to sacrifice pay to be with good workmates. Men with higher IQs were more individualistic and looked to longer-term incentives, such as promotion prospects, but they in fact ranked pay lower than did those of lower intelligence.[1]

The ideals taught in schools can influence both the choice of vocation and the spirit in which a man will do his life work. It would seem that money-making is not rated highly in Britain and that economic ambition may be squashed. Whether this is morally right or wrong is not here in question, but it is clear that the higher the value put on making money and 'getting on', the more efficiently will a *laissez-faire* economy run. What the schools teach may or may not match the contemporary moral ethos of the country, but they certainly do not seem to be stressing one of the values needed by our present economic system.

(b) *Equality of Opportunity*. Very closely allied with much of what has just been said is the value given to equality of opportunity. Again a comparison can be made between the USA and Britain. In the USA there is a belief that anyone can improve himself by his own efforts. There is difference of opinion as to whether there is, in fact, more upward social mobility in the USA than in Britain. A major comparative study (S. M. Lipset and R. Bendix, 1959) found the rates to be about the same in the two countries. But the really important thing is that men believe that they can rise easily up the social ladder. It is probably true to say that this belief is more strongly held in the USA than in Britain, though more now see a chance to rise in Britain as a result of the reforms implicit in the 1944 Education Act.

In the large public companies that are coming to be typical of British industry today nepotism would seem to be less important than it was, though it must be common in smaller firms, and in some industries, such as the woollen textile industry, there are still many

[1] L. T. Wilkins, 'Incentives and the Young Worker', *Occupational Psychology*, October 1949.

family firms. In a survey of the managers of twenty-eight firms, made in the Manchester area in 1954–5, R. V. Clements found only twenty-eight (or 4 per cent) out of a total of 646 managers who were what he called 'crown princes'.[1] These were men whose start in a firm could be ascribed to close family links with the ownership or management of the firm. It must be noted that this was not nepotism in its crudest sense since these men appeared to deserve their successful careers. They may have had an advantageous start to their lives in industry, but very often they had been educated and trained almost from childhood so that they would want and be able to run the family firm with success. The proportion of these instances seems small and on balance does not invalidate the statement that the incidence of nepotism has probably declined in British industry.

Formal educational qualifications, then, provide the entrée to the various levels of the labour force, and therefore the educational system has come to be seen as the key to equality of economic opportunity. Formerly the way to improve one's social position was by founding a small business and making a success of it, often with the help of one's family. Now that the size of economic unit has grown this is less often seen as the way. Today the ambitious youth enters a large corporation with the hope of working his way up the hierarchy of management. Large companies must, therefore, select their potential managers with care, and the stress has come to be laid on education as well as on qualities of personality. The chance to rise is still there, but has come to be centred on education. From which schools do our economic leaders come?

In the mid-1950s Rosemary Stewart (1956)[2] carried out a survey of the managers of fifty-one of the sixty-five British companies that had 10,000 or more employees and were not nationalized. Managers were defined as all those above the rank of foreman. Half of all managers had been educated at either a grammar or a public school. However, a greater proportion of senior managers had been at these secondary schools; a third went to public schools and a third to grammar schools. It seems that boys from such schools had more

[1] R. V. Clements, *Managers: A Study of their Careers in Industry*, London, 1958, espec. Ch. III.

[2] An abridgement of this book has been published as *Managers for To-morrow* (DSIR), London, 1957.

chance of achieving high positions in management than those who came up through the ranks. In fact, the trend seems to be moving further in this direction, as might be expected in view of the greater stress on selecting recruits to management who have formal qualifications. More than a fifth of those aged from thirty-five to thirty-nine, that is the more recent recruits, went to public schools as compared with only a tenth of those between fifty-five and fifty-nine. For the same age groups one in four of the younger group had university degrees, whereas only one in ten of the older men had. In Britain those below managerial rank rarely have formal qualifications.[1] In smaller companies there is less stress on educational qualifications, but even here at technician level emphasis is growing. It is by founding such companies that self-made men can make their start, and among such men formal educational qualifications may be rarer. We saw that in these smaller companies nepotism can perhaps occur more easily than in large public limited companies. Both these factors work against stress on educational qualifications in the management of many small companies.

Nevertheless the trend is towards an emphasis on education by industry and commerce. Equality of educational opportunity has, therefore, become linked with equality of economic opportunity. It has already been shown in the last chapter that in this country there are very much more restricted opportunities for higher education than in the USA. The universities of this country have an intense care for their academic standards. It could be that this leads to a restriction of the places available. A similar attitude will help to limit places in selective secondary schools. A wider educational avenue on the American pattern could lead to greater opportunity; standards might, but need not, fall if the narrow British road were widened. The connection between management and the selective secondary schools is growing closer, and therefore the bias inherent in any method of selection for these schools which was described in the last chapter stands in the way of equality of economic opportunity.

The hypothesis examined here was that three values were in-

[1] In a survey (P. W. Musgrave, *op. cit.*, *British Journal of Industrial Relations*, July 1966) carried out in two large British iron and steel companies in 1961, the author found that only 1 out of 365 foremen had the equivalent of a degree, 4 had HNC, 6 ONC, and 9 City & Guilds.

conditions. When the educational system has adjusted to produce the manpower with the qualifications and in the numbers that meet the needs of the economy, then equilibrium has been reached.

One proviso must be mentioned here. It is possible that ultimately the educational system will be capable of providing all the trained manpower that the economy demands. There are signs that this point has been reached, except in the case of some very specialized, high-grade scientific occupations, in the USA today, especially in those States, such as California, where a high proportion go into tertiary education. Under these circumstances any increase in the qualifications of those entering the economy will not be due to demands from employers, but be caused by a change in the view held by the populace at large about education as a good in itself.[1]

(i) *Equilibrium*. This position is never reached. The educational system tends towards it as successive changes occur. The quicker the reaction, the better will education serve the economy. However, strains are possible. The chronic shortage of scientists and mathematicians since 1945 is an example. The educational system has two responsibilities. It must make good the losses from the labour force due to normal retirement and to death; these are statistically predictable. But it also has to meet the needs of unforeseen innovations. There are two other difficulties. There is free vocational choice in Britain; a school may advise a career, but no one can compel a young person to enter any occupation. In addition, a state of full employment complicates the task, since there is no longer a pool of unemployed from which the economy may draw the labour it needs as was the case before 1939 when men and women at all levels changed their vocations in their search for work.

In the period of full employment since 1945 there has been constant talk of the shortage of highly educated and skilled manpower. It is well to be clear in what sense the word 'shortage' is being used. In the strict economic sense shortage implies that the supply of a given grade of labour falls short of the demand for it. This results in a rise in price; in the case of labour the wage or salary rises to ration out the supply. In view of the tones of urgency used in many recent discussions of these shortages a considerable rise in the level

[1] J. K. Folger and C. B. Nam, 'Trends in Education in Relation to the Occupational Structure', *Sociology of Education*, Fall 1964.

of salaries might be expected, especially in the case of scientists and mathematicians. Certainly in Britain for various reasons this has not always been so. Teachers of science and mathematics are in very short supply, but their salaries have risen little more than those of teachers of other subjects who are in far less short supply. 'Shortage' has been used in a second and not strictly economic sense to describe a state where not only the supply, but the demand, is too low. This condition may be caused by a lack of knowledge of what qualifications are actually required in a job or by dysfunctional attitudes towards the relevant branch of knowledge. Both of these forces have probably influenced the long neglect of science by British industry. The criterion of shortage used here may be comparison with the proportions of a type of labour with a given level of education employed in another industry or even in another country, or it may be based on some measurement of economic returns. In all these cases there are formidable statistical problems of calculation.

Can equilibrium be reached more quickly with or without Government intervention? In the nineteenth century many in Britain believed that 'the invisible hand' of the *laissez-faire* economists would force the schools to meet the needs of the economy. Only rarely have attempts been made in the twentieth century to interfere with the flow of labour from the educational system to the economy, and these have usually been as a result of war. Since 1954, however, the problem of shortages has grown so acute that Government intervention has become politically possible. Action has taken three main forms. Educational institutions have been given aid on condition that it will be used for a specific purpose; universities have received financial assistance to build laboratories. The Government has also given great publicity to deficiencies of manpower; the prominence given to scientific and technical education since 1956 may be quoted and a particular concern has been the drive to recruit more teachers. Lastly, there have been regular attempts to forecast the future demands for manpower so that educational institutions, particularly at the highest level, may try to match the expected needs, thereby easing the way to equilibrium between supply and demand.

(ii) *Forecasting*. At the national level the Government has issued several White Papers attempting to forecast the future needs of labour in the economy.[1] Some large firms make estimates of their future needs of managers and craftsmen, in which case analysis will be purely at a local level, though the same difficulties underlie forecasts by companies as those by the Government. The Government's estimates have been carefully compiled with the help of the industries concerned. Yet they have gone awry within the brief period of three years.

The reasons for these failures are both economic and educational. At a time of rapid technical change the educational system takes time to answer to the new needs of the economy even where its institutions are very adaptable. But apart from any educational consideration, assumptions of an economic nature underlie any attempt to foresee the needs for trained manpower. An industry that expresses a demand for a particular type of educated and skilled man may find that by the time the educational system has trained him he is no longer required. This may be due to the introduction of a new technique or to a change in the competitive strength of the industry in overseas markets. Again a basic assumption is that the wage structure will remain unaltered. An industry may offer a salary that influences a school leaver to begin a sandwich course at a College of Advanced Technology, but by the time he qualifies some four years later the salary in another industry may tempt the graduate away from the industry that he originally intended to enter. Lastly, it is not possible to say whether or not the forecast will affect the future supply of labour. Probably the most valuable effect of forecasts so far has been to give publicity to the shortage of trained manpower in certain fields, thereby influencing the direction of recruitment to the labour force. The need for scientists has been stimulated in industry and the knowledge of openings has been transmitted to the educational system. Despite this result forecasts do not yet appear to have been very successful tools of economic planning.[2] It must be made clear that a fully planned economy will have much the same economic and

[1] See, for instance, the triennial reports of the Committee of Scientific Manpower, set up by the Advisory Council on Scientific Policy, and also the series of Manpower Studies begun in 1964 by the Ministry of Labour.

[2] For some comments on the whole problem of forecasting manpower needs, see *Scientific and Technical Manpower* (1962), 1963, pp. 18–19; *Higher Education* (Robbins Report), 1963, pp. 71–3 and Appendix 4, p. 95.

educational problems in matching the supply of and the demand for labour. There is one major difference, namely that in many planned economies direction of labour replaces free choice of occupations.

The achievement of an equilibrium position between the supply of and the demand for labour is made more difficult by the growing realization of the educational needs of the economy. Over the last century in Britain an escalator effect has been at work; when plans for educational expansion have been made to meet one level of needs, a deeper level has been discovered leading to further needs. There seem to be two influences apart from that of technical change at work here to raise the demand for education. There is the natural tendency for education to create a desire for more education. But there are also various economic tendencies; for instance, the growing proportion of the labour force in maintenance work and in the tertiary sector perpetuates the rising demand for educated manpower with specific qualifications. If forecasting is almost impossible except in broad terms, we are again forced to take up the position that education can best help the economy not by attending to the exact numbers that are following a specific type of education, but by concentrating on giving a broad general curriculum that meets the needs of a technological age.

(iii) *The Pool of Capability and the Labour Force*. Before deciding that the educational system is carrying out this part of its economic function well, further consideration must be given to the pool of capability. In the last chapter this pool was analysed purely in terms of social selection; here its connection with the labour force will be examined. There is an upper limit to the numbers possessing a given level of capability in any country. The question arises whether the educational system is organized in such a way that manpower needs are met as nearly as the available supply of different levels of capability allows. There is no measure of 'capability' in the sense that the word is used here. The only possibility is to state the argument in terms of measured intelligence, whilst realizing that the case is open to criticism. It can be argued that, if the factor of capability could be isolated, its attributes would be very similar to those of measured intelligence. More particularly its distribution throughout the population would follow the same pattern as that for IQ. Each level of the labour force requires a minimum IQ. A manager must have a higher IQ than an operative in order to do his work. It seems that the minimum IQs required by the respective levels of the labour force are approximately as follows: senior executives 130; technologists, such as professional engineers, 120; technicians, such as junior laboratory workers, 110; skilled craftsmen, 100; semi-skilled and unskilled operatives less than 100. It is true that these are minimum IQs and a worker may decide to do a job which demands a lower IQ than he possesses.

The distribution of measured intelligence amongst the population falls along the curve of normal error and is therefore of the shape shown in Fig. I.

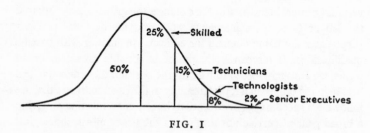

FIG. I

In each of the IQ ranges shown only a certain proportion of the population falls, and therefore there is a limit to the actual numbers capable of working at each of the levels of the labour force.

In an analysis of the possible effects of automation on education J. F. Coales (1958) has pointed out that where an educational system is selective and where each level of the educational system is strongly associated with a given level of the labour force, the cut-off points for selection for the different types of secondary school may be such that the supply of educated manpower does not match the needs of the economy. Using realistic assumptions Coales calculated that this may well be the case by 1975 for one important range of occupations. The level necessary to become a technician is that now provided in the main by the grammar school for which the minimum IQ is about 113, though there are large regional differences which bear little relation to the needs of the labour force. But it would appear that, unless the same education is given to those with an IQ of 110 and above, there is likely to be a shortage of those capable of becoming qualified technicians, the IQ range 113 to 120 not being large enough to fill the probable needs of industry. Though Coales' analysis made no allowance for the introduction of the comprehensive school, it does raise the whole problem of the relationship between the organization of secondary schooling and the flow of skill to the labour force.

(iv) *The Structure of Secondary Education and the Labour Force.* Secondary schools can be thought of as a graded series of take-off ramps into the labour force (J. E. Floud and A. H. Halsey, 1956). Although there is some overlapping each type of secondary school tends to lead into a definite level of occupations. This can be seen very clearly from the existence of predominant leaving ages for each school type. This age implies a level of education and very often the possession or otherwise of a formal qualification. Children tend to leave the secondary modern school at the legal minimum age of fifteen, the secondary technical school at sixteen after a five-year course leading to an external examination, the comprehensive school at fifteen or sixteen, and the grammar or public school at sixteen or eighteen after a higher level of examination.

The public school historically has served the professions and the needs of the Government at home and overseas. Particularly since 1945 it has come to have stronger connections with top management in commerce and industry; perhaps this new emphasis offsets the lack of openings in the former Empire to which young men from these schools might have expected to go. The grammar school has come to feed the lower levels of management; almost never do grammar school boys become foremen, which in Britain, unlike the USA, is not a career grade, but the highest level to which a capable and ambitious operative can aspire. The secondary technical school tends to prepare technicians and skilled craftsmen; some of the latter may hope to rise to junior managerial level. The secondary modern school is strongly associated with the operative and craftsmen level. Since in 1969 two-thirds of boys and just over two-thirds of girls left comprehensive schools at either fifteen or sixteen it would seem that, though some of their pupils are entering occupations of the same status as those from grammar schools, this new type of secondary school is coming to provide a take-off point into the labour force similar to those formerly supplied mainly by the modern and technical schools.

Prior to the 1944 Education Act many children of less wealthy parents could hope to rise up the labour force, certainly to the level of foreman, if not beyond, although they had left school at the legal minimum age. Now these more capable youths are selected at eleven plus for a grammar school education and therefore tend to enter the higher levels of the labour force. The process ensures a fuller use of the pool of capability, but it raises questions about the intellectual quality of the lower levels of the labour force. One important issue is what will be the future source from which foremen are to be recruited. Management may have to redefine the role of foreman and start to feed back ex-grammar school boys into the labour force at this level as junior supervisors with the chance of promotion.

If there is a shortage of educated manpower at any level of the labour force, then clearly the structure of the educational system must be arranged so that it gives the maximum of help or the minimum of hindrance to the economy. The schools must be organized so that they do all they can to develop capability and so that no one shall have his aspirations limited, as far as they are realistic. But, as Coales has pointed out, by 1975 this country may well be short of technicians because the secondary schools associated with this level of the labour force have tended to select only those with an IQ of 113 and above, whereas the work can be done by those with an IQ of around 110 and above. Those in the range from 110 to 113 are channelled off into the secondary modern schools or the lower streams of the comprehensive schools and into a lower level of employment.

(v) *Vocational Choice and Guidance.* The actual transition from school to job is vital, since it is at this point that the new recruits, as opposed to retrained adults, enter the labour force (M. P. Carter, 1966). Changes in the direction of recruitment in answer to new techniques can be made here. It is important to consider at what stage and by what means children are shown the occupational opportunities open to them. Vocational guidance now exists at all levels. In the universities there are Appointments Boards that link higher education to the economy. The public and grammar schools frequently have Careers Masters who specialize in giving advice on jobs. Finally, there is the Youth Employment Service, a Government-sponsored organization, that operates particularly for secondary modern, but also for grammar school leavers. This service was established by legislation whereby local authorities are permitted to incorporate the vocational guidance service into their educational service, if they wish. Where a local authority does not opt to do so, the Ministry of Labour is responsible. For this reason the service is not uniform in organization throughout the country. It is not therefore surprising to find that the Youth Employment Service does not wield great influence.

In the mid-1960s Youth Employment Officers only placed about 40 per cent of the younger leavers and about 30 per cent of the older leavers in their first jobs.[1] In Sheffield, Carter found that in 1959 just under two-thirds of the boys in his sample entered the jobs recommended by the Youth Employment Officers; as a result of job changes the proportion fell to a half. In the case of girls the proportion was still about three-quarters after a year, probably because of the rather narrower range of occupations available. Contact with the youths starts during their last year at school. However, the majority of young people have decided on an occupation before the Youth Employment Officer speaks to them and these choices are respected, although these decisions seem to be made in a very haphazard fashion. There is no guarantee that the chosen job suits the youth concerned, since many are influenced by parents, relations or school friends, whose detailed knowledge about occupations in general has been found to be scanty and unreliable.

The common use of the word 'choice' in this context is perhaps an unfortunate one, since the opportunities available to the majority of persons who are seeking work at any age are largely constrained by the locally available positions, which cover a very narrow range in, for example, a mining area. In addition, possible first choices are restricted by the pathways through which the young reach the age at which they leave school. By and large a child from a working-class background is fitted for a different range of occupations from a child from the middle class, and an education in a grammar school or the upper streams of a comprehensive school leads to a different level of

[1] *The Future Development of the Youth Employment Service*, London, HMSO, 1965, p. 14.

the labour force from that gained in a secondary modern school or the lower streams of a comprehensive school.[1]

As children grow older they gradually build up a knowledge of the occupational structure, in part learnt in, for instance, geography lessons, and come to anticipate their future occupational role. The self-concept of their own ability and personality, gained certainly in the first case very largely at school, is an important determinant of the level and type of occupation to which they begin to commit themselves. Sometimes a child may come to see himself as less capable than he might have been if, for example, he had not been placed in a low stream or in a secondary modern school. In such cases children in some senses make their first choice of occupation under the influence of a partly fictitious handicap.

Once the point of choice is reached, a process of exchange takes place in which the young person, with more or less rationality, balances the tangible and intangible rewards judged to flow from the various jobs then on offer against the tangible and intangible costs seen to be involved in doing each job. There are great variations in the age at which the decision must be made and in its irrevocability. The extremes are exemplified, on the one hand, by the temporary choice of such unskilled seasonal labour as hop-picking which requires little training and is known to be a short-term job and, on the other hand, by a medical career, which necessitates a decision early in secondary school to do a course biassed towards science subjects. This latter example also shows the increasing finality of many choices of managerial and professional careers, since the further the young person goes along the pathway towards his ultimate goal, the more irrevocable his choice becomes. At each stage he narrows his chance for manoeuvre. At fourteen he has the chance of becoming a doctor, dentist, or a pure or applied scientist. Ten years later his options have narrowed to becoming, perhaps, either an eye surgeon or an ear, nose and throat specialist.

It must be added that in Britain most workers are placed in jobs at all levels of the labour force by interview and without the help of any psychological testing. In these interviews personality as well as

[1] For the literature on the influences on a child prior to choosing an occupation see P. W. Musgrave, 'Family, School, Friends and Work: A Sociological Perspective', *Educational Research*, June 1967.

educational attainment is assessed. The interview is known to be a fickle tool and social background can unconsciously influence decisions. The aim of many interviewers is consciously to assess social factors. A public school education may be considered important for an industrial appointment on social rather than educational grounds. Social background can influence the work of the Youth Employment Officer in that he may consciously place secondary modern school leavers in jobs that match their family backgrounds. In both these cases the placings can be defended as matching the needs of the workers and the companies. However, it is clear that there is need for the closer integration of this service into the educational system, so that children can be helped to a wise choice by learning accurate details about themselves and possible jobs as early as possible.

C. Conclusion

In its economic function the educational system has to observe both quantitative and qualitative criteria. Schools inculcate ideals that can help or hinder the economy, but the curriculum best suited to the rapidly changing needs of a modern economy seems to be that preferred by most teachers on strictly educational grounds, namely a broad general education ensuring both literacy and numeracy pursued to as late an age as possible. To organize schooling in this way would also seem to assist the economy by inculcating an attitude favourable to change. The fundamental difficulties in accurately forecasting the needs of the labour force leads to the same conclusion. Therefore on the criteria of both quality and quantity the same type of curriculum is needed. However, the actual structure of the educational system has also to be considered. This may be dysfunctional in that the pool of capability may not be developed in the way that matches the needs of the economy, as mediated by the labour force. The situation can be made worse by institutions which are ancillary to the educational system, but which are not usually considered in Britain to be a part of it; such are apprenticeship and the method of giving vocational guidance.

It is apparent that there may be conflict between the ideals needed for a smoothly working economy and those inculcated by the ethos of the schools. A *laissez-faire* economy requires on the production side a positive attitude towards money-making and 'getting on', and on the consumption side there must be an eagerness to 'keep up with the Joneses'. These attitudes have not been greatly favoured by British teachers. Such conflicts may be due, as is probably true in this case, to autonomous developments rather than to policy decisions. It is none the less true that, if dysfunctional, these tensions must be discovered so that they may be resolved in the light of what the country wants as its educational aim.

It is fitting to end the functional analysis of the educational system contained in this part by indicating that political decisions in pursuit of aims involving one function that education can serve may lead to dysfunction in another sphere. This may happen fortuitously or because there was insufficient thought before the political decision was taken. In this chapter an example has been given. In the 1944 Act the main political aim was the provision of equality of educational opportunity, and the stress was laid on the function of selection. Undoubtedly this helped the economy by developing capability, but very little thought has ever been given to the way that the quality of the lower levels of the labour force will be altered. Yet in its economic function the educational system is responsible for the schooling of all levels of the labour force. One more example of conflicting functions must suffice. In a previous chapter it was indicated that an examination system which can in many ways help in the function of selection may hinder the development of the creativity that is so essential if the educational system is to fulfil its innovatory function.

Functional analysis of social institutions, carried out in as unbiassed a way as possible, can bring such conflicts to light. This can be done for social institutions in their existing forms, but it can also precede political decisions to alter institutions. This should help to prevent the creation of social institutions that are structured to increase conflict. Such an analysis will also show where conflict may emerge and thereby force a clear decision on political priorities. The functions of education are complex and closely interrelated. To change the educational system sets off a restructuring of these relationships. The tools needed for the functional analysis of the educational system have been provided in the third part of this book. It would give a clearer picture of the problems involved in such political decisions as the reorganization of the secondary school system, if the argument were to be carried as far as possible in these terms, before the final political decisions were made.

BIBLIOGRAPHY

A. The Economy

J. H. Dunning and C. J. Thomas, *British Industry* (2nd ed.), London, 1966.

P. W. Musgrave, *The Economic Structure*, London, 1969.

B. The Educational System and the Economy

E. Ashby, *Technology and the Academics*, London, 1958.

G. H. Bantock, *Education in an Industrial Society*, London, 1963.

M. P. Carter, *Into Work*, London, 1966 (Pelican).

J. F. Coales, 'Education for Automation', *British Journal of Educational Studies*, May 1958.

J. E. Floud and A. H. Halsey, 'Education, Social Mobility and the Labour Market', *The Yearbook of Education*, 1956 (also in A. H. Halsey, J. E. Floud and C. A. Anderson (eds.), *Education, Economy and Society*, New York, 1961).

E. Ginzberg, 'Education and National Efficiency in the USA', *The Yearbook of Education*, 1956 (also in A. H. Halsey, J. E. Floud and C. A. Anderson (eds.), *Education, Economy and Society*, New York, 1961).

C. J. Kerr, J. T. Dunlop, F. H. Harbison and C. A. Myers, *Industrialisation and Industrial Man*, London, 1962.

S. M. Lipset and R. Bendix, *Social Mobility in an Industrial Society*, London, 1959.

P. W. Musgrave, *Technical Change, the Labour Force and Education*, Oxford, 1967.

Oxford University Department of Education, *Technology and the Sixth Form Boy*, Oxford, 1963.

R. Stewart, *Management Succession*, London, 1956.

Indexes

Name Index

Anderson, H. H., 207n
Argles, M., 261n
Arnold, Thomas, 163, 330
Ashby, E., 326, 349
Ashley, B., Cohen, H., McIntyre, D. and Slatter, E., 225-6n

Bacchus, M. K., 232n
Bailyn, L., 131n, 135
Bantock, G. H., 323, 349
Barker, R. G. and Gump, P. V., 198n
Baron, G., 142n, 143n, 160, 163, 182; and Howell, D. A., 170n; and Tropp, A., 165, 182
Batley, R., O'Brien, O. and Parris, H., 168n
Belbin, C. E., 328n
Berger, P. L. and Luckmann, T., 23, 27n, 31, 185n, 186n
Bernbaum, G., Noble, G. and Whiteside, M. T., 154n
Bernstein, B., 68n, 78, 79, 99; and Henderson, D., 80n; and Young, D., 63n
Beveridge, Lord, 317
Biddle, B. J., Rosencrantz, H. A. and Rankin, E. F., 220n
Birch, A. H., 278n
Bird, C., 279n
Blyth, W. A. L., 90, 103, 110, 113, 119, 214n, 215, 217
Boocock, S. S., 23, 31; and Coleman, J. S., 196n

Bott, E., 38, 52
Bowker, G., 248, 265
Bracey, H. E., 172n
Brakken, E., 200n
Brennan, T. W., 278n
Brim, O. G. and Wheeler, S., 22, 31
Brookover, W., Thomas, S. and Paterson, A., 195n
Brown, R. (ed.), 257n
Brown, R. L. and O'Leary, M., 132n
Bunnicutt, C. W. (ed.), 186n
Burgin, T. and Edson, P., 249n

Campbell, F., 193n
Cannon, C., 156n
Carr-Saunders, A. M. and Wilson, P. A., 143
Carter, C. F. and Williams, B. R., 326n
Carter, M. P., 331, 332, 344, 345, 349
Cattell, R. B., 232
Chambers, R. C., 279n
Christensen, H. T. (ed.), 28n
Clark, B. R., 191n, 266
Clark, Sir F., 266
Clark, R., 308n, 336n
Clausen, J. A., 17, 31
Clements, R. V., 334
Coales, J. F., 342-3, 344, 349
Cohen, A. K., 26, 31

Coleman, J. S., 113, 116, 119, 175, 212, 258, 259, 263n, 265

Collier, K. G., 282n

Collins, A. *et al.*, 336n

Collins, M., 153n, 225n

Connell, R. W., 65n, 272, 283

Connell, W. F., Francis, E. P. and Skilbeck, E., 113n

Cooney, E. W. and Pollins, H., 278n

Copeman, G. H., 315n

Cotgrove, S., 306n

Dagar, E. Z., 28n

Dahrendorf, R., 57, 83

Dale, R. R., 305n

Dance, E. H., 270n

Dancy, J. C., 276n, 295n

Davis, A., 67, 69

Dennis, N., Henriques, F. and Slaughter, C., 38n

Dewey, J., 273

Dickson, G. E. *et al.*, 227n

Disraeli, B., 100

Dodd, C. H., 277n

Douglas, J. W. B., 44, 52, 74-5, 77n, 83, 114, 289, 292, 297, 299; and Ross, J. M., 49n; with Ross, J. M. and Simpson, H. R., 109n, 114n

Dowse, R. E. and Hughes, J., 269n

Duggan, E. P. and Stewart, W. A. C., 156n

Dunning, J. H. and Thomas, C. J., 319, 349

Dunphy, D. C., 106, 113, 119

Durkheim, E., 140, 251, 265

Ede, Chuter, 148

Eggleston, S. J., 100n, 114n, 168n

Eisenstadt, S. N., 50, 51n, 52, 105, 119

Eliot, T. S., 252, 265

Evans, K. M., 207n, 214, 215n, 217

Evetts, J., 284n

Ferez, J., 289

Finlayson, D. S. and Cohen, L., 235n

Fletcher, R., 37, 52

Florence, P. Sargent, 315

Floud, J. E., 230, 238, 294n; and Halsey, A. H., 299, 310, 343; with Halsey, A. H. and Martin, F. M., 74, 83, 299, 310; and Scott, W., 157, 159, 228n

Folger, J. K. and Nam, C. B., 338n

Ford, J., 100, 103, 206n, 211n

Fraser, E., 76, 83

Friedman, M. and Kuznets, S., 147n

Friedson, E., 120n, 127n

Furneaux, W. D., 302, 310

Galbraith, J. K., 261

Getzels, J. W. and Jackson, P. W., 262n

Ginzberg, E., 329, 349

Glass, D. V. (ed.), 34n, 59, 65n, 75n, 76n, 83, 153n, 211n, 279n, 294n

Gold, M., 210n

Golding, W., 46n

Goldman, R. J. and Taylor, F. M., 250n

Goldthorpe, J. H. and Lockwood, D., 61n

Goldthorpe, J. H., Lockwood, D., Bechhofer, F. and Platt, J., 61, 83

Granick, D., 330n

Greenstein, F. I., 268, 283

Guttsman, W. L., 275, 283

Halloran, J. D., Brown, R. L. and Chaney, D. C., 123n, 131n, 133n

Halsey, A. H., 159, 285, 287, 289,
310; with Floud, J. E. and
Anderson, C. A. (eds.), 46n,
86n, 206n, 217, 228n, 308n,
310, 349
Hargreaves, D., 97, 103, 112, 116,
124, 281
Harnqvist, K., 285, 287
Harris, C., 32, 52
Hebb, D. O., 77, 78
Hess, R. D. and Shipman, V. C.,
81n
Hicks, J. R., 56, 83, 337n
Himmelweit, H. T., 76n, 80,
122, 123–4, 128, 130, 131, 136,
211n, 303, 311; with Halsey,
A. H. and Oppenheim, A. N.,
65n; with Oppenheim, A. N.
and Vince, P., 122, 136; and
Swift, B., 102
Hoggart, R., 117, 119, 133–4,
252, 265, 273
Holly, D. N., 101, 281n
Homans, G., 280, 283
Hordley, L. and Lee, D. J., 306n
Horobin, G., Oldman, D. and
Bytheway, W., 298n
Hoselitz, B. F. and Moore, W. E.
(eds.), 72n
Hough, R. I., Summers, G. F.
and O'Meara, J., 51n
Howell, D. A., 169n
Hoyle, E., 218, 238
Humphrey, G. and Argyle, M.
(eds.), 217
Hunt, J. McV., 45n, 80n
Hunt, J. W., 270n

Jackson, B., 91n, 131n, 252n;
and Marsden, D., 75, 83, 172n,
211n, 254, 266
Jahoda, G., 64, 214, 217
James, Sir E., 280, 283
Jewkes, J., 262n
Johnstone, J. W. C., 125n

Kalton, G., 295
Katz, E. and Lazarsfeld, P. F.,
128, 129, 136
Kawwa, T., 249, 250n
Kelly, J., 280n
Kelsall, R. K., 34n, 223n, 277n
Kemeny, P. J., 98n, 301n
Kerr, C. J., Dunlop, J. T.,
Harbison, F. H. and Myers,
C. A., 322, 349
Keynes, J. M., 186, 264, 316, 317
King, R., 95–6, 103, 116, 126,
164n, 330
Klein, J., 46, 52, 175n
Klein, V., 117
Knapp, R. H. and Goodrich,
H. B., 263n
Kob, J., 219, 228n, 238
Kuhn, T. S., 184n

Lacey, C., 210, 211, 212, 217
Langeveld, M. J., 235, 238
Langton, K. P., 274n
Lasswell, H. D., 120, 126
Lawrence, E., 128n
Lawton, D., 78, 83
Leavis, F. R., 186, 264, 324
Lewis, R. and Maude, A., 139,
159
Lippitt, R. and White, R. K., 206,
217
Lippmann, W., 219
Lipset, S. M., 264n, 272, 283;
and Bendix, R., 58, 83, 333
Lipsitz, M., 273, 274n
Little, A. and Westergaard, J.,
305n
Littlejohn, W., 38n
Livingstone, R. W., 193n

McClelland, D. C., 72
McQuail, D., 120, 136; with
O'Sullivan, L. and Quine,
W. G., 270n
Manzer, R. A., 148, 159, 178, 182

Marsh, D. C., 56, 57, 83
Marshall, T. H., 140, 159
Martin, F. M., 65n, 74, 75n, 83
Marx, K., 57, 82, 319
Masters, P. L. and Hockey, S. W., 295n
Mays, J. B., 43, 52, 280n
Mead, M., 42, 46, 52, 247, 266
Merton, R. K., 180
Miller, T. W. G., 101n
Moreno, J. L., 213–14, 217
Morris, Henry, 167
Musgrave, P. W., 50n, 85, 89n, 94, 103, 122n, 156n, 183, 190n, 192n, 193n, 200, 244n, 269n, 312, 321–2n, 326, 335, 346n, 349; and Reid, G. R. B., 73n, 121n, 123n, 130n
Musgrove, F., 104, 117, 118, 119, 244n, 279, 283, 309, 311; and Taylor, P. H., 155n, 233, 238
Mussen, P. H., Langer, J. and Covington, M. (eds.), 103n

Naegele, K. D., 222n, 224n
Newcomb, T. H., Turner, R. H. and Converse, P. M., 279n, 280, 283
Newfield, J. G. H., 305n
Newson, E. and Newson, J., 25, 31, 68–9, 71, 83
Niblett, W. R., 173n
Nisbet, J. D., 45–6n; and Entwistle, N. J., 87n
Norwood, Sir Cyril, 163

Oldman, D., Bytheway, B. and Horobin, G., 46n
O'Leary, M., 132n
Opie, I. and Opie, P., 125n
Oppenheim, A. N., 211n
Orwell, G., 135, 301

Parsons, T., 35, 38, 52, 202, 217
Payne, G. L., 326n

Peschek, D. and Brand, J., 167n
Piaget, J., 77–8
Platt, R. and Parkes, J. S. (eds.), 44n

Reeves, M. (ed.), 176n
Reid, G. R. B., 130
Rex, J. and Moore, R., 250n
Richmond, W. K., 189, 200
Riesman, D., 230n
Riley, M. R. and Flowerman, S. H., 124
Robinson, W. P. and Rackstraw, S. J., 78n
Rohner, R. P., 29n
Rose, R., 267, 283
Roy, N. N., 149n
Rubinstein, D. and Simon, B., 166n
Runciman, W. G., 60, 62n, 83

Samuel, R. H. and Thomas, R. H., 193n
Saran, R., 168n
Schramm, W., Lyle, J. and Parker, E. B., 129, 136
Scott, E., 47n
Seers, D., 56n
Selleck, R. J. W. (ed.), 89n, 190n
Sewell, W. H. et al., 290n
Sillitoe, A., 259n
Skidelsky, R., 190, 201
Skinner, A. I., 225n
Smith, Adam, 312–13
Snow, C. P., 253, 266
Spinley, B. M., 70–1, 84, 230n, 273
Stacey, M., 278n
Stellway, H. W. F., 228n
Stewart, R., 334, 349
Strodtbeck, F. L., 186n
Sugarman, B., 111n, 112
Swift, D. F., 72, 75n, 84, 286n

Taylor, F. W., 320
Taylor, P. H., 229n

Taylor, W., 96, 103, 154, 159
Thomas, R. H. and Samuel, R. H., 271n
Thompson, D., 324
Toomey, D. M., 75n
Tropp, A., 139, 159
Tudhope, W. B., 220n
Turner, C. M., 97n
Turner, I. A. H., 125n
Turner, R. H., 86n, 206n

Veness, T., 300, 311
Vernon, P. E., 77, 84, 232, 238, 285, 286, 310

Waller, W., 139, 159, 219, 234n, 238
Ward, B., 122n
Webb, J., 213n
Weber, M., 63
Weinberg, I., 93, 103
West, D. J., 51n, 259n
Wheeler, D. K., 183, 201
Whiteside, M. T., Bernbaum, G. and Noble, G., 235n
Whyte, W. H., 173n
Wilensky, H. L., 132, 136, 141n, 151n
Wilkins, L. T., 333n

Wilkinson, R. H., 94n, 200n, 281–2n
Williams, Lady G., 262n
Williams, J., 250n
Williams, R., 254n, 324n
Williams, W. M., 38n, 51n, 222, 226
Willmott, P., 29, 31, 106, 119, 302; and Young, M., 40, 52
Wilson, B. R., 176n, 224
Wilson, M. D., 300n, 332n
Wiseman, S., 208n, 292n
Wolff, P. de, 285
Wylie, L., 18n

Yates, A. and Pidgeon, D. A., 300n
Young, D., 63n
Young, M. and Willmott, P., 39, 52
Young, M., 286n; and McGeery, P., 172, 182
Young, M. F. D., 257n
Yoxall, Sir J. H., 148

Zajonc, R. J., 122–3
Zeitlin, M., 273, 274n
Ziman, J., 184, 201
Znaniecki, F., 223

Subject Index

Aberdeen, 73, 121–3, 130–2, 268–269
ability, pool of, *see* capability; self-concepts of, 194–5, 346
academic success, 197, 203, 211; sub-culture of, 258, 259
academic teachers, 226, 227, 238
achievement, 72–3, 203–5
activity methods of teaching, 208, 298
adaptability, education for, 327, 328
adolescents, 36, 49–52, 104; formation of groups of, 49, 106–9, 216 (*see also* peer groups); leadership among, 280; relations between adults and, 118–119; and social class, 64, 65
advertising, 126, 144, 187, 261, 320
age: and peer groups, 109–12; of pupils, and self-image of teacher, 224; of pupils, and status of teacher, 153–5; and role, 18–20; in school class, 202–3; of teachers, and self-image, 228–9; and use of mass media, 129–30
aggression in children, social class and, 67, 69
aggressive heroes, of mass media, 123, 127, 130, 133, 135
Appointments Boards, 344
apprenticeship, 162, 251, 347; technical, 302

Approved Schools, 259
Australia, 47–8, 65, 106–9, 317
authoritarianism, 234–5, 273–4
authority, attitudes towards, 49–50, 70, 71, 229
automation, 321, 342
autonomous change, in educational system, 263–5, 309

behaviour, 71, 184–5
Bethnal Green, 39–41; adolescent groups in, 106–9, 115

Cabinet, the, 274, 276
California, tertiary education in, 308, 338
Cambridge, University of, 275, 276, 277
Cambridgeshire Village Colleges, 167
capability, pool of, 285–93, 309, 341–3
capitalism, in Britain, 312
careers masters, 344
Central Advisory Councils, 179–180
Certificate of Secondary Education (CSE), 177, 179, 191; in Commerce, 324
character: references to, 143–4, 174; school and development of, 95, 164
child-centred teachers, 226–7, 238

children: assessment of teachers by, 233; influence of, on teachers, 175–6; perception of social class by, 63–5; underground culture of, 125

Christianity, values of, 244, 245–6

churches, and education, 168, 170, 178

cinema, 130

City and Guilds courses, 306

Civil Service, 274, 277–8, 331

class, see social class

Colleges of Advanced Technology, 340

Colonial Service, 331

comics, 127, 128, 130, 135, 195

commitment, of labour force, 322, 329–36

Common Entrance Examination, 92, 295

Communists, 146, 274

competitive spirit, in schools, 205, 256, 330

comprehensive schools 88, 98–101, 166, 205, 343; education for leadership in, 282; leaving age from, 343; social class in, 114, 211, 281; sub-cultures in, 257; teachers in, 154, 235

conflict: or consensus, on values, 25–6; of parents with adolescents, 50, 125–6; of parents with teachers, 172; sociological analysis as means of detecting and lessening, 348

conformity: education for?, 237, 262; with peer group, 302; in public image of teachers, 220, 221, 223; in transmission of culture, 91, 247

conscience, 70, 71, 230

consensus: or conflict, on values, 25–6; political, 267–74

Conservative Party, 275, 276

consumption: education for discrimination in, 324; social class and pattern of, 55, 64

co-operation, 47, 204; in working-class ethos, 256

Corby, secondary schools in, 167–8

craftsmen, 323, 343

creativity: education and, 196, 199, 237, 262–3, 348

crime, in adolescence, 51

Crowther Report, 96n, 251, 253, 285, 291, 294n, 306, 307, 310, 311

culture: as an aspect of knowledge, 185–6; of different types of school, 89–101; education and, 242, 250–2; family and transmission of, 43, 52, 244, 250; of family and school, clash between, 43, 213, 230, 254; and maintenance of political consensus, 272; and personality, 47; teenage, see youth culture

curriculum, 173, 177, 183, 191–194; and behavioural patterns, 185–7; decisions about, 187–91; 'the hidden', 186; society and, 183–5, 194–200

curriculum experts, 192

Dainton Report, 197n

day release, of adolescents for education, 323

delinquency, 29, 115, 212; sub-culture of, 258, 259; TV and, 133

democracy: in classroom, 207; education and, 267, 272–3, 282

Department of Education and Science, 165–7, 178

deviance, 26, 71, 72, 75, 199

direct-grant schools, 169, 294, 295

Directors of Education, of local authorities, 167, 168

directors of large public companies, 315–16

discipline: at home, 68; in school, 206, 221, 236

discontinuity: between social institutions, 49–51; between values, 36

Duke of Edinburgh's Award, 331

Durham County Council, NUT and, 148

duty, in grammar and public school ethos, 256

dysfunction, 241, 242; in educational system, 255, 257, 260, 263, 296, 308

Early Leaving, HMSO, 302, 311

economic change: attitudes towards, 327–8; direction of, 317–21; and educational requirements, 338–41

economic function: of family, 33, 34–5; of education, 242, 321–49

economy, the British, 312–21

education: aims of, 323; attitudes towards, 74–7, 328–9; criteria of, 272; definitions of, 191–2, 194; general, advantages of, 327, 337, 341, 347; gestation period of investment in, 337

Education Acts: (1870), 158; (1902), 86, 161, 337; (1944), 87, 166, 178, 293, 333, 346

Educational Priority Areas, 89

elementary schools, 86, 90, 153

eleven-plus examination, 95, 98, 205, 296, 331

elite, the, 94, 205, 255, 275

embourgeoisement of working class, 60–2

employment: achievement of full, 316–17, 338; primary, second-ary, and tertiary sectors of, 313–14; sub-division of, 312–313, 317–18

equality of opportunity, 284, 333, 348

equilibrium, 338–41

ethnic groups, 248, 249–50

examinations, 194, 195; and careers, 95, 259; and creativity, 262, 348; external, 176–7, 188, 190–1, 199, 343

extended family, 37, 39, 40, 41, 42

family: adolescents and, 117–19; culture of school and of, 43, 213, 230, 254; and political socialization, 268, 269, 274; size of, 37, 44–5; and socialization, 27–8, 35–6, 41–52; and transmission of culture, 43, 52, 244, 250; and transmission of knowledge, 185–6

feedback, in socialization, 23

finance: of education, 165; of independent schools, 171; of teaching materials, 191

forecasting needs for labour, 339–40, 347

foreigners, TV and stereotypes for, 135

foremen, 75, 321, 343, 344

France, 162, 289–90, 325

'fun culture', 116, 258

Future Development of the Youth Employment Service, The, HMSO, 345n

games, 92–3, 111, 162, 164, 196, 197, 205, 258

'gangs' of adolescents, 50, 107, 216

General Certificate of Education (GCE), 162, 176, 197, 303

General Teaching Council, Scotland, 142

geographical distribution, of secondary school provision, 288–90, 307

geographical mobility, 38, 210, 222

Germany, 162, 305, 321, 325; education in, under Nazis, 193, 251, 271; militarism in education in (1906), 271; technical education in, 261–2

girls, and peer groups, 107, 108, 113, 210

governing bodies of schools, 161, 168, 169–71, 181

government: and flow of labour from educational system to economy, 339; percentage of scientists in, UK and USA, 326

graduate teachers, 227, 228, 235; and choice of teaching as career, 224, 225; in different types of school, 153, 155, 223; teacher training not compulsory for, 142, 151

grammar schools, 86, 88, 95–6, 161, 197; education for leadership at, 277, 279; entry to, 67, 205, 300, 308–9; entry to university from, 294; geographical differences in provision of, 288–90, 307; IQ at, 292, 299; leaving age from, 301, 302, 343; parents' attitudes towards, 74–7; social class in, 81, 210; teachers in, 154, 155, 223; values of, 254, 256, 270, 330

groups, primary, 32

headmasters, 163–4, 170, 171, 174

headteachers, 173–4

high schools, USA, 205, 210; sub-cultures in, 116, 175, 212, 258

history, national bias in teaching of, 270, 271

hobbies, social class and, 114

Holland, 325

House of Lords, 274, 275

house system in schools, 96, 162

ideology of society, and curriculum, 190

image: public, of teachers, 219–223, 237; self-, of teachers, 219, 223–31, 238

immigrant groups, 229, 247–50, 257, 265

income, and social class, 55, 56–7, 61, 64

independent schools, 85–6, 88, 169, 257, 293–6; governing bodies of, 170–1; IQ at, 292, 295; parents and, 89, 172; teachers in, 154, 169; see also progressive schools, public schools

India, democracy in, 272

Industrial Training Act (1964), 262, 323

industry: changing nature of, 318–21; education and, 261, 328; percentage of scientists employed in (UK and USA), 326

initiative, 69

innovation, innovators, 242, 245, 260–5

insecurity: in role of teacher, 236; of slum children, 70

Inspectors of Schools (HMIs), 142, 145–6, 149, 165, 232

institutions: autonomous change in, 263–5, 309; lives and values of, 242

intellectual discipleship, 95, 251

intelligence: code of language and development of, 77–80, 82; in leaders, 279, 280, 281, 282–3; and use of mass media, 131 intelligence quotient (IQ), 285–6, 297, 333; family size and, 44–5; range of, at different types of school, 292, 295; range of, for different levels of labour force, 342; social class, and educational attainments at same level of, 291, 299–305, 307, 309–10; tests of, 87, 99

interpersonal socialization, 17, 23–6

interviews, assessment by, 346–7

iron and steel industry, 321

isolates: in school class, 214, 215; and TV, 124, 125

Israel, youth activity in two types of co-operative farm in, 51

kindergartens, 169

knowledge, 183–5; required for industrial work, 322; required for professions, 141; stock of, and behavioural patterns, 185–7; stock of, divided among social classes, 256–7

labour: direction of, in planned economies, 341; division of, 312–13, 317–18; skilled and unskilled, 318, 342

labour force, 312–14; pool of capability in, 341–3

Labour Party, 275, 276, 278

language: reflects complexity of culture, 187; restricted and elaborated codes of, 78–80, 81, 195; in transmission of culture, 246–7, 248

Latin, 193, 256

Latin America, 272

lawyers, in political elite, 275

leaders: local, 274, 278–9; national, 274, 275–8

leadership, 206–7; selection and training for, 255, 267, 275–82

leisure, 115, 132

literacy, 133–4

local authorities: education of officers of, 279; and religious instruction, 178; and schools, 162, 165, 167–9; and teachers, 148, 181

management: hierarchy of, 334; problems of, 336; techniques of, 320–1

managers, education of, 334–5, 343

Manchester, 166

Manpower Studies, 319n, 340n

manufacturing establishments, 314–16

marriage, 34; age at, 105; between teachers, 222–3; social mobility in, 59

mass media, 30, 120–36, 187

mathematics, 306–7, 324, 339

Men, Steel, and Technical Change, DSIR, 318n

merit, equals IQ plus effort, 286

middle class: changes in, 63; sub-culture of, 61, 78, 164, 254–5

Middlesex, 168

minorities, democracy and, 267

missionary teachers, 227

mobility, *see* geographical mobility, social mobility

money-making spirit, 330, 333, 346

morality, professional, 144, 158

mother–child relationship, 33, 37; in different social classes, 67–9, 71

motivation: for leadership, 281–2; of pupils, curriculum and, 195; for teaching, 224–5

motor cycles, peer groups and, 108, 111

mutual steering, in interpersonal socialization, 23–4, 47–8

National Certificates, 306, 307
National Union of Teachers (NUT), 143, 147–9, 168, 178, 179
Newcastle Commission (1861), 191–2
New Guinea, 42, 46
Newsom Report, 222n, 259n
nuclear family, 37–8, 39, 40, 42
Nuffield Science Teaching Project, 196
numeracy, 253, 327
nursery schools, 48

occupation: family and choice of, 44; and social class, 55, 56, 57, 64
one-parent families, 28
opinion leaders, 128–9
Opposition, Leader of, 267
Oxford, University of, 275, 276, 277; Department of Education, 324, 349

Parent–Teacher Associations, 171 172, 173
parents: attitudes towards education of, 74–7; on governing bodies, 170; and teachers, 171–173, 181; and TV for children, 122
Parliament, 274, 276
peer groups, 49; conformity in 302; and mass media, 123, 124, 136; school classes as, 208–12; in socialization, 29–30, 104–19
pensions, for teachers, 149
perception, 77–80, 82
personality: family and school in development of, 46–8, 95, 203, 204; social class and, 69–73, 80, 82; of teachers, 231–3; and use of intelligence, 285–6
physical education, 156

Plowden Report, 89n, 170n, 172, 173n, 229, 298
political function of education, 242, 267–83
politics, 148, 178, 273, 331
pop music, 111, 123, 130, 132, 195
power, social class and, 57
prefects, 281, 282
preparatory schools, 92–3, 295
primary schools, 87, 90–2, 102, 255, 293; boards of managers of, 161; parent–teacher associations at, 172; peer groups in, 110–11, 210; streaming and IQ in, 296–8, 307; teachers in, 154–5, 228, 251
professions, the, 140, 146–9, 151–152, 275; code of conduct in, 143–5, 152, 158; conditions of service in, 149–50; control of entry to, 141–3, 188; freedom to practise, 145–6; schools and, 95, 330, 331, 343; teaching as, 139–41, 150–2
progressive culture, in primary schools, 91–2
progressive schools, 169, 198, 203–4
Protestant ethic, 73
public schools, 86, 93–5, 102, 162, 244, 293–6; curriculum of, 199–200; education for leadership at, 255, 275, 276, 277, 279, 280–1; entry to university from, 294; leaving age from, 343; managers from, 334–5; old boys' clubs of, 106, 331; values of, 270, 330
punishment, 24–5, 68; see also sanctions

qualifications, for professions, 143

radio, 127, 128
reading, TV and, 128

recipe knowledge, 185
regional sub-cultures, 252–3
registration: of independent schools, 169; of teachers, 142
religious instruction, 177–8, 189, 245–6
research: in education, 189; industry and, 260–1, 319–20, 326
resocialization of adults, 198
retraining, in industry, 328, 337
rewards: immediate and deferred, 70, 71, 73, 80, 195, 196, 273; in socialization, 24–5
Robbins Report, 66, 77n, 285, 287n, 289n, 303, 304n, 305n, 309, 310, 340n
role models, 27, 121, 126, 136; for girls, 130
role-set, 180; of teacher, 180–1, 231, 233
roles (mutual behaviour expectations), 17–26; ascribed and achieved, 20; in children's play, 36, 46; instrumental and expressive, 38–9; latent, 195; mediating, 222; in peer groups, 109; of teachers, 218–38
Roman Catholics, 168
rural sub-culture, 252, 253

Samoa, 42, 43
sanctions: in child-rearing, 68; in peer groups, 108, 111, 124, 136, 209; in professions, 145, 147; in schools, 91, 94, 197, 206, 230; in socialization, 24–5, 27
sandwich courses, 162
scholarships, to grammar schools, 86, 87, 99, 254
school class, as a social system, 202–13
school leaving age, 100, 301–2, 303, 343
school stories, 135

school system, 85–7; changes in, 87–9
school textbooks, 188, 192–3, 270, 271
schoolmasters, 153, 154
schools: British idea of, 161–5; cultures of different types of, 89–101, 255–7; cultures of family and of, 43, 213, 230, 254; education in basic skills at, 42; peer groups and, 116–17; in political socialization, 268–9; in socialization, 28–9, 30, 102; teachers in, 160–1, 165–81; see also comprehensive, independent, preparatory, primary, progressive, public, and secondary schools
Schools Council, 114n, 177, 179, 190
science: in curriculum, 189, 191; industries based on, 319; pure and applied, attitudes towards, 263, 324–5, 326–7; sex difference in percentage studying (sixth form), 288; sub-culture of? 253; teachers of, 339
science fiction, on TV, 195
Scientific and Technical Manpower, HMSO, 340
Scotland, 38, 64, 85n, 95, 142, 143, 163, 197, 224–5
Scottish Mental Survey, 44–5
secondary modern schools, 96–7, 282; adjustment to failure in, 99, 205; clash of values in, 213, 256, 331; IQ at, 292; leaving age from, 114, 343; streaming at, 97, 116, 124; teachers in, 154, 223, 232–3; transfer to grammar or technical schools from, 300
secondary schools, 87, 163; entry to, 298–301, 307; governing bodies of, 169–70; and labour

force, 343–4; peer groups in, 111–12; *see also* grammar, secondary modern, *and* secondary technical schools

secondary technical schools, 88, 97–8, 260, 300–1; IQ at, 292; leaving age from, 343

self-discipline, in different social classes, 69, 71

self-reliance, 47, 73

service, ideal of, 330, 331

sex, 33, 50, 105; family and, 33; and personality, 46; separation into groups by, 110–11, 215

sex differences: in expected personality of teachers, 232; in percentage leaving school with two A levels, 287; in political interests, 269; in reaction to mass media, 138–1; in reading, 128; in reasons for choice of teaching as career, 224, 225; in self-image of teachers, 229; in status of teachers, 152–3; in subjects studied in sixth form, 287–8

sex roles, in peer groups, 105, 109, 112, 113–15

sixth forms, 95, 176; attitudes of boys in, towards science and technology, 324–5; numbers of places in, provided by independent schools, 294; selection at entry into, 302–4; specialization in, 197, 261; subjects studied in, 287–8

skills, portable, 59

social class, 53–4, 60–3; and attitude towards education, 74–82, 299; children and, 63–5; indices of, 54–8; and infant rearing, 67–9; and intellectual attainments (with same IQ), 291, 299–305, 307, 309–10; and language code, 77–80; and

peer groups, 114–15; and personality, 69–73, 80, 82; and school leaving age, 301, 308; and socialization, 27, 28, 52; of teachers, 156–7, 222; and use of mass media, 131

social class learning, 65–7, 82–3, 213, 254, 257, 290–1, 297

social distance, 60

social mobility, 38, 58–60, 64, 75, 254–5; 'cooling out' of those with excessive aspirations for, 308; education and, 82, 309; of teachers, 156–7, 236; in UK and USA, 333

social selection function of education, 242, 293–311

social structure, 18, 23; and available roles, 20; public schools and, 199–200

socialization (learning of roles), 17–26; family in, 27–8, 35–6, 41–52; mass media in, 134–6; occupational, 231; peer groups in, 29–30, 125; political, 268–274; school in, 28–9, 30, 102; social class and, 53–83

society: and the curriculum, 183–5, 194–200

sociogram, 214

sociometry, of school class, 213–17

solidarity, in working-class ethos, 256

specialization: in employment, 317–18; in school subjects, 197–8, 253, 261

speech, social class and, 54

'splash' period, of adolescent or young adult, 117, 118

sport, peer groups and, 111; *see also* games

stability, balance between change and, 244, 245

state, the: and education, 151, 165; and professions, 145

Statistics of Education (*Annual*), 155n, 294n, 295n

status, 57, 62; academic success and, 211; competition for, 205; of different sciences and technologies, 325; in peer groups, 112, 125, 129; personal, 106; of professions, 144; of teachers, *see under* teachers

Steel Workers and Technical Progress, OEEC, 328n

stereotypes, 219; education to alter, 249; mass media and, 135, 185; of teachers, 220, 223, 238

— streaming, 209; in comprehensive schools, 101, 206, 257; dysfunctional effects of, 309; and IQ, 292; in primary schools, 296–8, 307; in secondary modern schools, 97, 116, 124

strikes, by teachers, 144–5, 147–8, 151, 159

structural perspective, of socialization, 17–22

sub-cultures: of immigrants, 229, 231; regional, 252–3; of social classes, 65–6, 82, 254–5; of types of educational institution, 264, 265; of types of school, 89–101, 255–7; vocational, 260; within schools, 175, 258–60; within universities, 253

subject taught, and status of teacher, 155–6

success in life, criteria of, 329–33

suggestibility, 273

Superannuation Act (1918), 149

Sweden, 287, 325

teachers: in the classroom, 202–217; graduate, *see* graduate teachers; ideal types of, 226–231; in a profession, 139–52, 158–9; pupils' attitudes to-

wards, 70, 195; role of, 218–38; in the school, 160–1, 165–81; shortage of, 339; sociometric studies of, 215; status of, 149, 151, 152–7, 158, 228, 229

teachers' centres, 198

teachers' training colleges, 232, 305; *see also* training

teaching: adjusting to, 231–7; materials for, 191; skills in, 226

technical colleges, 260, 303, 305

technical education, 261, 306–7, 323, 339

technicians, 285, 302, 342–3, 344

technologists, 285, 342

technology, attitudes of sixth-form boys to science and, 324–5

teenage culture, *see* youth culture

television (TV), 30, 118, 121–3, 124, 128, 195; as topic in peer groups, 111, 134

tolerance, 101, 267; length of education and, 264, 273

trade cycle, 316

trade unions, 147, 331; education of leaders of, 275, 278

Trades Union Congress, 149

traditional culture, in primary schools, 90–1

training: as distinct from education, 194; of teachers, 151, 153, 226–7, 305

Treasury Bulletin for Industry, 320n

twins, IQ of, 45

unemployment, 317

United States of America (USA): education of leaders in, 278, 279; employers of scientists in, 326; high schools in, 116, 175, 205, 210, 212, 258; money-making spirit in, 330; parents and schools in, 172; 'return to learning' in, 189; social mobility in, 333; stereotype of teacher in, 220; TV in, 122, 124; universities in, 287, 290, 330, 335

universities: academic standards of, 335; Arts faculties of, 309; entry to, 197, 287, 294; and examinations, 176, 188; managers with degrees from, 335; the new, 176, 261; as sources of change, 263–4; status of different subjects in, 155; status of teachers in, 152, 158; in USA, 287, 290, 330, 335

USSR, 251, 270, 279

values, clash of, 28–9, 36

vocational aspirations, 211, 299–300, 332–3

vocational education, status of, 199, 257

vocational guidance, 332, 344–7

vocational sub-cultures, 332, 344–7

Wales, 289, 290

wealth, inherited: and social class, 55

'Westerns', 127

women: social class and treatment of, 65; social mobility of, 59; untapped pool of capability in, 288

Workers' Educational Association, 271

working class: embourgeoisement of? 60–2; sub-culture of, 69, 76, 80, 133

Yearbook of Education, 152, 159, 225n

youth clubs, 108–9; effects of type of leadership in, 206–207

youth culture, 95, 112, 114, 117, 123, 124, 132; in USA, 116, 212

Youth Employment Service, 332, 344–5, 347